Introduction to International Environmental Law

Timo Koivurova

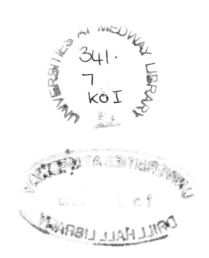

Routledge
Taylor & Francis Group

LONDON AND NEW YORK

First published 2012 by Tietosanoma oy
This revised and translated work published in 2014
by Routledge
2 Park Square, Milton Park, Abingdon, Oxon OX14 4RN

and by Routledge
711 Third Avenue, New York, NY 10017

Routledge is an imprint of the Taylor & Francis Group, an informa business

© 2014 Timo Koivurova

British Library Cataloguing in Publication Data
A catalogue record for this book is available from the British Library.

Library of Congress Cataloging in Publication Data
Koivurova, Timo.
[Johdatus kansainv?liseen ymp?rist?oikeuteen. English]
Introduction to international environmental law / Timo Koivurova.
pages cm
Includes bibliographical references.
ISBN 978-0-415-81653-3 (hardback) – ISBN 978-0-415-81574-1 (pbk) –
ISBN 978-1-315-85159-4 (ebk) 1. Environmental law, International.
I. Title.
K3585.K6513 2014
344.04'6–dc23
2013026365

ISBN: 978-0-415-81653-3 (hbk)
ISBN: 978-0-415-81574-1 (pbk)
ISBN: 978-1-315-85159-4 (ebk)

Typeset in Bembo
by Cenveo Publisher Servi

Contents

List of figures

Acknowledgements

Grateful acknowledgement is made to all the owners and copyright holders of the images that appear in this book, and in particular to the following for permission to reprint images from the sources indicated:

Rebecca M. Bratspies for Figure 1.1, Graffiti protest against US oil company Texaco in Quito, the capital of Ecuador in 2003.

ITOPF for Figure 2.1, Oil tanker catastrophes have often given rise to a pressure to regulate.

UNECE for Figure 3.1, The fourth meeting of the parties to the Espoo Convention took place in Bucharest, Romania, 19–21 May 2008.

Melissa K. Scanlan for Figure 4.1, A private beach at Lake Michigan in the USA.

Ellen Desmet for Figure 4.2, Protest by indigenous people living in the Peruvian Amazon rainforest in Iquitos, May 2009.

Andrew Jackson for Figure 4.3, Demonstrators dressed as penguins outside a meeting related to the Antarctic Treaty in Bonn in April 1991.

HyBIS RUV, National Oceanography Centre, Southampton for Figure 4.4, The Beebe hydrothermal vent, 5,000 metres deep in the Caribbean Sea near the Cayman Islands.

European Commission for Figure 5.1, Regional fisheries management organizations for highly migratory fish stocks (tuna and other species) and for non-tuna species. Eurostat/GISCO Source RFMO data: European Commission Administrative boundaries: © EuroGeographics, © FAO (UN), © TurkStat.

Andrea Calmet for Figure 5.2, Forest destroyed to make way for illegal gold mines in Madre de Dios, Peru.

Emmanuelle Bournay, UNEP/GRID-Arendal for Figure 5.3, An assessment of the development of skin cancer cases in relation to UV radiation in the world.

Michael Gerrard for Figure 6.1, A tomb vault sinking in the sea in the Majuro atoll in the Marshall Islands in 2010.

IISD/Earth Negotiations Bulletin for Figure 7.1, The representatives of Finland and Cape Verde during a recess in a preparatory meeting for Rio +20 in New York on 19 March 2012; and Figure 7.3, The chairs of the meetings of the parties to the Basel, Rotterdam and Stockholm Conventions made their historic decision on 24 February 2010 in Bali, Indonesia. Photographs courtesy of IISD/Earth Negotiations Bulletin (http://www.iisd.ca/unepgc/unepss11/).

Azote Images/Stockholm Resilience Centre for Figure 7.2, The boundaries of our planet.

Vernon Rive for Figure 7.4, During the Durban Climate Conference on 10 December 2011, civic organizations demonstrated outside the plenary hall.

Every effort has been made to trace the copyright holders but if any have been inadvertently overlooked the publishers will be pleased to make the necessary arrangement at the first opportunity.

List of acronyms

ACIA	Arctic Climate Impact Assessment
AEPS	Arctic Environmental Protection Strategy
AHJWG	The Ad Hoc Joint Working Group on enhanced cooperation and coordination between the Basel, Stockholm and Rotterdam Conventions
AMAP	Arctic Monitoring and Assessment Programme
ASCOBANS	Agreement on the Conservation of Small Cetaceans of the Baltic, North East Atlantic, Irish and North Seas
ATCM	Antarctic Treaty Consultative Meeting
ATS	Antarctic Treaty System
BASIC	Brazil, South Africa, India and China
BAT	best available technology
BEP	best environmental practice
BINGO	business and industry non-governmental organization
BSAP	Baltic Sea Action Plan
BSPA	Baltic Sea Protection Areas (Helsinki Commission)
CDM	clean development mechanism
CJEU	Court of Justice of the European Union
CFC	chlorofluorocarbons (compounds containing chlorine, fluorine and carbon)
CITES	Convention on International Trade in Endangered Species of Wild Fauna and Flora
CLCS	Commission on the Limits of the Continental Shelf
CRAMRA	Convention on the Regulation of Antarctic Mineral Resource Activities
CRC	Chemical Review Committee
CSCE	Conference on Security and Co-operation in Europe
CSD	Commission on Sustainable Development
DDA	Doha Development Agenda
EC	European Communities
EEA	European Economic Area
EEC	European Economic Community
EIA	environmental impact assessment

EMEP	European Monitoring and Evaluation Programme (for long-range transmission of air pollution)
ENGO	environmental NGO
EPA	United States Environmental Protection Agency
EU	European Union
FAO	UN Food and Agriculture Organization
GATT	General Agreement on Tariffs and Trade
GEF	Global Environment Facility
HCFC	hydrochlorofluorocarbons (compounds containing hydrogen, chlorine, fluorine and carbon)
HELCOM	Helsinki Commission (The Baltic Marine Environment Protection Commission)
HFC	hydrofluorocarbons (compounds containing hydrogen, fluorine and carbon)
IAEA	International Atomic Energy Agency
ICC	International Criminal Court
ICCPR	International Covenant on Civil and Political Rights
ICESCR	International Covenant on Economic, Social and Cultural Rights
ICJ	UN International Court of Justice
IGO	intergovernmental organization
ILA	International Law Association
ILC	International Law Commission
ILO	International Labour Organization
IMF	International Monetary Fund
IMO	International Maritime Organization
IPBES	Intergovernmental Science-Policy Platform on Biodiversity and Ecosystem Services
IPCC	Intergovernmental Panel on Climate Change
IPO	indigenous people's organizations
IPPC	International Plant Protection Convention
ISA	International Seabed Authority
IUCN	International Union for Conservation of Nature
IWC	International Whaling Commission
JI	joint implementation
LGMA	local government and municipal authorities
LRTAP	long-range transboundary air pollution
MA	Millennium Ecosystem Assessment
MARPOL	(marine pollution) International Convention for the Prevention of Pollution from Ships
MCPFE	Ministerial Conference on the Protection of Forests in Europe
MOU	memorandum of understanding
MOX	mixed oxide fuel
NASA	National Aeronautics and Space Administration (in USA)
NEAFC	North East Atlantic Fisheries Commission

NGO	non-governmental organization
NIEO	New International Economic Order
OECD	Organisation for Economic Co-operation and Development
OPEC	Organization of the Petroleum Exporting Countries
OSPAR	(Oslo and Paris) Convention for the Protection of the Marine Environment of the North-East Atlantic
PCIJ	Permanent Court of International Justice
PIC	prior informed consent
POP	persistent organic pollutants
PRTR	Pollutant Release and Transfer Register
R2P	responsibility to protect
REDD	Reducing Emissions from Deforestation and Forest Degradation
RINGO	research and independent NGO
SBSTA	Subsidiary Body for Scientific and Technological Advice
SBSTTA	Subsidiary Body for Scientific, Technical and Technological Advice (in the Biodiversity Regime)
SEA	strategic environmental assessment
SOLAS	Safety of Life at Sea
SPS	Agreement Sanitary and Phytosanitary Agreement (WTO)
TEK	traditional ecological knowledge
TUNGO	trade union NGO
UN	United Nations
UNCED	United Nations Conference on Environment and Development
UNCLOS	United Nations Convention on the Law of the Sea
UNDP	United Nations Development Programme
UNECE	United Nations Economic Commission for Europe
UNEP	United Nations Environment Programme
UNHRC	United Nations Human Rights Council
UNTC	United Nations Treaty Collection
WEO	World Environmental Organization
WMO	World Meteorological Organization
WSSD	World Summit on Sustainable Development
WTO	World Trade Organization
WWF	World Wide Fund for Nature
YOUNGO	youth NGO

To the reader

Familiarity with international law – or one of its branches, international environmental law – is, in my experience, not part of the general knowledge of most people who read newspapers and watch the news on television. The press reflects a world-view in which conflicts and superpowers control the harsh reality of international politics. If a country happens to be small, it is well advised to maintain good relations with the centres of power. During the Cold War, this kind of pragmatic attitude was essential. The battle for dominion between the superpower blocs of the United States and the Soviet Union and the race for nuclear armament prevailed to the extent that international rules were not the first thing one thought of studying. The mainstream based its international relations philosophy on realist views of international politics where states and groups of states were the main actors, and their military-economic power defined their status on the world political map; there was hardly room for the rules of international law.

This world-view is gradually becoming history. Today, the mainstream research in international relationships is based on many theories that acknowledge the role of rules in the behaviour of governments and other actors. This step forward in scientific research, however, has not yet been adopted by journalists who continue to transmit the 'realist' world-view to the general public in their reports and broadcasts.

When the Russians planted their flag on the seabed in the Lomonosov Ridge below the North Pole in August 2007, scholars of international relations and geography all over the world gave interviews declaring that the intergovernmental power game on the Arctic natural resources had begun. As climate change is accelerating the melting of the Arctic sea ice, the rich and politically secure energy resources of this new ocean become increasingly accessible for exploitation.

For anyone engaged in international law, this was a good indication of just how powerfully the media models our world-view. Many leading academics, including myself, wrote articles to try to counter this misinterpretation; my own article appeared in the leading Finnish newspaper *Helsingin Sanomat*. It was not a case of an intergovernmental 'power game', but a process regulated by the UN Convention on the Law of the Sea (UNCLOS). This Convention obliges its member states, within ten years from becoming members, to submit scientific-technological information to the Commission on the Limits of the Continental Shelf (CLCS) if their continental shelf reaches more than 200 nautical miles (370 kilometres) from the shore. In fact, Russia has so far observed the Convention in an exemplary way: it was the first state to deliver its submission to the Commission in 2001 and has since collected sufficient scientific information for a further submission.

The misinterpretation was also due to the fact that experts, too, were ignorant of some of the context. Talking to international relations colleagues and geographers, I realized that many of them were not even aware of the UN Convention on the Law of the Sea; this Convention, also called the 'constitution of the oceans', regulates almost all human activity in marine areas. These colleagues from other fields gradually began to realize that the UN Convention on the Law of the Sea was actually the main reason why governments were conducting this continental shelf research.

Although experts today appreciate why continental shelf research is conducted, the media still have not adjusted their interpretation of events. The more dramatic an interpretation invented by a self-appointed expert – for example, that the Cold War never ended in the Arctic – the more likely it seems that even quality media such as the BBC and *The Guardian* will report it. An ordinary educated reader is therefore left with good reason to fear an armed conflict in the Arctic. The potential for armed conflict can never be fully excluded in international politics, but it is highly improbable in the Arctic.

Meanwhile, a massive dramatic 'real' change is taking place in the Arctic, partly hidden under the conflict narrative. The ice cover of the Arctic Ocean is receding and thinning at an accelerating pace, and the permafrost in the High North and the Greenlandic ice-sheet are melting. In the midst of all this, economic actors are competing for the opportunity to exploit Arctic oil resources. The changes in the Arctic are both global and local. If methane is released from under the permafrost, or if the ice covering Greenland melts more rapidly, climate change will also accelerate and sea levels will rise globally. The receding ice will allow companies to drill for oil in an extremely vulnerable Arctic environment where the consequences of an oil spill would be catastrophic, since oil disperses very slowly in cold and icy sea water.

While the media offers a very conflict-centred world-view, it is important to write in a comprehensible way about the essential role played by international regulations in international relations. The rules of international law and international environmental law are significant in the 'real' world of international relations, even if they are often too tedious for the media to observe. Textbooks are mainly written for students and so it is my intention to present matters as generally as possible, sometimes perhaps bordering on simplification; this is not necessarily a drawback. It is my hope that this book could be read by a broad range of readers, too, besides lawyers and law students.

Many English-language textbooks tend to devote several pages to going through the contents of hundreds of international treaties, instead of inspiring the student to find these agreements and to read them for themselves. It is my view that if the reader who is interested in the subject is given a general view of it and the tools to make sense of it, he or she will learn much more efficiently. International environmental law and politics speak for themselves.

The reader could benefit from reading a general textbook on international law before starting to read *Introduction to International Environmental Law*, as international environmental law is part of general international law. Examples of suitable textbooks are *Handbook of International Law* by Anthony Aust and *Public International Law* by Alina Kaczorowska.

This book offers a mainstream account of international environmental law; that is, it describes how the majority of those engaged in the field interpret a certain agreement or understand a certain concept or case. It should be recognized, however, that international environmental law can and should be interpreted in different ways. The leading experts in the field disagree on many points, although they rely on the same sources of law. An essential part of a lawyer's proficiency is being able to justify an issue from various points of view.

Finally, I must state that I will always remain a student of international environmental law. When one thinks one has achieved the 'correct' view, one will no longer learn. This is the problem with being considered an expert: in contradicting cases where there are differing views, we come to expect a clear and definitive opinion from an expert as to the obligations that international environmental law establishes for governments and other actors. A judge is required to resolve the conflict, and attorneys are required to defend the interests of their clients, whereas a scholar can maintain the attitude of a lifelong student, remaining open to differing viewpoints.

Writing this book was a good example. The book was reviewed by some of the leading experts in the field; I disagreed with them on certain matters and agreed with them on others. I learnt a lot from them. The best way to learn is often to challenge an author's view, always making sure that you can justify your disagreement. I therefore urge the reader to disagree with me as often as possible. I also urge the reader to find as convincing legal grounds as possible for why they may think I am wrong.

This book does not attempt to present all the comprehensive regulations relating to international environmental law. Many of the existing English-language textbooks are volumes of over 1,000 pages which describe and analyse an enormous number of regulations relating to international environmental law. The extensive material is then organized into specific sections of international environmental law, which is most suited to experts. In contrast, an introductory book such as this one is free to concentrate on the basics of the subject. The primary aim of this book is to provide a generalized account of international environmental law, since the 'industrial' rate at which new international regulations are made makes it difficult to make sense of and penetrate these enormous detailed texts. Unlike other textbooks, this one is intended to be easily comprehensible, rather than provide an exhaustive overview of all the regulations in the field.

This book has several features intended to help the reader better understand the sometimes abstract reality of international environmental law.

- In the example boxes, I attempt to illustrate how international environmental law works in practice and/or concretize abstract ideas.
- Photos and illustrations also serve to concretize ideas and offer another perspective to the topic under discussion.
- Data boxes are provided to clarify essential concepts.

The book does not contain footnotes, tables of treaties or a bibliography – features that we legal scholars are used to. This is simply because the book is intended for a broader audience, many of whom are used to reading the main text without interruptions. With the use of endnotes, the reader is free to concentrate on the main text. Sections on further reading and recommended websites at the end of each chapter point the reader to sources of further information on those parts of international environmental law that may be found to be of interest. Information on treaties and other international instruments is included in the main text and they are properly cited when they appear; the full name of the instrument and its source appear in the respective endnote at the end of each chapter.

This book is a veritable project of calling for me. For a long time already, I have felt the need to write a new kind of popular introduction into international environmental law, but being a busy research professor, I am also aware of the lack of time. I gained new motivation after giving a course on international environmental law in the University of New South Wales in Sydney, Australia, where I was a visiting professor in 2011. I started work on the book in August 2011, working as intensely as other commitments allowed. I wrote it in Finnish at first for publishers Tietosanoma, after which Routledge became interested. For this English-language edition, I have amended the book considerably with the help of colleagues from all four corners of our planet. It was important to target the book to an international public, not only a Finnish one.

The book reflects its author, although many people helped me write it. It is not easy to put into words how grateful I am towards all those who helped. It was my goal from the start to write an introductory textbook to motivate a student to learn more, rather than an exhaustive presentation of the subject. Instead of addressing lawyers only, I wanted to give a basic view to anyone interested in the environment. I trust I have achieved these two goals. I greatly appreciate my editor, Nana Sironen, who was of enormous assistance in making the original Finnish book easier to read and more popular. I also want to thank Routledge for translating the work into English and for all the help provided by Damian Mitchell and Fiona Briden.

I sent the manuscript to quite a number of my fellow academics to read, and they made incredibly useful comments. This English version, to which I have made a fair amount of revisions, received feedback from Don Anton,

Nigel Bankes, Neil Craik, Meinhard Doelle, Sébastien Duyck, Inna Ignatieva, Rachael Lorna Johnstone, Qin Tianbao and Robin Warner.

All these wonderful colleagues corrected errors and challenged me to reconsider the contents and structure of the book. We had our disagreements, which was good: one can only learn when one dares to disagree. I learnt a lot, and I believe the comments have improved my book significantly. Thank you so much!

My colleagues in the Northern Institute for Environmental and Minority Law and in the Arctic Centre encouraged me in many ways during the project – thank you, my great workmates.

As always, my parents, my sister and my in-laws sustained me in every way in this project as well, understanding the scholar who often wandered in a world of his own. Thank you all!

My dear wife Anniina and our great kids Joonas and Vilja sustained me in the writing process, although it cut into our time together. I guess the children were happy: although Dad was writing, at least he was at home.

I feel privileged and blessed to have a vocation I find useful and interesting. I hope this book will inspire others to consider how we relate to our shared environment.

Timo Koivurova
Rovaniemi, at the end of 2012.

Introduction

The existing state system regulated by international law has evolved slowly over several centuries. The birth of the international politico-legal system is often dated back to the Peace of Westphalia of 1648 which ended the Thirty Years' War and initiated the development of the state-based system in Europe. The goal of this state-based international political system has been to maintain peace among independent states. The idea that the international community could pursue shared law and politics in order to address worldwide problems together is a comparatively modern one: the foundation of the United Nations in 1945 made the development of international political and legal cooperation possible.

Although such international political and legal collaboration was made possible, international law still maintains a political community that essentially seeks to secure the independence of its political units, and peace between them. At the same time, the pressure to create politics and laws that are truly global is increasing in various fields, be it controlling and eliminating weapons of mass destruction, preventing human rights abuses, averting global pandemics or controlling and preventing global environmental hazards. The need to create such common structures for global policy is hindered by Westphalian structures that seek to safeguard the rights and interests of each individual sovereign state. This can be seen in the context of global environmental problems, which would require effective policies and laws restraining the actions of sovereign states.

International environmental law faces a very rapidly changing world characterized by an escalating trend of political power applied outside conventional governmental structures: in global and regional international organizations or in multinational companies. International environmental governance attempts to create administrative structures that are capable of change and able to administer constantly changing environmental problems.

The private sector is making decisions that are increasingly significant politically, so environmental regulations are more and more often targeted directly towards companies. International environmental problems have a direct impact on us all; therefore, increasing numbers of non-governmental actors are demanding rights to participate and influence how such problems are managed.

One of the most important developments in world history has been the emergence of the state as the central form of global political organization. The rules by which a group of people can strive to form a state are defined in international law. The group shall control a certain territory; it shall have an effective government and be able to interact with other sovereign states. Mainstream opinion is that recognition by other states is no longer a prerequisite for the status of a state, although it is, of course, important: a state will have limited scope of action in foreign policy if it is recognized by just a handful of other states. A good example is Taiwan (the Republic of China), which is recognized by a little over 20 states, even if it clearly meets the criteria of statehood.[1]

Over time, almost all the land on earth has fallen under the sovereign dominion of states. Coastal states have also gradually increased their jurisdiction over marine areas. The nearly 200 organized states whose rights and duties are mainly regulated by classical international law constitute a challenge to international environmental law: each one of them is essentially in charge of environmental protection in their own territories. The basic principle of international law is that states can create laws for themselves and no institution can create a law that is binding upon them without their consent. Environmental protection (legislative and enforcement powers) is therefore shared between independent territorial states. This, of course, contradicts the fact that pollutants or ecosystems do not observe the boundaries between states.

International environmental law seeks to find ways for these sovereign states to prevent transboundary environmental problems or to administer shared ecosystems jointly. Tension is created by the fact that classical international law guarantees legislative and enforcement powers to territorial political communities, the boundaries of which are artificial from the perspective of pollution or natural ecosystems. For their part, actors committed to international environmental protection endeavour to find ways of helping states understand what is in their long-term best interests – as well as in the short term. It is interesting that international environmental law has been able to make a significant challenge to long-held principles of classical international law in a very short period of time.[2]

Structure of the book

Chapter 1 considers the basic issues in international environmental law. Why is international environmental law necessary, and can it meet the challenges posed by aggravating regional and global environmental problems? Should international environmental law set legal obligations for companies directly instead of states, since it is mainly companies that are generating pollution and causing environmental problems? The chapter also examines the character of international environmental law as part of general international law and how international law becomes part of national law.

Chapter 2 reviews the history of international environmental law. This branch of law is usually considered solely in the context of the development of environmental regulations, but it is helpful to start by understanding the broader context of the development of international environmental law: as part of the more general development of international law and politics. This will help us to appreciate just how brief the timescale is within which international environmental law has been able to create politico-legal institutions to develop environmental protection. International environmental law is faced with increasingly difficult and extensive environmental problems (such as ozone depletion, climate change, losses to biological diversity). It has therefore been necessary to try and develop regulations and structures that will help the entire world community take measures to solve the problems that threaten us all.

International environmental law has challenged classical international law about the ways in which international law is enacted and by whom. Chapter 3 surveys these new ways of enacting law. First, it examines the difference between soft law and hard law, after which it considers the primary and various subsidiary sources of international law in turn. The concept of the 'regime' is particularly important in this chapter and throughout the book.

A regime is broadly a type of international permanent management body based on an international environmental agreement and established by its parties. Through regimes, governments endeavour to control reactions to a changing environmental problem. Over the years, governments have started to develop treaty regimes to control international environmental problems. The reason is that environmental problems usually call for a permanent management system, established by intergovernmental agreements. Many environmental problems cannot be solved; they can only be minimized, as they result from socially acceptable economic activity.

A treaty regime[3] should also be capable of the flexibility to make efficient decisions in order to react to a changing, sometimes aggravating environmental problem. This is why 'meetings of the parties' (representing all the state parties to the treaty) are established which can, together with other organs in the regime, quickly make both non-binding and legally binding decisions to tackle an environmental problem.

Chapter 4 illustrates the extent to which classical international law has influenced international environmental law. The principles of general international law define the legal status of various areas of the world; consequently, they define who has the authority to protect or not to protect the environment within those areas. The principles of international environmental law which hold the most authority are those based on the state structure of classical international law: central to the regulation are issues secondary to global environmental protection, such as the regulation of transboundary pollution. Preventing and controlling many of the world's environmental problems, however, requires genuinely global environmental governance that can influence states' domestic environmental policy and laws. Principles are evolving within international environmental law intended to resolve global and regional environmental problems. Although the legal status of these principles is not quite established yet, they still have relevance to modern international environmental regulation. International environmental law has also benefited from recent developments in environmental law domestically: international environmental regulations have adopted new approaches (such as the ecosystem approach) and means of control (such as emissions trading and environmental impact assessment) which originated in a national context.

Chapter 5 briefly examines specific topics within international environmental law. The chapter addresses environmental problems related to the atmosphere and biodiversity losses in particular through treaty regimes that include almost all world states. However, international environmental law is a highly fragmented[4] branch of law compared with the regulatory system protecting free trade which is also examined in this chapter. The chapter also considers various ways of categorizing international environmental law, and looks at the main branches and sub-branches that have evolved over time.

Chapter 6 examines responsibility for environmental damage. International environmental agreements seldom include rules for who compensates whom for environmental damage and how. Although the liability rules in general international law also apply to transboundary environmental damage, they seldom have any practical significance. This is typical in international environmental law: contracting parties generally tend to concentrate their scarce resources on preventing environmental damage rather than on clarifying the rules of restitution.

Chapter 7 offers a consideration of the extent to which international environmental law has been able to challenge classical international law. International environmental regimes, for instance, have met with some success in reacting to the special challenges created by environmental problems, despite the powerful Westphalian structure of classical international law. However, specific rules for compensating environmental damage have not been created despite considerable efforts. This chapter also surveys the overhaul of the institutional structure of international environmental protection, one of the main goals during the two-year process that led to the Rio +20 at the end of June 2012, the 20-year follow-up to the 1992 Rio conference. An improved structure is vital, as overlapping work between different environmental governance institutions wastes scarce resources and complicates environmental protection. A final consideration of this chapter is whether increased measures can be established within international environmental law to help combat the most difficult contemporary environmental problem – the most challenging to respond to politically: climate change.

The chapters end with questions and research tasks to help the reader consider the themes in each chapter from their own viewpoint. These can be used for independent or group study.

Researching international environmental law

The sources of law doctrine (see Chapter 3) provide the basic tools for establishing which government-ratified written instruments are international treaties and which of them are non-binding soft-law instruments, as well as which kind of government statement is relevant in terms of the development of customary international law.

Research has changed radically since the mid-1990s in all branches of academia. In legal scholarship as well, the internet and electronic databases have transformed legal research. The change is not quite as dramatic in domestic law as it is in international law. A scholar of national law already had fairly easy access to the sources of law (court decisions, legislation and its preparatory work, for example) before the era of information technology. Probably the greatest change for a scholar of national law is that he or she no longer needs to go to a physical library, as most of the material is available in electronic databases.

For a scholar of international law, the change has been enormous. The decisions of the International Court of Justice of the United Nations were previously available only in certain libraries, and usually years after the decisions were made. International treaty collections and other instruments were available in select publications such as *International Legal Materials* (ILM), in treaty collections or professional journals. Detailed research into the development of, say, international labour law, maritime rules or human rights, often necessitated a journey to the country in which the international organization or other institution was based. Moreover, it was not certain that one could access all the material, due to the non-disclosure rules of various organizations that were in place.

A Canadian colleague of mine studied international maritime rules in the early 1980s. He had to start by flying to London to visit the headquarters of the International Maritime Organization (IMO) and then identify the appropriate contacts who could lead him to the documents he needed. He copied all the relevant material, and as this was so substantial, he had to send a large part of the material to Canada by sea freight. Today, that same academic can sit in his study and print all of the documents he needs from the internet.

This book is partly intended to inspire the reader to research international environmental law sources for themselves. If you have access to a library's electronic database, that really is all that you need. However, in today's research, it is essential not just to know search words and basic search procedures, but also to know the most likely source for each kind of information. For example, decisions by the International Court of Justice can be found in the official home page of the Court. It is always worth your while to use the official sites in order to verify that what you are looking at is the exact and entire decision in question.

International treaties can be found in several databases. One of the most reliable ones is the United Nations Treaty Collection[5] (UNTC), accessible through many libraries. One of the most useful features of this database is that it also contains a separate section showing which states are party to each treaty. Another useful source is the UN International Law Commission's site,[6] which contains vast amounts of useful legal materials, of relevance to international environmental law.

If you are studying a specific issue in international environmental law and are looking to find out more about it, the quickest way of finding all the relevant information on the subject is to read a textbook or a more advanced book on the subject. If another scholar has already done most of the research, why do it again? This book also provides you with advice on relevant literature and related web links at the end of each chapter. There is one common and dangerous pitfall to be avoided by modern researchers: internet search engines make it easy to find websites, articles and agreements on any given subject. The danger is that various interest groups maintain websites and publish material which may look like a reliable neutral source but may be of questionable quality. It is important to check the ownership and control of the website you are looking at, who made it and the qualifications and allegiances of the author. It is also important to find websites that can help direct you towards primary sources on international environmental law.

Notes

1 Taiwan has diplomatic relations with 22 UN member states (and with the Holy See). Mainland China (the People's Republic of China (PRC)) perceives Taiwan as one of its provinces, and reacts negatively for any factual or legal recognition of Taiwan as a state.

2 See further Chapter 7 ('The divergence of international environmental law from international law') for further analysis of this tension.

3 In this book, I use the term 'treaty regime' to refer to the entire process initiated by a certain environmental treaty. I use the name or acronym of the treaty if I refer to the treaty alone. The regime is a useful concept for legal scholars for several reasons:

- It makes it more obvious that international environmental regulation is not only a question of interpreting an original agreement; it implies a kind of a mini organization that is constantly changing in various ways.
- Having evolved within the research of international relations, the concept has given scholars of international environmental law an opportunity to understand the significance of soft-law rules as part of the operation of the regime.

- The 'regime' is based on the idea of constantly changing regulation. Scientific discovery of the environmental problems regulated by international environmental law is constantly changing. It is therefore important to perceive the regimes based on an international environmental agreement, as management mechanisms in a transient state.
- International environmental regimes are often influenced by actors other than governments.
- As the concept guides one to consider the change in the regime, one will also have to consider how a regime could be improved.

4 This book uses the concept of fragmentation. Fragmentation of international law means the division of the legal system into various sectors, each one of which often has their own unique goal and values that can contradict with other branches of international law. International trade law pursues free trade between the states in the world, whereas international environmental law pursues protection and sustainable use of the global and regional environment. International law has long been fragmented, but there is also fragmentation within international environmental law. There are already lawyers who specialize in the details of agreements and regulations against climate change, or drops in biodiversity, for example.

5 http://treaties.un.org/

6 http://www.un.org/law/ilc/

1 Basic issues in international environmental law

Before looking at the scope of international environmental law in detail, we should consider the basic issues.

To understand the system of international environmental law, we need to have a general understanding of the nature of international law. In this chapter, we will focus primarily on the factors that have influenced the development of international environmental law. We will then be able to review international environmental law's potential to resolve regional and even global environmental problems. As international law is a legal system controlled by states, we will see that there is good reason to question its capacity to regulate environmentally destructive activities in a world in which it is not primarily states but multinational businesses operating within an increasingly global market which are the worst polluters.

The main function of international environmental law

International environmental law is an extremely challenging branch of law and difficult to organize into a coherent whole. If there were a global, international environmental organization comparable to the World Trade Organization (WTO), with its automatic dispute settlement procedures, international environmental law could be viewed in a more unified light. But in international environmental law, there are just a number of loosely connected international environmental and other organizations, self-standing international environmental agreements and piecemeal governmental practices related to the use of the environment, united by an effort to promote international environmental protection or sustainable use of natural resources. However, as we will see in Chapter 4, efforts to protect the environment have resulted in the development of a significant number of principles, which have brought some coherence to international environmental law.

As with all environmental regulation, international environmental law can only strive to control and minimize pollution damage[1] we have caused. It cannot control natural disasters such as volcanic eruptions or earthquakes and the environmental damage they cause. International environmental regulation[2] seeks to control and minimize the harmful results of humankind's impact on the environment, such as the use of harmful substances that deteriorate air quality or interfere with the functioning of ecosystems.

The line between international and national environmental law becomes blurred as the amount of environmental regulation increases. The central issues in international environmental regulation – what gives it international character – are environmental problems that no government can control independently: issues such as air pollution drifting to other national or international territories, for example. Yet, increasingly, international environmental law harmonizes the way national environmental protection systems function, and impacts on our everyday lives, even if we are not aware of it.

When you fill up your car, the climate change regime has already influenced your fuel options as well as its price. Just by opening your refrigerator, you would never realize that the refrigerants used now are different from the ones used before the regime to restore the ozone layer commenced. The energy consumption options of European one-family houses are today largely defined by EU environmental regulation.[3] When you travel abroad, you are personally responsible for ensuring that any exotic objects that you may wish to bring home (coral jewellery, for example) are not prohibited or subject to a licensing system under the Convention on International Trade in Endangered Species of Wild Fauna and Flora (CITES).

The need for international regulation

The best way to recognize the importance of international environmental law is to consider why international law in general is necessary. The legal system of each country functions within certain geographical boundaries. Each government can only pass and enforce its laws within its sovereign territory – which extends to the outer limit of its territorial waters. It also has jurisdiction over matters in its airspace or in outer space, but only within the limits of international law. A country's parliament can regulate its citizens or companies both domestically and when they operate abroad. However, when a problem is not limited to the jurisdiction of a single country, intergovernmental cooperation is required.

Environmental problems have no respect for territorial borders. If the boundary waters of two countries are contaminated, those countries will need to cooperate, as neither one can manage the problem alone. If prevailing airflows carry heavy metals from one area to another, those in the polluted area are motivated to influence the policies of the countries in the offending jurisdiction. If an environmental problem is caused by multiple countries and affects them all, global solutions should be sought.

Today, we are aware that international environmental problems concern us all. Anyone following current affairs knows that climate change is altering the world we know irrevocably and that biological diversity is reducing at an accelerating rate. Many governments are aware that the best national environmental policy can be to try to influence a neighbouring country's environmental protection measures or its industrial policy, especially if this country is focused intensely on economic growth. We know that pollution does not respect boundaries and that solutions to our own environmental problems can often only be found internationally.

It is not just a question of how we protect our own national environment. Life on our planet is in actual danger. The scientific community tells us that our world is changing at an alarming rate. Although it is still possible for us to reduce greenhouse gas emissions and manage to get climate change under control, in the long term, there is still a significant risk that human impact will exceed the point of rapid climate change acceleration and natural feedback mechanisms will become a vicious cycle (for instance, global warming could increase the amount of water vapour – a significant greenhouse gas – in the atmosphere, which would then lead to further warming, and so on).

If we asked what kind of a political community the world should have in order to resolve global problems effectively, many people would answer that it should be a global government or at least an international administrative system with the power to enjoin governments to observe the obligations of international law. No such system exists now or in the foreseeable future. There is only a deficient community of governments with a regulatory system called international law. Many international environmental problems are the kind of global problems that call for joint and efficient actions by all humankind: for instance, the reduction of greenhouse gas emissions in the atmosphere. A world government would be a good idea for meeting climate change challenges, but as it does not exist, the only way to solve global and regional environmental problems is to purposefully develop international environmental law.

The nature of international law and environmental law

International environmental law forms part of international law.[4] How international environmental law is enacted depends on the rules defined in general international law. The rules on state responsibility in general international law also apply to all branches of international law, including international environmental law.

Economic, military and environmental changes create a pressure to review and develop international law. International law could be said to register the minimum consensus reached in the international community, stabilizing the international operating environment; international law can only rarely be referred to as a changing force in the operation of the international community.

International environmental treaties often work in a more instrumentalist way than the more traditional areas of international law. Decisions in certain branches of international environmental law are made through treaty regimes – to regulate whaling, for example, or to protect the unique ecosystems in Antarctica. This is closer to the way national legal systems work. One case decided by a domestic judiciary can change the entire basis of a society, or a statute drafted by a legislator can change the behaviour of the people. Similarly, decisions by the Court of Justice of the European Union[5] (CJEU) have influenced the direction of the integration process.

As international law lacks the usual elements of a municipal legal system such as a legislature and an executive, any meaningful changes in the world community cannot be achieved quickly or easily. There is no world government with executive power, no court system with mandatory jurisdiction, no world parliament to enact legislation that binds all states. On a global scale, there is no real political community that could stretch its loyalty and solidarity to all humankind, so it is only natural that there is no full-scale legal system either.

International law – and hence international environmental law – occupies the middle ground between idealism and realism. There are often very high expectations demanded from international law. The UN General Assembly, for instance, asked the International Court of Justice (ICJ) for an advisory opinion on whether threatening the use of nuclear weapons or using them violates international law. The International Court of Justice refused to state whether the use of nuclear weapons should be forbidden entirely or permitted by international law in the extreme case that the very existence of a state is threatened.[6] Many people expect international law to be able to end violent conflicts and to force all warring parties to observe the laws of war, or that the International Criminal Court should be able to capture and prosecute every war criminal.

For its part, international environmental law is expected to prevent climate change, the loss of biological diversity and the production and spreading of persistent organic pollutants (POPs). These are not realistic expectations in a world where the actors in international politics are made up of nearly 200 states as well as international organizations.

Despite this, international law can still be considered to have achieved much. The world has not, after all, turned out to be the scene of a no-rules power game as described by the Cold War realists – rather the opposite. The bulk of rules produced by governments and intergovernmental organizations are expanding at an exponential rate. It is remarkable that under international law different countries, cultures, religions, races and civilizations have organized themselves into an international community that speaks the common language of international law.

International environmental law, too, has accomplished a great deal. The community of states reacted to the first global environmental problem, ozone depletion, very quickly, and ahead of their original timeline. It now seems that the ozone layer is gradually being restored, although the ozone regime faces new challenges. While the action against climate change is certainly not before time, it does at least demonstrate that the international community is trying to do something about what is a massive environmental problem.

Factors affecting the development of international environmental law

To understand why a certain environmental regime was negotiated, or why it is in a state of change, we need first to understand the decisive factors in international environmental policy and law.

Science is an essential factor in international environmental law, much more so than in other branches of international law. Scientific understanding and knowledge are constantly changing, and this affects international environmental regimes in many ways. A good example of the changes in science is the concept of the 'ecosystem', a fairly novel concept that evolved gradually in the scientific literature of the 1930s.[7] An ecosystem refers to a functioning regional community of living organisms and non-living environmental factors.

It was long thought that ecosystems had an equilibrium that could be upset through pollution caused by humans: if the pollution ceased, it was thought that the ecosystem would recover its original equilibrium. We now understand that the ecosystems themselves experience great changes – even without human influence. This is why the concept of adaptive management is becoming prevalent in environmental governance; it is a model to adapt decision-making so that the dynamic change in ecosystems is taken into account.

International environmental regimes are largely based on such an adaptive management model. For example, many fish resource management regimes have been influenced by what we have learned about ecosystems. While the renewal of fish from one year to another was previously established by researching the extent of a species in a certain area, fish are now understood to be just one part of a wider ecosystem. The replenishment of fish stocks should, then, take into account the well-being of the entire ecosystem, of which the fish are just one part.

Science can also have a much more direct impact on how international environmental regimes develop. For example, in the ozone regime, science bore a direct influence on the decisions the parties made to restore the ozone layer. The climate regime unfortunately lacks a similar direct influence, because states negotiate the wording of popular reports by the Intergovernmental Panel on Climate Change (IPCC), which are made for decision-makers. Although these summaries are based on scientific data compiled by the IPCC, the summaries provide opportunities to water down scientific results, and are often the only sources the decision-makers have access to or the time to read.

Dedicated **interest groups** have different ways of influencing our understanding of environmental problems, and they have the means of lobbying states to act for or against the cause of environmental protection. For example, in 1988, the Convention on the Regulation of Antarctic Mineral Resource Activities[8] was negotiated to permit mining in Antarctica, with stringent environmental regulations, but partly as a result of lobbying by Greenpeace, two key states pulled out of the agreement. The Antarctic Environmental Protocol was then negotiated in 1991, prohibiting mining in Antarctica for 50 years.

Economic interest groups have financed various climate research projects in order to cast doubt on the contribution of human activities to climate change. Their aims are to protect entrenched economic systems depending on resources such as oil. One of the arguments of such interest groups is that environmental protection can undermine economic development and result in job losses in some areas.

International environmental regulation develops in line with changing prevailing **values and opinions**. When the whaling regime started in 1946, the objective was to secure sustainable whaling. When science proved that whaling was putting whales at risk of extinction, a ban on all commercial whaling was enacted in 1982. Although many whale populations have now recovered so much so that commercial whaling could start again without posing any threat to the sustainability of whale stocks, the values of many human communities have altered to the extent that it would be politically difficult to lift the ban. Television documentaries and films have instilled a sense of familiarity and affection for such animals and, as a result, large sections of the public employ more energy and resources to protect them than other less familiar species. Large mammals generally arouse the public's emotions in the West, and although ecologists say that all species are equally important parts of the ecological system, it is easier to mobilize public support to protect these so-called charismatic megafaunas.

The **development of international law** itself has changed people's attitudes. Individuals and civic organizations are no longer reluctant to participate in decisions affecting their environment, but increasingly perceive that it is their human right to do so. International human rights systems both globally and regionally urge decision-makers and industry to engage with the public in decisions concerning the state of the environment. It is no longer an interest restricted to industry and the authorities, but a human right guaranteed by international conventions.

Another motivation for states to pursue a policy of international environmental protection relates to **security policy**. During the Cold War especially, any cooperation between the United States and the Soviet Union (international environmental protection included) helped increase trust between the superpower blocs.

The establishment of the 1959 Antarctic Treaty is a good example: Antarctica was demilitarized and existing sovereignty claims were suspended. The United States and the Soviet Union were in the same position: they were both conducting a lot of scientific research in the area; neither one had claimed sovereignty in the continent; and both of them objected to the earlier sovereignty claims of other states (see Chapter 4, 'State jurisdiction', p. 90). As a result, while diplomacy in almost every other matter was suspended, they were in agreement on Antarctica and pursued a common solution to reserve Antarctica as a haven of science, peace and environmental protection.[9]

The other polar area, the Arctic, was a key strategic territory during the Cold War, because of the geographical proximity of both the Soviet Union and the United States and because nuclear submarines in the area could carry and release long-range nuclear missiles across the Arctic Ocean and threaten strategic targets. With this undoubtedly in mind, in his Murmansk speech in 1987, Soviet Secretary-General Mikhail Gorbachev proposed that the Arctic be reserved as an area of cooperation. Finland took heed of the proposal and suggested that all eight Arctic governments implement a policy of cooperative environmental protection. The process culminated in the Arctic Environmental Protection Strategy (AEPS) which was initiated in 1991. Earlier in the Cold War, efforts to create mutual trust had resulted in a trans-East-West agreement on environmental protection: in 1973 Denmark, Norway, Canada and the Cold War rivals the USA and the USSR signed the International Agreement on the Conservation of Polar Bears.[10]

So we see that many factors influence the development of an international environmental regime, as the case of the whaling regime well demonstrates.

The 1946 International Convention for the Regulation of Whaling is administered by the International Whaling Commission (IWC). It was established to promote sustainable whaling in the same way that fishing conventions administer various fish species: fishing is controlled only enough to secure the natural renewal of a certain fish population in a certain area from year to year.

Scientific research has allowed us to gradually increase our knowledge about whales, and we now understand whales to be intelligent animals with advanced mutual communication. Strong public organizations started to advocate the protection of whales and other animals, and government policies began to reflect this new perspective on whales.

In 1982, the IWC prohibited all commercial whaling (the prohibition came into force in hunting season 1985–86), which divided the treaty system: some governments pursued a total ban on whaling, while others wanted to continue whaling. Those who wished to continue the practice assumed various strategies: Canada withdrew from the agreement, while Norway filed a protest, as it considered that the prohibition was not based on scientific assessment. Having protested, Norway was free to continue whaling legally, which became the basis for diplomatic wrangling between Norway on one side and Finland and Sweden on the other regarding the hunting of minke whales. Japan, too, filed a protest but withdrew it when the United States threatened to apply trade sanctions and cut the Japanese fishing quota in its waters. Japan continues whaling, claiming that this is purely for the purposes of scientific research and within the limits of the agreement. Iceland withdrew from the IWC in 1992, but after a number of contentious and very close votes was readmitted in 2002 with a reservation to the whaling ban – a reservation to which half of the IWC states in attendance formally objected. The whaling agreement also permits traditional hunting by indigenous peoples.

The whaling regime has reached stalemate. More and more governments want to put an end to whaling, but those that support it stick to their opinions. This can be seen in the annual meetings of the IWC where the governments for and against whaling have accused each other of recruiting compliant countries into the commission and influencing their votes by promising to grant or threatening to withhold financial aid.

Australia recently initiated contentious proceedings against Japan before the International Court of Justice, asking it to declare that Japan is in violation of the whaling agreement. The Australian argument is that Japanese whaling is not intended for the purposes of scientific research but is in fact a smokescreen for harvesting whale meat to sell for food. The International Court of Justice has much to decide, and its decision may direct the development of whaling-related international law.

Although the scientific committee of the treaty regime has recommended limited whaling, it no longer seems to be a scientific issue but an issue of how governments and individuals relate to whales: are whales a natural resource that can and should be used for food, or are they an intelligent and sociable species that man should protect for future human generations? Or should man protect whales regardless of his own interests, just for the sake of the whales themselves?

Multiple actors

International law is a state-oriented legal system. States and their organizations can establish legally binding rules and agree international treaties. Similarly, it is primarily the practices and attitudes of states and their mutual organizations that have a bearing when deciding whether a rule has evolved into a rule of international customary law that binds states.

In contrast, international environmental law has challenged the idea that only governments can steer foreign policy. The de facto power of non-governmental actors is a key contributing factor in the creation and implementation of international environmental law, although it is governments that formally ratify the agreements and implement the rules of environmental treaties. This trend began on a large scale at the time of the preparations for the Rio UN environmental conference in 1992. Agenda 21 recorded the world community's plan for promoting sustainable development in the twenty-first century. A key element of the plan, initiated in 1989 and endorsed by 178 governments, is Section III, which strengthens the role of major groups such as women, children and youth, indigenous peoples, non-governmental organizations, local authorities, trade unions, business and industry, the scientific and technological community, and farmers in promoting sustainable development.

In any environmental regime or in negotiations for any international environmental agreement, non-governmental actors have used actual power in a number of different ways. Epistemic communities of scholars – communities that share roughly the same way of classifying the world intellectually – have significant influence over government representatives in the way regulations are developed on the basis of the latest environmental research. Environmental organizations have many strategies to influence the values and information base of the representatives of governments. The central organizations of business and industry often attempt to counter the arguments of these environmental organizations, turning the discourse towards the economic consequences of regulation, the country's competitive strength and possible job losses, for example. The secretariats of international environmental agreements for their part can influence what issues come under discussion and how, as they set the agenda and draft the preliminary texts of each environmental treaty.

Although the representatives of governments are the ones who formally make the decisions in environmental treaty negotiations and the agreements are usually ratified by national systems, there are in fact a large number of actors contributing towards the contents of environmental treaties.

How can small non-governmental actors influence global environmental negotiations?

Cooperation in Arctic environmental protection was initiated in 1991 with the Arctic Environmental Protection Strategy (AEPS), which later evolved into the Arctic Council. The Arctic Council is a soft-law cooperative body made up of the governments of eight Arctic states (five Nordic states, Russia, Canada and the USA). Indigenous groups have a unique status in the Arctic Council: they are permanent participants, and must be consulted by the Arctic states in all decision-making. Arctic cooperation concentrated from the start on producing information about the threats posed to vulnerable ecosystems mostly by long-range transboundary pollution.

A working group of the Arctic Council, the Arctic Monitoring and Assessment Programme (AMAP), showed in its 1997 assessment that persistent organic pollutants or POP compounds end up in the Arctic due to the so-called 'grasshopper effect'. These harmful compounds are especially detrimental to the indigenous peoples in the Arctic, whose traditional food sources comprise some of the most seriously contaminated animals (see Chapter 4, 'Long-range transboundary air pollution', p. 113).

It was interesting to see the creative impact of the coalition between indigenous groups and the scientific community at the global 2001 Stockholm Convention on POPs. Scientific assessments on environmental problems in the abstract are often insufficient and it often requires an explicit link to the human consequences for people to absorb the true impact. For example, ozone depletion became a much more acute environmental problem once it had been concretely proven that it was one of the causes of skin cancer in humans. AMAP scientific assessments on the danger to the Arctic and its indigenous peoples from POPs alone might not have been sufficient to have influenced governments' representatives were it not for the activism of the indigenous peoples most at risk.

It was therefore important that the Arctic indigenous peoples actively communicated the AMAP group's findings to the representatives in the negotiations.

They gave the environmental problem a human face and reminded the state negotiators of the injustice of emitting POP compounds: for example, victims included pregnant Inuit women living in an area where POP compounds are not even produced. Since effectively it was the foetuses of the Inuit women that would suffer from transboundary POPs pollution, the indigenous groups managed to present the environmental problem as an issue of intergenerational injustice.

The coalition between the scientific community and the indigenous peoples was possible because these actor groups had already previously collaborated through the activities of the Arctic Council.

The influence of international environmental law

The need for international law and regulation is obvious, but we should also ask ourselves whether these rules are effective. This is a matter of great debate, with certain schools of international relations alleging that rules in international politics have hardly any bearing.

As there is no global state, what incentives are there for governments to keep the promises they have made each other in a treaty? Many people think that governments' foreign policies are a mixture of self-defence and pursuit for power, influenced by factors such as the size of the country, its resources, military power and population.

This perspective tends to forget that even if there is no global state, it is the states themselves that create the rules of international law. It can be presumed that if states themselves create the rules via their explicit (treaty) or implicit (customary law) consent, we should also be able to expect that they would feel compelled to follow them.

National implementation of international environmental law

National implementation of international environmental law is a precondition for international environmental law to be effective and have any global influence. Only nation-states have the requisite legislative and enforcement powers to fully implement the obligations of international environmental law, even if other actors can be of some assistance.

In many states, international environmental law rules are 'internalized' as part of their domestic legal order. If the civil servants and the judiciary are accustomed to applying and administering only national legal rules, it stands to reason that international environmental rules will be better observed if they are first made part of the domestic legal order. There are no clear-cut dualist or monist systems, but it is possible to pin down the basic characteristics of a system: in some states (such as the United Kingdom) rules such as international treaties must be incorporated as part of national law or they are not legally binding domestically, while in others international law rules almost automatically become part of national law (the Netherlands, for example).

Dualist vs monist systems

Although there are no 'pure' dualist or monist models, the systems in various countries can be roughly divided as follows.

The dualist model is based on the idea that international law and national law are separate and independent legal systems with separate roles. If a state has assumed a constitutional dualist model, international law must expressly be made part of its national legal system in order to become domestically binding. For example, a state, before ratifying an international convention, amends its own laws to correspond to the obligations of the international convention. Many countries 'internalize' an international convention by a separate enforcement act or statute when they become party to it.

The monist model is based on the idea that international law is already and automatically a part of domestic law; therefore no special measures to incorporate international law are required. In each case, international conventions bind the states committed to them on the international legal plane, irrespective of whether the state employs a dualist or monist constitutional model.

Sometimes it is not enough just to incorporate international environmental rules into a national legal system, even if this is a good starting point. Often it is necessary to provide further regulations and measures to really ensure that measures such as international environmental treaties, for example, are implemented nationally. Most international environmental treaties specify what kind of national implementation measures are required – for instance, the establishment of competent authorities with specific duties, or the prohibition and criminalization of trade that contravenes a treaty's provisions – but sometimes states are expected to come up with their own ways to implement the treaty obligations. Under the Vienna Convention on the Law of Treaties as well as customary law of treaties, states are required to observe in good faith every treaty that is binding on them (*pacta sunt servanda*, Article 26[11]). There are various measures a state can put in place to implement treaty provisions nationally. In some extreme cases criminal law can be implemented, penalizing and prosecuting behaviour that violates an essential provision of an international environmental treaty.

Some international environmental treaties may pose problems to national implementation since it is not clear what their open-ended, loose provisions expect from the states. Often international treaty provisions, especially those negotiated between most major world states, are the result of numerous compromises, resulting in provisions that remain ambiguous and open-ended. An example of one such compromise is expressed in Article 8(j) of the Convention on Biological Diversity:[12]

> Each contracting Party shall, as far as possible and as appropriate ...
>   Subject to its national legislation, respect, preserve and maintain knowledge, innovations and practices of indigenous and local communities

embodying traditional lifestyles relevant for the conservation and sustainable use of biological diversity and promote their wider application with the approval and involvement of the holders of such knowledge, innovations and practices and encourage the equitable sharing of the benefits arising from the utilization of such knowledge, innovations and practices.

The Convention on Biological Diversity is now binding almost all over the world as almost all of the world's states are parties – but this is at the expense of its substantive content. The more states that are party to an environmental treaty, the more the process has to meet their multiple and varying demands, including the demands of those who are opposed to strict environmental regulation. The result of this is that it can become difficult to determine exactly what it is that the negotiating states have actually agreed.

In the case of Article 8 (which concerns the use of indigenous and local communities' traditional knowledge in promoting biological diversity) it is clear that the outcome is a result of many conflicting interests, with the result clearly very much a compromise. For example, each government is obliged to implement the obligations of this Article (a) as far as possible, (b) as appropriate, and (c) subject to national legislation. We should, however, note that a specific working group is developing this article in the biological diversity regime.[13] The development of Article 8(j) by the working group is a good example of the gradual developmental process of international environmental regimes in practice: even vague provisions can be given substantive content in a continuing process with the collaboration of other actors, such as indigenous representatives, thereby helping national civil servants devise measures to implement a given treaty provision.

How can we ensure states comply with international environmental rules?

After the Cold War in particular, research in international relations has been increasingly interested in why governments comply with 'promises written on a piece of paper'. This is due to increased empirical evidence of governments actually complying with international agreements and the decisions of international organizations.

The reality of how environmental treaties are applied is often rather bureaucratic. Most environmental treaties are applied in a routine manner; frequently those that are responsible for their application are unaware that the obligation actually originated in an environmental treaty at all. This is especially true in dualist countries where international obligations are internalized in the national legislation. A local official thinks he or she is applying national environmental law, whereas it is in fact a regulation in an international environmental treaty that has been incorporated into domestic environmental law. In the case of an EU member state, the process of application of a certain legal obligation from an environmental treaty is very long and complex. The EU itself is often the party (together with its member states) to an environmental treaty. The EU then implements the treaty through legislative acts (usually directives), which are then implemented in the various member states under domestic law.

For an individual official, there is a great responsibility in applying an international agreement. If a ministry in state A contacts a fellow party to an agreement, state B, to discuss a case of pollution damage potentially caused by that state, it is a challenging situation for officials in state B, as the reputation of their state in the international community is at stake.

An interesting older example of the pressure to comply with international environmental law can be seen in the case of the *Enskeri*, a Finnish tanker. Neste Oy's tanker the *Enskeri* was on its way to dump a large amount of arsenic on the high seas in the southern Atlantic in 1975. The matter was publicized at a time when the UN Convention on the Law of the Sea was being negotiated, and it aroused an enormous spate of criticism against Finland, as the operation was probably against Finland's international environmental obligations. As a result, Finland stepped back from the dumping.[14]

The question of how states' compliance of international environmental treaties could be improved has been the subject of much scholarly debate. The so-called facilitative school argues that contracting parties to an international environmental treaty should be aided and assisted by the treaty community to meet their obligations. Underlying this approach is the presumption that states do not intentionally breach their treaty commitments, but they do so rather because of lack of resources or knowledge. Downs[15] and his colleagues in the enforcement school counter this by arguing that international environmental treaties may well be observed primarily because the obligations they establish are so weak (such as those established by the Convention on Biological Diversity). Their argument is that when international obligations start to hurt (so-called deep obligations) states' own primary interests, they will no longer observe these treaties.[16]

Both schools therefore argue for different approaches for the observation of treaty regimes (even those treaty regimes that lay down deep obligations) in order to make sure that treaty obligations are respected and observed. The facilitative school seeks to encourage treaty parties to focus their efforts in assisting those states that have problems in complying, and to only penalize them as a last resort. Since the enforcement school presumes that states violate deep commitments intentionally, they argue for treaty regimes to establish strict compliance committees with the authority to punish any violations, thereby retaining the trust of the parties that do abide by the terms of the treaty.

As we will see in this book, it is the facilitative school that has had the most influence on how the treaty regimes try to make sure that their obligations are observed by contracting states. Actual penalties have been imposed only very rarely in the practice of international environmental treaty regimes. Yet, it is important to keep in mind the warning from the enforcement school: the more the obligations demand from states, the less we should expect them to abide by the provisions. It is crucial to find a solution to this dilemma since there are clearly problems in ensuring the mitigation obligations of the most ambitious international environmental treaty regime to date, the climate change regime, are observed. To date many states have either not observed the legally binding reduction obligations assumed in the Kyoto Protocol, or have opted out of the Protocol (Canada, for example) or its second commitment period (the Russian Federation). Moreover, the United States did not even become a party to the Kyoto Protocol, and major greenhouse gas-emitting developing states such as China[17] and India have no binding reduction obligation at all.[18]

Can international environmental law really resolve environmental problems?

There is an important distinction to be made between compliance with an environmental treaty and whether the treaty has the capacity to solve an international environmental problem in the first place. The risk is that the conflicting interests of the parties negotiating an environmental treaty can result in such compromised obligations that they are too weak to solve the problem that the treaty is intended to address. For example, in 1997, the negotiations resulting in the Kyoto Protocol linked to the UN Framework Convention on Climate Change were a diplomatic accomplishment in their time, but it was already known that the proposed 5 per cent reduction in greenhouse gas emissions from the levels registered in 1990 would not be sufficient to stop global warming and prevent climate change.

Another risk is that the environmental treaties that governments negotiate remain so ambiguous as to allow the parties enough room to interpret the rules in order to suit their own interests. Furthermore, environmental treaties rarely regulate military operations; governments have frequently specifically eliminated armed forces from the scope of application of an environmental treaty. This is problematic, since military operations are detrimental to the environment during times of peace as well as in times of war.

On the whole, we have reason to exercise a healthy degree of scepticism about the ways in which states have endeavoured to solve international environmental problems. Empirical research indicates that the ecological status of our environment is in a state of continual deterioration despite the enormous number of environmental treaties and other instruments directed towards environmental protection. This does not, however, mean that environmental treaties are meaningless. Many environmental problems have been contained and even eliminated by such agreements. Governments have proved themselves capable of reacting efficiently and quickly to a global environmental problem: the emissions of ozone-depleting CFC gases (chlorofluorocarbons) have been successfully reduced by the Montreal Protocol and its amendments (and adjustments) and, as a result, the ozone layer is expected to be restored in a couple of decades.

Whether we think that international environmental law is capable of providing solutions to environmental problems depends on the perspective with which we approach the question. For a lawyer, the effectiveness of international environmental law is primarily considered by evaluating whether or not governments are complying with the rules of international environmental agreements. For a natural scientist, however, the issue is different: the capacity of international environmental agreements to solve an environmental problem carries more weight.

US professor Oran Young expresses it well: we can never know for sure whether an environmental problem will be solved by a particular agreement, as the world is full of interrelated environmental problems. We cannot learn much about the effect of an environmental agreement just by studying how its rules have been complied with; governments are, after all, able to create agreements that barely bind them to do anything at all. According to Young, the crucial factor is whether an environmental regime creates around it a body of enthusiastic actors who are committed to solving the particular environmental problem. For example, in some cases senior-ranking government officials have become 'ambassadors' in their respective countries for the treaties they have helped to negotiate. Partly as a result of their support, the rules of the environmental treaty are then gradually incorporated into their respective domestic environmental policy.

Responsibilities of states and businesses

International environmental law, like all branches of international law, is a state-centred system. States make the rules of international law, and are in turn expected to implement them. However, the international community is moving increasingly towards a global economic system, especially since the Cold War. Large corporations are no longer seen as the flagships of any particular nation as they have shareholders all over the world and their top management is often recruited globally. It is the duty of the management to secure maximum profit for the company's shareholders in a global market.

The free movement of investments, utilities and services around the world has fundamentally changed the international order. This freedom of movement has been made possible through multilateral agreements between governments. Above all, the World Trade Organization (WTO), with its almost globally binding agreements and very efficient legal dispute settlement process, has gradually made most of the world a global market place. The immense speed at which international trade law has been generated has resulted in a world increasingly controlled by private industry, mainly multinational corporations.

The cost of environmental protection to businesses

There is good reason to ask why states and their taxpayers should be responsible for environmental protection if environmental damage is caused by multinational businesses with global shareholders, employees and strategies. Before open markets, a state was able to control the operations of companies through its political and legal system. This was because big businesses did not actually need to compete, since there were fewer competitors fighting for market share. Economic globalization has completely changed this.

We find ourselves, therefore, in a very different global situation now. Multinational businesses have become increasingly competitive, and are able to determine factors such as which country offers them the cheapest labour, the safest operational environment, and the least environmental obligations in order to enhance profits.[19] Environmental protection poses a significant expense for companies, so those states that mandate or enforce only minimal environmental obligations (or, for example, low labour standards, weak tax requirements, lax anti-corruption measures) are potentially more attractive to companies to locate within their jurisdiction. Some experts argue that this has already caused competition between countries to reduce environmental protection measures (the 'race to the bottom').

Ships are being withdrawn from the registries of those countries that set stricter rules related to their condition and operation. Certain so-called 'flag of convenience' states set no strict requirements on ships, and collect high tax revenue by offering ships the opportunity to register with limited oversight. As the regulation of seafaring is essentially based on the principle that the flag state has jurisdiction, it can be difficult to bring these states to account for failing to regulate and control the extent to which ships are fulfilling safety and environmental protection standards.

Companies that continue to operate in countries with stricter environmental controls face unequal competition as rivals based in countries with less strict environmental controls can potentially be more competitive. Shouldn't international environmental law regulate companies instead of states? Wouldn't it be better if international agreements were concluded by businesses in order to lay down identical environmental obligations to all those who operate in a particular market segment?

The 'polluter pays' principle

International environmental law is not an independent legal system, as we have seen above, but one of several branches of international law (such as international human rights, international law of the sea, and international trade law). The primary subjects of international law are states: as sovereign actors in the international community they are entitled to conclude treaties, and have (in principle) international-legal operational responsibility within their territory. The principle of no-harm in international law requires states to regulate their polluting operations carefully in order to avoid causing environmental damage to territories belonging to other states or to areas beyond national jurisdiction.

The 'polluter pays' principle has been applied within certain treaties in order to make private enterprises or industry sectors accountable for environmental damage. Such agreements primarily concern certain high-risk operations such as nuclear power plants or oil transportation, and even then they have only a limited effect. A small number of treaties have even been made to allow for compensation claims from victims of environmental accidents in the legal system of the country of their choice. Private enterprises have been heavily involved in efforts to reduce greenhouse gas emissions, although they are not directly involved in the negotiations; climate regime is, after all, ultimately a matter for agreement by states.

Generally, a company can only be held legally accountable for environmental damage through the national legal system. How this happens in practice depends on the rules relating to transboundary damage. For instance, Article 3 of the Nordic Environmental Protection Convention[20] states:

> Any person who is affected or may be affected by a nuisance caused by environmentally harmful activities in another Contracting State shall have the right to bring before the appropriate Court or Administrative Authority of that State the question of the permissibility of such activities including the question of measures to prevent damage, and to appeal against the decision of the Court or the Administrative Authority to the same extent and on the same terms as a legal entity of the State in which the activities are being carried out.
>
> The provisions of the first paragraph of this Article shall be equally applicable in the case of proceedings concerning compensation for damage caused by environmentally harmful activities. The question of compensation shall not be judged by rules which are less favourable to the injured party than the rules of compensation of the state in which the activities are being carried out.

Anyone affected can, then, take a claim of compensation for transboundary environmental damage to a court in the state in which the damaging activities are being conducted.

Figure 1.1 Graffiti protest against US oil company Texaco in Quito, the capital of Ecuador in 2003. Texaco's present owner Chevron was in 2011 found liable for compensation totalling $18 billion for environmental damage in the Amazon. Texaco drilled for oil in the rainforest areas of Northern Ecuador in the 1970s and 1980s. According to environmental organizations, the drilling resulted in contamination of the soil and water in the area and violated the rights of the indigenous peoples. Chevron is now adopting various legal strategies to seek to prevent the enforcement of the ruling and to take it to a court of arbitration. (Photo © Rebecca M. Bratspies)

Increasing the motivation of business for environmental protection

In general terms, we can see that international environmental law is still strongly based on treaties negotiated between states. These treaties are used by states to try to solve international environmental problems, according to the rules of international law: states being the only actors that can make legally binding rules. The system of international law does not easily capture the reality where companies operate in a global market place.

The reality is not quite as gloomy. Although environmental treaties are concluded between states, they do also oblige businesses to observe stricter environmental regulations. A state enforces an international treaty's environmental protection measures at national level and, in turn, national legislation obligates companies to implement these measures in a number of ways. Increased cooperation between states can help to respond to the problem of the 'race to the bottom': they have the power to control and determine the ways in which companies operate in order to solve these global problems. This will require improved commitment from businesses. There is increasing discussion regarding ways in which companies could participate more fully in the operation of international environmental regimes and contribute to the development of international environmental rules.

Many enterprises and industry sectors already factor environmental protection into their strategies of their own accord as part of their corporate social responsibility policy, reflecting increasing public concern for our environment.[21] An environmental disaster can be catastrophic for a multinational company, its management and its shareholders in many ways, – and can result in a decline in its market value, with the associated negative public perception.

The financing and insurance sectors have – for obvious reasons – long been keen to become more involved with international environmental protection. Reliability and reputation are of paramount importance for banks and other financial institutions in terms of competitive strength. Insurance companies are especially worried about the effects of climate change, as their liabilities are increased.

Equator principles

Some very innovative initiatives have been created to try to increase the willingness of businesses to protect the environment. The so-called Equator Principles constitute a set of standards aimed at environmental protection. Private commercial banks that give loans can elect to pledge to follow these principles. The Equator Principles have now been adopted by 72 banks in 27 countries, and their joint share of loans in the emerging markets is 70 per cent.

If a bank commits to these principles, it pledges itself to ensure, *inter alia*, that the industrial or infrastructural projects it finances are first subjected to a close environmental assessment. The banks that have signed up to the principles have created their own system of supervision to ensure that the principles are upheld. An affected party can submit a complaint about the environmental impact of a financed project, many of which must also undergo through independent expert monitoring. A community of non-governmental organizations called Banktrack monitors banks' compliance with the principles.

What motivates banks to create their own rules for environmental protection? The answer is simple: reliability and reputation are key to the competitive strength of a bank; banks therefore adopt the Equator Principles for their own interests to increase their competitive power.

Questions and research tasks

1   What would you consider to be the most efficient strategy for environmental protection? Should, for instance, the focus be on enforcement of existing international environmental law? Should ways be found to better motivate multinational companies to protect the environment more efficiently? If you choose this option, how could companies be motivated? What other options would you emphasize?

2   Try to find a website that gives an objective discussion of the whaling treaty system. Then find a scientific article that you think gives a neutral account of ways in which the whaling system might be developed.

3   Consider institutions where you might expect to find good, topical articles and comment on the development of international environmental law. Find the homepages and explore the resources.

Notes

1   Contamination and pollution are used here as general terms to refer to harmful impact on the environment from human activity, understood in a wide sense. The UN Convention on the Law of the Sea, for instance, defines pollution of the marine environment for its purposes in Article 1 (4): "'pollution of the marine environment' means the introduction by man, directly or indirectly, of substances or energy into the marine environment, including estuaries, which results or is likely to result in such deleterious effects as harm to living resources and marine life, hazards to human health, hindrance to marine activities, including fishing and other legitimate uses of the sea, impairment of quality for use of sea water and reduction of amenities'. An agreement generally needs to consider what kinds of environmental impact it can be applied to. A good example is the so-called Espoo Convention (Convention on Environmental Impact Assessment in a Transboundary Context). Article 1(vii) states: "'Impact' means any effect caused by a proposed activity on the environment including human health and safety, flora, fauna, soil, air, water, climate, landscape and historical monuments or other physical structures or the interaction among these factors; it also includes effects on cultural heritage or socio-economic conditions resulting from alterations to those factors.' It is worth considering whether or not this definition includes the reduction of natural diversity.

2   By international environmental regulation, I refer to intentional actions by governments to change human behaviour by legally binding and so-called soft-law rules. Soft-law instruments (e.g. declarations or action programmes) do not strictly bind governments legally, but signal political or moral commitment. International environmental law is a broader notion than international environmental regulation, since it also comprises other ways in which rules and principles develop. When governments react to each other's actions, it can be deemed after a certain time that a principle within international customary law has evolved. It has not been expressly created by states, but it has evolved gradually as a combined outcome of the practices and legal views of governments.

3   Directive 2010/31/EU of the European Parliament and of the Council, of 19 May 2010, on the energy performance of buildings, http://eur-lex.europa.eu/LexUriServ/LexUriServ.do?uri=CELEX:32010L0031:EN:NOT

4   International environmental law is a branch of international law, though research in international environmental law is more and more diverging from mainstream

research in international law. International law has expanded enormously during the past few decades, but it can still be defined as a legal system that mainly regulates intergovernmental relationships. International environmental law has challenged this government-oriented structure of classical international law. Private international law for its part concentrates on international legal relationships between private bodies (citizens, companies). It defines, *inter alia*, the national legislation which applies to private legal relationships.

5 This book does not discuss EU environmental law and regulation as part of international environmental law, though some scholars do. The EU is so clearly a legal system of its own, *sui generis*, that its environmental law is discussed separately under Chapter 4 ('Limits of territorial sovereignty', pp. 94–104).

6 The Court did point out that in almost every case, international law, including international environmental law, prohibits the threat or use of nuclear weapons.

7 See Frank Benjamin Golley, *A History of the Ecosystem Concept in Ecology: More than the Sum of the Parts*, New Haven, CT: Yale University Press, 2012.

8 See http://sedac.ciesin.org/entri/texts/acrc/cramra.txt.html

9 The Antarctic Treaty, 1 December 1959, Washington DC, http://www.ats.aq/e/ats.htm

10 See http://sedac.ciesin.org/entri/texts/polar.bears.1973.html

11 http://untreaty.un.org/ilc/texts/instruments/english/conventions/1_1_1969.pdf

12 Convention on Biological Diversity, http://www.cbd.int/convention/text/. The United Nations Environment Programme (UNEP) convened the Ad Hoc Working Group of Experts on Biological Diversity in November 1988 to explore the need for an international convention on biological diversity. The Convention was opened for signature on 5 June 1992 at the United Nations Conference on Environment and Development (the Rio 'Earth Summit') and it entered into force on 29 December 1993.

13 See http://www.cbd.int/traditional/

14 Holger Rotkirch, 'Tapaus Enskeri', in Timo Koivurova (ed.) *Kansainvälistyvä oikeus. Kari Hakapään juhlakirja*, pp. 441–60, Lapin yliopiston oikeustieteellisiä julkaisuja, series C41, 2005.

15 G.W. Downs, D.M. Rocke and P.N. Barsoom, 'Is the Good News About Compliance Good News About Co-Operation?', at http://www.nyu.edu/gsas/dept/politics/faculty/downs/goodnews.pdf

16 Interestingly, the climate change regime's compliance committee is made up of two branches: facilitative and enforcement.

17 China is currently the biggest greenhouse gas emitter of all states. See the respected International Energy Statistics as compiled by the US Energy Information Administration, http://www.eia.gov/cfapps/ipdbproject/IEDIndex3.cfm?tid=90&pid=44&aid=8

18 See further Chapter 7 for a review of the latest developments of the climate regime.

19 Note that most of the environmental legislation in a state where a multinational company is registered will apply to the company, although it can often be difficult to bring the company to account if it operates on the other side of the world.

20 Nordic Environmental Protection Convention (Norway, Sweden, Finland and Denmark), Stockholm, 1974, http://sedac.ciesin.org/entri/texts/acrc/Nordic.txt.html

21 There is an increasing use by the companies of mitigation hierarchy and net positive impact methodologies to conserve biodiversity. See the IUCN report on Rio Tinto, which takes up both concepts, at http://data.iucn.org/dbtw-wpd/edocs/2012-049.pdf

Further reading

Alam, S., Bhuiyan, H., Chowdhury, T.M.R. and Techera, E.J., *The Routledge Handbook of International Environmental Law*, London: Routledge, 2012.

Beyerlin U. and Marauhn, T., *International Environmental Law*, Oxford: Hart Publishing, 2011.

Birnie, P., Boyle, A. and Redgwell, C., *International Law and the Environment*, 3rd rev. edn, Oxford: Oxford University Press, 2009.

Bodansky, D., *The Art and Craft of International Environmental Law*, Cambridge, MA: Harvard University Press, reprint edn, 2011.

Chayes, A. and Chayes, A.H., *The New Sovereignty: Compliance with International Regulatory Agreements*, rev. edn, Cambridge, MA: Harvard University Press, 1998.

Downs, G.W., Rocke, D.M. and Barsoom, P.N., 'Is the Good News About Compliance Good News About Co-Operation?', http://www.nyu.edu/gsas/dept/politics/faculty/downs/goodnews.pdf.

Hunter, D., Salzman, J. and Zaelke, D., *International Environmental Law and Policy*, 4th edn, New York: Foundation Press, 2011.

Koivurova, T. and Pölönen, I. 'Transboundary Environmental Impact Assessment in the Case of the Baltic Sea Gas Pipeline', *International Journal of Marine and Coastal Law*, 25, 2010, pp. 151–81. (Also in *German Yearbook of International Law*, 52, 2009, pp. 293–326.)

Louka, E., *International Environmental Law: Fairness, Effectiveness, and World Order*, Cambridge: Cambridge University Press, 2006.

Sands, P., *Principles of International Environmental Law*, Cambridge: Cambridge University Press, 2003.

Shaw, M.N., *International Law*, 6th edn, Cambridge: Cambridge University Press, 2008.

Siegele, L. and Ward, H., 'Corporate Social Responsibility: A Step Towards Stronger Involvement of Business in MEA Implementation?', *Review of European Community & International Environmental Law*, 16(2), July 2007, pp. 135–44.

Yang, T., 'The Relationship Between Domestic and International Environmental Law', in R. Martella and B. Grosko (eds) *International Environmental Law: The Practitioner's Guide to the Laws of the Planet*, American Bar Association, 2013.

Young, O., *The Institutional Dimensions of Environmental Change: Fit, Interplay, and Scale*, Cambridge, MA: MIT Press, 2002.

Websites

Convention on Biological Diversity (CBD): http://www.cbd.int

International Institute for Sustainable Development, The Earth Negotiations Bulletin: www.iisd.ca

International Union for Conservation of Nature (IUCN), Law Commission: http://www.iucn.org/about/union/commissions/cel/

The Equator Principles: http://www.equator-principles.com/

The Rockefeller University: http://phe.rockefeller.edu/verification/

United Nations Environment Programme (UNEP), legal matters: http://www.unep.org/law/

United Nations International Law Commission: http://www.un.org/law/ilc/

World Wide Fund for Nature (WWF): http://www.wwf.org

2 The history of international environmental law

It is fascinating to think that there are many different ways in which we can interpret our past. Considered from the perspective of international political science, our history is full of war and aggression: the First World War was followed swiftly by the Second World War and then the Cold War. And when we thought there would be no more, the War on Terror began.

International lawyers see things differently: they do not deny the existence of these wars or claim that there won't be any more. The tradition in international law looks at our history as one long learning experience rather than as proof that the world has not changed. The same period of time that international political science views as filled with aggression is seen, in international law, as steady progress towards a more regulated international community.

The greatest challenge for those engaged in international law is not the absence of international cooperation but somewhat the reverse: the fact that the body of regulation is increasing too rapidly and beginning to fragment. On the other hand, we must acknowledge that all these rules have not been sufficient to eliminate international conflicts and problems. Similarly, agreements are being made at an accelerating pace in the field of international environment protection, yet still environmental problems continue to escalate.

This chapter reviews the history of international environmental law. The development of international environmental law is considered in the context of wider influential developments in international politics and law. Finally, we draw some conclusions as to the major trends that have shaped the evolution of international environmental law.

The development of international environmental law as part of the evolution of international politics and law

International environmental regulation has naturally developed in the context of the general development of international relations, although it is often discussed discretely in textbooks. International law textbooks survey international environmental law as if it were an entirely separate branch within international law and politics. The Second World War, the Cold War and the extremely rapid liberalization of world trade, especially since the World Trade Organization (WTO) was established in 1995, have undoubtedly affected the way international environmental policy is made.

Long before the actual international environmental protection movement began, states and groups of states had already agreed on numerous measures to protect individual animal species and ecosystems. The main objectives were either the sustainable use of marine resources (mainly various fish and whale species) or the conservation of animals that were useful to man. Among the first early protective measures was the 1902 Convention for the Protection of Birds Useful to Agriculture, which is considered the first multilateral environmental treaty.[1] There were also several transboundary river treaties which included articles on environmental protection, such as the 1909 International Boundary Waters Treaty between the USA and Canada, for example. One early intergovernmental environmental protection project, the International Convention for the Prevention of Pollution of the Sea by Oil, perhaps the most ambitious of its time, was targeted towards minimizing oil emissions into the sea in 1954.

The UN and increasing international cooperation

It is essential to consider environmental protection measures before and after the Second World War in the context of the international politics of the time. After the war, the focus of international politics was on the establishment of the first truly global intergovernmental organization (IGO). Having learnt from the experiences of the war, the governments of the world established the universal organization, the United Nations (UN), whose main objective was to prevent wars between its member states.

The League of Nations, which operated between the World Wars, only included some of the international community (the USA, for instance, was not included). Although aimed at preventing wars by establishing obligations of arbitration on states that were on the brink of war, the League of Nations did not go so far as to prohibit war as the last resort of foreign policy or to create a mechanism for intervention in the event of the threat of war. The UN sought to learn from the limitations of the League of Nations and charged five permanent members of the Security Council with the maintenance of international peace and security (the USSR, the USA, France, the United Kingdom and China). However, for a long time, the Cold War between the Soviet bloc and the United States prevented any meaningful intervention by the UN in wars between states.

The UN was more successful when it started promoting human rights. The atrocities of the Second World War meant that people no longer trusted government policy alone to shape the development of their communities, and so the UN Charter expressing the commitment to promoting human rights was established (Articles 1(3) and 55). This was followed in 1948 by the UN Universal Declaration of Human Rights.[2] Over the years, many binding international human rights agreements have been concluded under the auspices of the UN. Not one of these international agreements, however, explicitly refers to the right to a decent or healthy environment, although some regional human rights agreements, such as the African Charter on Human and People's Rights, do expressly mention the right to a healthy environment.[3]

This goes to show how little attention was paid to environmental protection in the aftermath of the Second World War. This was understandable, as at this period in time the significance to human communities of ecosystems and the biosphere was not yet widely understood and the international community was concerned with other priorities. On the other hand, events of the Second World War demonstrated only too well that humankind had developed terrible powers of destruction that could eliminate our entire world. For in inventing atomic weapons, such as those used by the United States on Hiroshima and Nagasaki, Japan, we had created the potential to destroy life on our planet as we know it.

The rise of the former colonies

The evolution of human rights saw the colonial policies of European governments being questioned. The UN Charter had declared that all peoples are equal. In the 1950s, many African and Asian colonies took matters into their own hands and fought for independence from their European colonial rulers. The resulting paradigm shift in the participants in the international community saw a change in the nature of international law itself; it guaranteed sovereignty and independence to all those colonies that sought it.

As African and Asian countries became independent, they formed a stronger voice in international politics and law. This was especially manifest in the UN General Assembly, where each of the UN member states have one vote; the developing countries as a group were able to work for the reversal of colonization and to promote the so-called New International Economic Order (NIEO). One important result was that these newly independent developing countries were able to claim permanent sovereignty over the natural resources in their territories. Many of these newly independent developing countries now began to nationalize projects in their territories under which Western companies had previously exploited their natural resources. The former colonizing Western states responded by demanding compensation to their companies for the losses incurred, but the developing countries were not prepared to pay.

The influence of African and Asian governments increased in international politics and law in the 1960s and 1970s. At a time when interest in environmental protection was being awakened with initiatives such as the Declaration of the United Nations Conference on the Human Environment in 1972,[4] developing countries continued to concentrate on promoting the implementation of the NIEO. In 1973, the Organization of Petroleum Exporting

Countries (OPEC) caused a worldwide panic by refusing to transport oil to Western states whose economies were fundamentally dependent upon it.

Several international environmental agreements were concluded between the late 1960s and the late 1970s in which the developing countries played no significant role in negotiations. However, these developing nations did play an active part in the negotiations for the 'constitution of the oceans' – the UN Convention on the Law of the Sea (UNCLOS) – between 1973 and 1982. The negotiation process was probably the most ambitious that the international community has ever attempted. Part XII of the Convention concerns the protection of the marine environment and is still the only global agreement that concentrates on the environment of 70 per cent of the Earth's surface. Part XII is intended to define how operations that threaten the maritime environment could be conducted in a sustainable way. The UNCLOS also specifically considers the interests and concerns of developing countries.

The emergence of multilateral environmental protection

Various sporadic multilateral agreements – also in the realm of environmental protection – were concluded before the UN Conference on the Human Environment in Stockholm in 1972, but it can be argued that the Stockholm Conference was the first to join together existing and planned international environmental regulatory processes under one umbrella with its declaration and action plan. The establishment of the UN Environment Programme (UNEP) made it possible to organize international environmental regulation into a dedicated separate stream from the institutional perspective as well.

It was only after the Stockholm Conference, in the mid-1970s, that the first textbooks in international environmental law, in Spanish and in English, began to appear. These textbooks had a significant impact in terms of simplifying a complex reality: the first step in distinguishing international environmental law from general international law as an academic discipline.

Between the late 1960s and the early 1980s, several multilateral environmental agreements were negotiated. Nuclear power was considered a problematic source of energy from a very early stage. Even with the utmost diligence, nuclear disasters can still happen, as the Fukushima power plant disaster demonstrated in 2011. As early as 1960, the members of the Organisation for Economic Co-operation and Development (OECD) agreed a regional convention on nuclear liability.[5] In 1963, the Vienna Convention on Civil Liability for Nuclear Damage was agreed under the auspices of the International Atomic Energy Agency (IAEA),[6] and in 1971, the International Maritime Organization (IMO) adopted the Convention relating to Civil Liability in the Field of Maritime Carriage of Nuclear Material[7] (the Convention entered into force 20 years later in 1991).

At the time, the primary focus was on the development of marine environmental law, both regionally (the Baltic Marine Environment Protection Convention in 1974, for example) and above all globally. This period culminated in the ratification of the UN Convention on the Law of the Sea, Part XII of which relates to the protection of the marine environment. Prior to this and until the early 1970s, protection of the marine environment focused primarily on oil pollution from tankers: the first such convention was the 1954 International Convention for the Prevention of Pollution of the Sea by Oil,[8] followed by the Convention on Civil Liability for Oil Pollution Damage[9] and the International Convention Relating to Intervention on the High Seas in Cases of Oil Pollution Casualties.[10]

This most recent Convention was motivated largely by the first major oil disaster, in 1967, when the *Torrey Canyon* tanker grounded off the Cornish coast in England. Around 170 million litres of oil were spilled into the sea. The efforts to disperse the oil with chemicals resulted in serious environmental damage and the British finally decided to bomb the tanker in order to burn the oil on the high seas. The *Torrey Canyon* case also saw the first negotiations relating to liability for damages for oil spills in the light of the catastrophic pollution damage caused to the Cornish coast.

Figure 2.1 Oil tanker catastrophes have often given rise to a pressure to regulate.
(Photo © ITOPF)

The major global agreements relating to the protection of the marine environment were the London 1972 Convention on the Prevention of Marine Pollution by Dumping of Wastes and Other Matter[11] and the 1973 International Convention for the Prevention of Pollution from Ships, complemented with a Protocol in 1978 (together known as MARPOL).[12] The MARPOL regime aims to reduce and minimize marine pollution from ships, both from accidents and from routine operations. The Convention contains six annexes that concentrate on controlling and preventing oil, noxious liquid substances carried in bulk, and harmful substances in packaged form from being spilled into the sea. The Convention also aims at controlling contamination by solid waste and sewage, as well as air pollution caused by ships.

The adoption of the UNCLOS was a significant accomplishment because it created general overarching principles in relation to all activities that pollute the sea. The regulation of no other part of the biosphere has matched it, although a law of the atmosphere was discussed without result in the mid-1980s (it was to have included regulation on ozone depletion, climate change and the prevention of airborne pollutants).[13]

Global development has impacted on other areas of nature protection as well. The 1971 Ramsar Convention[14] created the basis for protecting wetlands important for waterfowl, whereas the 1972 World Heritage Convention[15] protects natural heritage sites. The Bonn and Bern Conventions of 1979 aim at protecting migratory wild animals[16] and European wildlife.[17] CITES[18] from 1975 and its annexes aim to protect species of flora and fauna by limiting their international trade: the idea is that if organisms or parts of organisms cannot be traded commercially, the economic motivation to collect or hunt endangered species will be eliminated: in essence, eliminating demand will eliminate supply.

The first real phase of international environmental regulation was tentative; the initial objective was to protect the environment from great threats such as oil tankers, nuclear power plants and intentional waste dumping. At the same time, however, hybrid organizations such as the International Union for Conservation of Nature (IUCN)[19] began to create a separate discipline of international environmental law soon after the Stockholm Conference with a single clear objective: to prevent and eventually eliminate international environmental problems. The establishment of the UNEP institutionally helped establish international environmental protection as a separate discipline of international politics and law.

Phases in the development of international environmental law

Global awakening to environmental problems and the change in the economic system

During the 1980s, the international community came to acknowledge that humankind was responsible for causing serious, global, long-term environmental problems. The extensive hole in the ozone layer protecting the earth from ultraviolet radiation, which was first confirmed over Antarctica, forced us to admit that industrial operations can have far-reaching consequences. Awareness of climate change and the rapid depletion of biodiversity also increased during this period.

The preparation process for the 1992 UN Conference on the Environment in Rio was different from the 1972 Stockholm process: it evolved into a veritable battle between the richer North, which was pushing for stricter environmental protection, and the poorer South, which prioritized its economic progress. The developing countries were happy with the loose wording of the UN-established Brundtland Commission that human communities should aim for 'sustainable development'. The industrial countries' agenda was considered rather hypocritical by the developing countries: the industrial countries were, after all, the ones that had caused both global and local environmental problems, and they had the resources, the technology and the know-how to mitigate these problems.

The industrial countries managed to negotiate a relatively ambitious Rio Declaration, the Agenda 21 (a plan for promoting environmental protection during the next century), the Framework Convention on Climate Change[20] to combat climate change, the Convention on Biological Diversity[21] to combat the loss of natural diversity, and the non-binding forest principles, but the developing countries were still able to promote their own interests during the negotiations. Essential to the developing countries were the right to development and to a greater stake in future negotiations to address the world's environmental problems. For the developing countries, the top priority was to combat poverty, since poverty results in an unsustainable future and intensifies environmental problems.

The Rio 1992 Conference took place at a time when the idea prevailed that a new fair world order based on international law could be attained. The dissolution of the Soviet Union and the end of the Cold War had dismissed socialism as a viable system and resulted in a global change in both security and economic systems. The two-pole world turned into a world dominated by the USA. The UN Security Council finally started to function as it was supposed to: to intervene in wars and threats of war. US troops led the UN Security Council mandated forces to eject Iraqi troops when they invaded Kuwait in 1990.

The special status of the United States was already evident in the Rio 1992 Convention. The USA refused to sign the Convention on Biological Diversity and made interpretive statements regarding certain principles of the Rio Declaration. During Bill Clinton's two presidential terms, the USA assumed a more international foreign policy, and the Clinton administration was active in the negotiations leading to the adoption of the Kyoto Protocol. However, disappointingly, the next US President, George W. Bush, refused to ratify the Kyoto Protocol.[22]

Probably the most profound change was the one that took place in the global economic system after the fall of the Soviet Union. The free trade system based on capitalist principles permitted goods, capital and services to cross borders. The establishment of the World Trade Organization (WTO) in 1995 was an enormous force towards global removal of market boundaries. It was complemented by regional free trade areas such as the European Community (EC/EU). However, the breakthrough of free trade caused problems for international environmental protection. Unilateral measures to promote environmental protection were more frequently considered as a form of economic protectionism, and as such potentially prohibited by the WTO rules and principles.

The beginnings of international environmental law

In the second phase, the actors in international environmental politics were faced with highly complex environmental problems. This phase in history was dominated primarily by a focus on so-called diffuse pollution: pollution that springs from many small sources and grows into a severe contamination problem, which is not distinctly traceable to any single source. The problems that emerged in the 1980s required huge volumes of scientific research and bodies that were able to analyse and make sense of this vast wealth of information; one such body was the Intergovernmental Panel on Climate Change (IPCC). The era was also characterized by the emergence of genuinely global environmental problems: ozone depletion, climate change and loss of biodiversity are problems that were not caused by any single country or actor, but they affect us all.

Pollution by many small sources is difficult to regulate, as no single government or identifiable factory can be deemed responsible for the pollution. There are just so many factories, cars and energy plants that discharge air pollutants, each on its own producing a negligible contribution, but creating significant cumulative damage and often transboundary damage, where air currents carry pollutants to other regions, causing problems such as acid rain, for example.

The first regional environmental treaty system to address such a pollution problem was adopted under the United Nations Economic Commission for Europe (UNECE) in 1979: the Convention on Long-range Transboundary Air Pollution (LRTAP).[23] The LRTAP process was initiated by the 1975 Conference on Security and Cooperation in Europe (CSCE) (and the fifth Chapter in its Final Act). The LRTAP Convention set an example for environmental regulation generally: in 1979, the LRTAP Convention was adopted which only contained general obligations; it has since been supplemented by several protocols. By supplementing an initial Convention with numerous protocols, we can ensure that we begin environmental regulation early and make it more specified and intensified as our knowledge about the environment increases.

The focus of environmental regulation relatively soon turned to global environmental problems: climate change and ozone depletion. In 1985, the Vienna Convention[24] sought to address ozone depletion by means of general obligations, but the discovery of a vast Antarctic ozone hole really awakened people to the problem later the same year. The reduction and elimination of chlorofluorocarbons or CFC compounds has proceeded rapidly since the 1987 Montreal Protocol.[25]

Climate change, loss of biodiversity and the poor state of the world's forests were on the UN agenda when the 20-year follow-up meeting to the Stockholm Conference was arranged in Rio de Janeiro in 1992. There was still some scepticism as to the scientific evidence for climate change, so the World Meteorological Organization (WMO) and the UNEP established the Intergovernmental Panel on Climate Change (IPCC) in 1988.

The separate negotiating processes proceeded rapidly before the Rio Summit, but developing countries now assumed a much more active role than in the Stockholm Conference. A major confrontation between the richer North and the poorer South related to the protection of tropical rainforests – 'the lungs of our planet'. As these forests are of utmost importance for both biological diversity and for combating climate change – and as they are being destroyed at an accelerating rate – it was essential from the point of view of the North to reach an agreement to allow for better protection of the rainforests. From the perspective of the developing countries, however, this was viewed as a neo-colonialist strategy to limit their economic growth. Since the 1992 UNCED took place in Brazil, the home of the Amazon rainforest, it was apparent that no easy solution could be found. The industrial countries' objective to protect the rainforests by means of a strict climate agreement or a binding forest agreement was not achieved. However, much was accomplished in Rio among the 178 participating states:

1   The Rio Declaration: the most authoritative declaration thus far, which records the principles of international environmental law. A significant point is that the Rio Declaration actually reflects a compromise between the poorer South and the richer North.
2   Agenda 21, which records an environmental protection action plan for the next century in a total of 40 chapters.
3   Non-binding forest principles: there was an effort to negotiate an international agreement, but the political will was lacking.
4   Opening the Framework Convention on Climate Change for signature.
5   Opening the Convention on Biological Diversity for signature.

The Rio Conference further achieved a tentative agreement on the conservation and management of straddling fish stocks and highly migratory fish stocks[26] and on negotiations for an agreement to combat desertification;[27] these international agreements were adopted in 1994 and 1995. An example of institutional development in Rio was the establishment of the Commission on Sustainable Development (CSD).

The Rio Environment Conference in 1992 was historic in many ways. For the first time, the entire international community was able to agree on principles to promote environmental protection and sustainable development; it was also able to conclude an ambitious action plan, Agenda 21, to resolve sustainable development problems. The conference adopted strategies to implement international environmental agreements more effectively. The 1997 Earth Summit +5 follow-up meeting recognized that it was high time to make the transition from negotiating agreements to actually implementing them.

Challenges for solving environmental problems

Progress after the Rio conference has been disappointing. The follow-up conference to Rio was held in Johannesburg, South Africa in 2002. It did achieve a declaration and an agenda, but they were very modest compared with the accomplishments of Rio. It was no longer clear what 'sustainable development' was: it had gradually become a term enveloping social, economic and environmental sustainability, but in reality governments and communities still appeared to prioritize economic development above all else.

However, there is another way of looking at it. Although targets and measures for sustainable development were recorded in Rio, it proved difficult to translate them into action. The follow-up conference in Johannesburg was preceded by many preparatory meetings at which the obstacles to sustainable development were discussed, such as poverty, population growth, decreasing development aid, and increasing consumption in both industrial and developing countries. Increasing anti-terrorism policies and measures in the light of the 'War on Terror' can also be seen as a threat to global cooperation and have made their own contribution to environmental damage.

It is often difficult to move from words to actions in international environmental law, despite acknowledgement that the functioning of the ecosystems and the biosphere creates the basis for our entire human existence. This has become evident in the lack of global cooperation to combat climate change – without doubt the greatest contemporary environmental problem threatening humankind. The UN climate treaty system has lurched from one crisis to another and culminated in the failure of the Copenhagen 2009 Climate Change Conference. The objective for Copenhagen was for powerful limitations on greenhouse gas emissions to finally be agreed, but the only outcome was the legally non-binding Copenhagen Accord. In 2011, the Durban Climate Change Conference revived hopes of more effective measures, although the Durban decisions, too, postponed the implementation of the necessary actions. The twenty-first century has seen more practical action: the focus has finally begun to move from negotiating international environmental agreements to implementing and applying them.

Solving environmental problems internationally is no easy matter. It is not that we lack the inventiveness to create environmentally sustainable development. Our methods for environmental management are developing all the time as we understand more and more about the ecosystems and their complex nature, in particular. Environmental sciences have made extraordinary progress. We have also become aware of how dependent humankind is on the ecosystem services provided by our environment: in, for example, the regulation of the composition of our atmosphere and water systems. The natural environment performs an incredible role in our survival, accomplishing natural miracles beyond the feats of human engineering.

The major difficulty we have in resolving environmental problems is due primarily to our overriding focus on continuous economic growth. We have become intensely aware of the change in the world's geopolitical balance. China and India, among other countries, are seeking to emulate the levels of development of the West, and their relative power in world politics will continue to grow over the next decades.

Recent economic crises, both global and within the EU, have shown the intense fear evoked by the threat of financial meltdown as well as the considerable resources that governments are still able to find to invest in mitigating the situation. Yet scientific assessments of the consequences of climate change and the depletion of biodiversity border on the type of scenario encountered in a sci-fi film, but they do not seem to have anything like the same impact on the way our governments function. Decision-makers still do not seem to fully understand why environmental protection is so important. This is one reason why environmental protection work has started to focus on increasing our awareness of the immeasurable value of the services provided by ecosystems.

The maturity of international environmental law

In the 1990s, a significant number of environmental treaties on a great variety of issues were adopted. Although it was becoming clear that the proportion of environmental regulation does not necessarily correlate with an improvement in the quality of the environment, there were still gaps to be filled. Many treaties were complemented, amended and updated in the 1990s and the 2000s by new protocols: for instance, the Framework Convention on Climate Change was updated by the 1997 Kyoto Protocol, and the Biodiversity Convention by the 2000 Biosafety Protocol;[28] and many other amendments were incorporated through memorandums of understanding (MOU). Several agreements were comprehensively renewed, such as the Baltic Sea Convention[29] in 1992, for instance. The Oslo 1972 Convention on dumping and the Paris 1974 Convention on land-based sources of marine pollution were combined in 1992 into the Convention for the Protection of the Marine Environment of the North-East Atlantic (OSPAR).[30]

The 1990s witnessed the adoption of the environmental conventions of the UN Economic Commission for Europe (with the exception of LRTAP, which relates to long-range transboundary air pollution). The Espoo Convention on Environmental Impact Assessment in a Transboundary Context[31] was adopted in 1991, and two Helsinki Conventions in 1992: the Convention on the Protection and Use of Transboundary Watercourses and International Lakes[32] and the Convention on the Transboundary Effects of Industrial Accidents.[33] The Aarhus Convention[34] was signed in 1998, which grants rights to information, to public participation and the right to appeal against environmental decisions. The experience of the UNECE on environmental agreements has been important for other areas of the world as well; its membership includes a wide spectrum of states from North America and Western Europe to Eastern Europe, the Caucasus and central Asia. A vital protocol on environmental protection[35] was accepted in the Antarctic Treaty in 1991, *inter alia*, prohibiting mining in the continent for 50 years. New global environmental agreements included the Stockholm Convention, tackling the problem of persistent organic pollutants[36] (POPs) in 2001, and the Rotterdam 1998 Convention on the Prior Informed Consent Procedure for Certain Hazardous Chemicals and Pesticides in International Trade.[37]

The Rio ten-year follow-up in Johannesburg – the so-called World Summit on Sustainable Development (WSSD) – illustrated the current direction of international environmental regulation. No agreements were adopted in Johannesburg but it was confirmed that the Rio Principles and Agenda 21 would continue to guide the international community toward sustainable development. The Johannesburg Declaration on Sustainable Development and the Plan of Implemention were adopted in the WSSD. Another major achievement was the so-called partnership agreement, which helped such diverse international actors as businesses, indigenous peoples and states promote sustainable development in practical ways.

It should be remembered that the processes for sustainable development began before the WSSD. The WTO initiated the Doha Development Agenda (DDA) in 2001 and it is still ongoing, as its progress has been challenged by many complex issues, such as those related to free trade in agricultural products (and to the subsidies that industrial countries grant their agricultural enterprises). The International Conference on Financing for Development (Monterrey Conference) discussed the financing for sustainable development, together with the WTO, the IMF and the World Bank.

As we saw above, in comparison with the Rio Conference, Johannesburg was a disappointment to many. The only accomplishments were a general declaration and an agenda. Johannesburg, though, saw the beginning of progression from words to deeds. It was vital to connect the start of the Doha Development Agenda with a discussion about the future of environmental protection; Monterrey actually considered improving the financing for sustainable development; and Johannesburg started to construct a new multiple actor model for the creation of sustainable development. Of course, it is easier to adopt principles and agendas than to actually finance and implement them in practice.

I see this as the beginning of a new phase – a phase of maturity in international environmental law. This is also evident in recent international environmental agreements. The focus is no longer on agreeing new conventions or protocols but on putting them into practice both internationally (by amendments, MOU documents, or major international meetings) and domestically (by means of national agendas and implementation through legislation).

Governments also seem to be taking environmental rules more seriously, as is evidenced by an increased willingness to protect their own environment through the international courts of justice.[38] Before 1993, when Hungary and Slovakia submitted a dispute concerning environmental damage caused to the Danube through their joint dam project,[39] the International Court of Justice had not processed many environmental disputes. Since then, the Court has made one more ruling on environmental law and two further cases are pending.

Environmental disputes between neighbours

Pollution can be the cause of environmental disputes between neighbouring countries, because it is possible to give credible evidence of another country's responsibility for the environmental damage caused.

For example, in the *Pulp Mills on the River Uruguay* case (*Argentina v Uruguay*) decided in 2010, the International Court of Justice addressed the environmental impact on the boundary river between Uruguay and Argentina of the pulp mills on the Uruguayan side.[40] The Court has now considered and is currently processing other cases concerning pollution between neighbouring states.

The *Aerial Herbicide Spraying* case[41] concerns the actions of the Colombian government in the destruction of cocoa and poppy crops by aerial herbicide spraying near the Ecuadorian border. Ecuador claims that the toxic herbicides have caused massive damage to the environment, crops and the health of humans.

The difficult neighbourly relations between Costa Rica and Nicaragua have already spawned three ICJ cases, the first of which was decided in 2009.[42] Two further cases are pending. In the first, Costa Rica complains (*inter alia*) that Nicaragua's dredging of the Costa Rican Colorado river and construction of a canal is being carried out in a manner that is causing damage to Costa Rican territory, including the wetlands and national wildlife protection areas.[43] In 2011, Nicaragua instituted the third contentious proceedings between the two countries at the ICJ, arguing that Costa Rica, in carrying out major construction works along the border area, is threatening to destroy the San Juan river: 'its fragile ecosystem, including the adjacent biosphere reserves and internationally protected wetlands that depend upon the clean and uninterrupted flow of the River for their survival' (para. 4).[44]

Of course, such cases are often only partly about environmental protection. There are other issues at stake as well: defining the boundaries between the states, securing economic interests, protecting possessions, and being awarded compensation.

The Rio +20 follow-up conference (20–22 June 2012) was the first UN environmental conference with two distinct themes intended to develop the agenda of sustainable development: the green economy and institutional changes. The focal point in Rio +20 was on helping international environmental protection work in a more coordinated way, avoiding overlapping work by various environmental regimes. In an ideal world, this will help save scarce resources and avoid contests between regimes as to who should be responsible for each environmental protection operation. Another objective was to identify synergies among international environmental regimes in order to make best use of existing know-how by combining operations instead of wasting resources. This is particularly expedient because the environmental problems administered by the various different regimes are often interconnected – that is, they should be administered in a coordinated way (see, for instance, Chapter 5, 'Connections between ozone depletion and climate change', p. 168).

The preparatory process for Rio +20 clearly expressed the need to improve the status and resources of the UN Environment Programme (UNEP). Unfortunately, this follow-up meeting was only able to make cosmetic changes: for example, UNEP's membership base was to be expanded and the 'High Level Political Forum' was created along the same lines as the Commission on Sustainable Development. The conference published a somewhat general document, entitled *The Future We Want*.[45] In many ways Rio +20 must be seen as a disappointment, perhaps even a type of mid-life crisis for international environmental law. The outcome document pretty much repeats what has already been agreed before and the institutional changes for the improvement of international environmental governance are moderate. Yet there are those who argue that we can see positive things in Rio +20, in particular the voluntary commitment from different types of actors to advance sustainable development.

Conclusions on the development of international environmental law

If we examine the evolution of international environmental law more closely, we can detect some contrasting trends. There is no denying that of any branch of international law and policy, international environmental law has seen enormous progress. The number of international treaties and soft-law instruments is breathtaking, taking into consideration the comparatively short period of time in which the discipline has developed. The sheer number of treaties and other instruments has become problematic in itself; as a result, many treaty regimes are actually carrying out overlapping work. Consequently, in the last decade or so there have been increasing calls to move towards the implementation of existing international environmental obligations, and trying to come up with ways of avoiding overlaps and finding synergies between treaty regimes.

There were high hopes from Rio +20 that international environmental governance could be strengthened at an institutional level, in particular to address the increasing fragmentation and overlapping work within international environmental law. Some small changes were adopted, but states were not yet ready to even upgrade UNEP to a UN specialized agency (despite the fact that almost every other policy area has its own such agency). UNEP was established after the 1972 Stockholm Conference and it still serves as the main institutional body for the advancement of international environmental protection; the Commission on Sustainable Development was established after the 1992 UNCED, but this was a weak Commission, now due to be replaced. From the institutional perspective, the main progress has been with treaty regimes,[46] which have created innovative ways to deal with all kinds of environmental problems.

The political momentum and direction for international environmental law have been steered by major UN environment and development conferences, where declarations and action plans have been adopted. It is difficult to say exactly what the significance of these UN conferences has been. The 1992 UNCED has often been regarded as the seminal conference since, at the time at least, it demonstrated major states and other stakeholders to be taking environmental protection seriously. The follow-ups to the UNCED have been disappointing to many. However, from a more positive perspective we can see them as conferences where the international community has sought to deal with a much more challenging issue: how to put the Rio Principles and Agenda 21 into action. Yet, after the widely felt disappointment in Rio +20, it seems pertinent to ask whether UN conferences really are the best forum for providing political direction for international environmental protection. Many are asking whether there are better investments to be made than in convening such large-scale conferences.

International environmental law has progressed in the way that it deals with environmental problems. For instance, we are now seeking more holistic solutions, the prime example being the Convention on Biological Diversity, which enables the international community to unite efforts to protect various species and habitats, which prior to the biodiversity regime were dealt with in only a fragmented manner. Though for the most part attempts by states to curb and control the release of persistent organic pollutants are restricted to a regional level, in 2001 they came together to negotiate and conclude a global Stockholm Convention, on the basis of which global measures against POPs are now possible. Increasingly, we are seeing states being prepared not only to seek regional solutions to environmental problems, but to aim for global solutions.

A new way of making sustainable development politics

Finnish President Tarja Halonen, together with Namibian President Sam Nujoma, led the preparatory process for the UN Millennium Summit. The Millennium Declaration was adopted by the UN General Assembly and 189 governments committed themselves to its goals. It contains eight very specific objectives, including the objective to halve the global proportion of those whose income is less than one dollar a day between 1990 and 2015, and the objective to guarantee primary schooling to all children, boys and girls alike, by 2015. The implementation of these summit goals was subsequently reviewed in the 2005 World Summit and in the 2010 Summit on the Millennium Goals.

This represents a new model for the advancement of sustainable development: by adopting a single politically binding document, which nevertheless defines precise targets and deadlines for reaching them.

The World Summit on Sustainable Development in Johannesburg in 2002 (WSSD) confirmed the millennium goals but new environmental goals were also adopted, such as that by 2020 we will only use and produce chemicals that will not have significant adverse effects on human health and the environment; and that by 2010, we would achieve a significant reduction in the current rate of loss of biological diversity. Unfortunately, however, this second goal was not achieved.

There are critics of such distinct goal-setting, as it is clear from the outset that they will be difficult to achieve. On the other hand, this kind of genuinely global politics with precise goals certainly gives the international community a very practical direction, at least promoting a change for the better. The Rio +20 conference preparation concentrated on principles of sustainable development that focused on specific goals.

It is not easy to assess how the inclusion of international environmental protection in the general sustainable development agenda has promoted environmental protection itself. But environmental protection cannot and should not be separated from the wider goals of sustainable development. Arranging the Rio 20-year follow-up conference was in itself a way of implementing the environment-friendly Agenda 21 that commenced for real in Rio. However, it can be argued that the concept of sustainable development has become rather watered down over the years. Social and economic agendas have diverted our attention from the fact that functioning ecosystems are the prerequisite for human development. Perhaps sustainable development is too broad a term and too easily accepted, and this has led to initiatives that are economically beneficial in the short term, but questionable from the long-term perspective of the environment.

One advantage of the sustainable development agenda has been that international lawyers have recognized that their issues and concerns cannot be considered in isolation. The values and objectives of free trade, with its often immediate financial benefits, should be considered within the context of our dependence on nature's ecosystems and the services they provide. The Rio 1992 Declaration Principle 4 states that sustainable development cannot be achieved if environmental protection is considered in isolation from the general development process. This is evident in an increase in environmental impact assessments: projects and plans detrimental to the environment and even political programmes and legislation in the making are increasingly subject to the demands of the environmental impact assessment (EIA) and the strategic environmental assessment (SEA).

On the other hand, an international environmental lawyer must understand that the solution that seems best from an environmental perspective is not necessarily the best one – if, for example, a local population is to be deported from an area designated as protected, violating their basic human rights. It is too early to say that all the branches of international law (human rights norms, international environmental law and free trade law) are merging to a single common sustainable development law, but this is one possible trend.

To summarize, we can argue that the evolution of international environmental law has seen both successes and failures. International environmental law has certainly progressed at least in the way it reacts to international environmental problems; it has contributed to a reduction in the harm caused by international environmental problems. A vast number of international environmental agreements are now being practically implemented. International environmental law has given rise to significant and meaningful research, but this cannot solve environmental problems alone. Despite all our best intentions, the condition of the environment has actually deteriorated over the same period wherein international environmental law has evolved.

Milestones in the development of international environmental law

1909   The International Boundary Waters Treaty is signed between USA and Canada; it includes environmental protection.

1941   The *Trail Smelter* tribunal of arbitration announces that states are not permitted to pollute each other's territories.

1948   The International Union for Conservation of Nature (IUCN) is established (membership includes states, governments, and civic organizations).

1954   The first extensive, multilateral international environmental treaty is concluded (International Convention for the Prevention of Pollution of the Sea by Oil).

1962   Rachel Carson's book *Silent Spring* is published; it raises extensive discussion on the use of pesticides and on environmental protection generally.

1972   The UN Conference on the Human Environment takes place in Stockholm.

1971   The only global environmental agreement that deals with a particular
        ecosystem (Convention on Wetlands of International Importance
        especially as Waterfowl Habitat) is adopted in Ramsar, Iran.
1974   The Nordic Environmental Protection Convention and the
        Convention on the Protection of the Baltic Sea are signed.
1979   The first extensive regional convention limiting air pollution is
        concluded (Convention on Long-range Transboundary Air Pol-
        lution); the framework convention model (with the subsequent
        protocols added to a framework treaty) are introduced.
1982   The Whaling Commission, based on the Whaling Convention signed
        in 1946, prohibits commercial whaling (although the original inten-
        tion was sustainable and organized whaling).
1985   The first treaty regime addressing a global environmental problem,
and   the ozone regime, starts with the Vienna Convention and the
1987   Montreal Protocol.
1989   The first of the chemicals conventions (The Basel Convention on the
        Control of Transboundary Movements of Hazardous Wastes and
        their Disposal) is adopted in Basel, Switzerland.
1991   Eight Arctic governments (five Nordic countries, USSR/Russia,
        Canada and USA) commence the Arctic Environmental Protection
        Strategy.
1991   The parties to the Antarctic Treaty decide to prohibit mining and sign
        an Environmental Protection Protocol.
1991   The Convention on Environmental Impact Assessment in a Trans-
        boundary Context is signed in Espoo.
1992   The Rio Earth Summit, UNCED (Stockholm 1972 Conference 20-
        year follow-up conference) produces conventions on climate change
        and biodiversity and adopts the Rio Principles and the Agenda 21
        environmental strategy (and the Forest Principles).
1992   The New Baltic Sea Convention is signed.
1997   The Kyoto Protocol is adopted; the industrial countries legally commit
        to cutting their greenhouse gas emissions.
1998   The Convention to promote environmental democracy (access to
        information, public participation in decision-making and access to
        justice in environmental matters) is adopted in Aarhus, Denmark.
2000   The Protocol on Biosafety is adopted in Montreal, Canada.
2001   The global POPs Convention, aimed at controlling and reducing
        persistent organic pollutants, is adopted and opened for signature in
        Stockholm.
2002   The World Summit on Sustainable Development, the ten-year follow-
        up conference to the Rio Earth Summit takes place in Johannesburg,
        South Africa; it produces a declaration and a plan of implementation.
2003   The Protocol on Strategic Environmental Assessment (SEA) is adopted
        to the Espoo Convention in Kiev, Ukraine.
2003   The Framework Convention for the Protection of the Marine Envi-
        ronment of the Caspian Sea is adopted in Tehran.

2003   The amended version of the African Convention on the Conservation of Nature is adopted.

2006   The Framework Convention for the Protection of the Environment in Central Asia is adopted.

2007   The Baltic Sea Action Plan, to control the protection of the Baltic Sea until 2021, is adopted.

2009   A legal commitment for combating climate change is expected from the Copenhagen Climate Change Conference. In its absence, a last-moment non-binding Copenhagen Accord is cobbled together under the leadership of the USA.

2010   The Nagoya Protocol to the Convention on Biological Diversity (controlling access to and equitable sharing of the benefits arising from genetic resources within national jurisdiction – genetic material that is or can be valuable) is opened for signature.

2012   The Rio 20-year follow-up conference (Rio +20) takes place. Its central themes are green economy and institutional decisions.

Questions and research tasks

1   Many experts see the UNCED as the pinnacle of international environmental politics and law. Why do they think so? Why, on the other hand, do some critics consider it a failure, although the conference adopted two conventions, a declaration, Agenda 21 and the Forest Principles? How do you consider the UNCED to have influenced the participation in international environmental politics of actors other than states? What about Rio +20? Read Tzeming Yang's ASIL Insights piece, 'The UN Rio +20 Conference on Sustainable Development – What Happened?', and Gro Harlem Brundtland's discussion piece 'Rio +20 didn't go far enough – what now?' How would you evaluate the merits of the Rio +20 after reading these two very different views on what the conference achieved or not.

2   What do you find most important about the UN conferences? Consider other ways in which international environmental protection and sustainable development could be promoted globally. Find the Earth Charter Initiative on the internet. Could this be a prospect for the international community? How would you evaluate what should be the role of the most powerful current international organization, the World Trade Organization, in environmental protection?

3   Was the emergence of sustainable development in the 1980s an inevitable trend, or could another general principle have been better or more realistic from the point of view of environmental protection? Find the World Charter for Nature drafted by the International Union for Conservation of Nature (IUCN) online. It was approved by the UN General Assembly in 1982. Could its principles have functioned in the Rio Earth Summit

as well? Could the Draft International Covenant on Environment and Development from the IUCN introduce better principles?

4   Comment on the institutional infrastructure for global environmental protection. What are its strengths and weaknesses and how can it be improved?

Notes

1   Convention for the Protection of Birds Useful to Agriculture, http://eelink. net/~asilwildlife/bird_1902.html
2   Universal Declaration of Human Rights, http://www.un.org/en/documents/udhr/ index.shtml
3   See African Charter on Human and People's Rights, Article 24, and Additional Protocol to the American Convention on Human Rights in the Area of Economic, Social and Cultural Rights, Article 11.
4   Declaration of the United Nations Conference on the Human Environment, Stockholm, 1972, http://www.unep.org/Documents.Multilingual/Default.asp?do cumentid=97&articleid=1503 Interestingly, the first Principle refers to a sort of human right to an unpolluted environment, more clearly than any other international declarations have done before or since.
5   See Convention on Third Party Liability in the Field of Nuclear Energy of 29 July 1960, as amended by the Additional Protocol of 28 January 1964 and by the Protocol of 16 November 1982, http://www.oecd-nea.org/law/nlparis_conv. html
6   The international liability regime was embodied primarily in two instruments: the Vienna Convention on Civil Liability for Nuclear Damage of 1963 and the Paris Convention on Third Party Liability in the Field of Nuclear Energy of 1960 linked by the Joint Protocol adopted in 1988. In September 1997, delegates from over 80 states adopted a Protocol to amend the 1963 Vienna Convention on Civil Liability for Nuclear Damage and also adopted a Convention on Supplementary Compensation for Nuclear Damage. See further http://www.iaea.org/Publications/ Documents/Conventions/liability.html
7   Convention relating to Civil Liability in the Field of Maritime Carriage of Nuclear Material (NUCLEAR), http://www.imo.org/About/Conventions/ ListOfConventions/Pages/Convention-relating-to-Civil-Liability-in-the-Field-of-Maritime-Carriage-of-Nuclear-Material-(NUCLEAR).aspx
8   International Convention for the Prevention of Pollution of the Sea by Oil, 1954, http://www.unescap.org/drpad/vc/orientation/legal/3_marine.htm#_1_1
9   International Convention on Civil Liability for Oil Pollution Damage (CLC), 1969, http://www.imo.org/about/conventions/listofconventions/pages/international-convention-on-civil-liability-for-oil-pollution-damage-(clc).aspx
10 International Convention Relating to Intervention on the High Seas in Cases of Oil Pollution Casualties, 1969, http://www.imo.org/about/conventions/listof-conventions/pages/international-convention-relating-to-intervention-on-the-high-seas-in-cases-of-oil-pollution-casualties.aspx
11 Convention on the Prevention of Marine Pollution by Dumping of Wastes and Other Matter: adoption 13 November 1972; entry into force 30 August 1975; 1996 Protocol: adoption 7 November 1996; entry into force 24 March 2006. See http:// www.imo.org/about/conventions/listofconventions/pages/convention-on-the-prevention-of-marine-pollution-by-dumping-of-wastes-and-other-matter.aspx
12 International Convention for the Prevention of Pollution from Ships (MARPOL): adoption 1973 (Convention), 1978 (1978 Protocol), 1997 (Protocol – Annex VI);

entry into force: 2 October 1983 (Annexes I and II). See http://www.imo.org/
about/conventions/listofconventions/pages/international-convention-for-the-
prevention-of-pollution-from-ships-(marpol).aspx

13 See further Chapter 5.
14 The Convention on Wetlands of International Importance especially as Waterfowl
    Habitat (Ramsar Convention), 1971, http://jncc.defra.gov.uk/page-1369
15 Convention Concerning the Protection of the World Cultural and Natural
    Heritage, 1972, http://whc.unesco.org/en/conventiontext/
16 The Convention on the Conservation of Migratory Species of Wild Animals (also
    known as CMS or Bonn Convention), http://www.cms.int/about/intro.htm
17 Convention on the Conservation of European Wildlife and Natural Habitats (Bern
    Convention), http://www.coe.int/t/dg4/cultureheritage/nature/bern/default_
    en.asp
18 Convention on International Trade in Endangered Species of Wild Fauna and
    Flora (CITES), 1975, http://www.cites.org/eng/disc/what.php
19 The International Union for Conservation of Nature is not an intergovernmental
    organization in the conventional sense but neither is it a non-governmental organ-
    ization, as its membership includes governments, ministries, intergovernmental
    organizations and civic organizations. It has therefore been able to initiate the
    negotiations for several international environmental agreements with its ideas.
20 UN Framework Convention on Climate Change, http://unfccc.int/essential_
    background/convention/items/2627.php
21 Convention on Biological Diversity, http://www.cbd.int/
22 Kyoto Protocol to UN Framework Convention on Climate Change, http://
    unfccc.int/kyoto_protocol/items/2830.php
23 Convention on Long-range Transboundary Air Pollution, 1979, http://www.
    unece.org/env/lrtap/
24 The Vienna Convention for the Protection of the Ozone Layer was adopted in
    and entered into force on 22 September 1988. See http://ozone.unep.org/new_
    site/en/vienna_convention.php
25 Montreal Protocol on Substances that Deplete the Ozone Layer, http://ozone.
    unep.org/new_site/en/montreal_protocol.php
26 Agreement for the Implementation of the Provisions of the UNCLOS for the
    Conservation and Management of Straddling Fish Stocks and Highly Migratory
    Fish Stocks, http://www.un.org/Depts/los/convention_agreements/convention_
    overview_fish_stocks.htm
27 UN Convention to Combat Desertification in Those Countries Experiencing
    Serious Drought and/or Desertification, especially in Africa, Paris 1994, http://
    treaties.un.org/pages/ViewDetails.aspx?src=TREATY&mtdsg_no=XXVII-
    10&chapter=27&lang=en
28 Cartagena Protocol on Biosafety related to the Biodiversity Convention, 2000,
    http://bch.cbd.int/protocol/
29 Convention on the Protection of the Marine Environment of the Baltic Sea Area,
    http://www.helcom.fi/Convention/en_GB/text/
30 Convention for the Protection of the Marine Environment of the North-East
    Atlantic (OSPAR), 1992, http://www.ospar.org/
31 Convention on Environmental Impact Assessment in a Transboundary Context.
    Protocol on Strategic Environmental Assessment (SEA), Kyiv 2003, http://www.
    unece.org/env/eia/
32 Convention on the Protection and Use of Transboundary Watercourses and
    International Lakes, 1999, http://www.unece.org/env/water/
33 Convention on the Transboundary Effects of Industrial Accidents, 1992, http://
    www.unece.org/env/teia.html

34 Convention on Access to Information, Public Participation in Decision-making and Access to Justice in Environmental Matters, 1998, http://www.unece.org/env/pp/welcome.html

35 Protocol on Environmental Protection to the Antarctic Treaty, 1991, http://www.antarctica.ac.uk/about_antarctica/geopolitical/treaty/update_1991.php

36 Stockholm Convention on Persistent Organic Pollutants, 2001, http://chm.pops.int/default.aspx

37 Rotterdam Convention on the Prior Informed Consent Procedure for Certain Hazardous Chemicals and Pesticides in International Trade, 1998, http://www.pic.int/

38 There are few international courts of justice or arbitration courts into which a state can issue proceedings against another state. The fundamental rule is that legal settlement requires that both states consent to a legal procedure (see Chapter 3, 'Secondary sources of law', p. 80).

39 See the judgment at the *Gabčíkovo-Nagymaros* project (Hungary/Slovakia), at the ICJ's website at http://www.icj-cij.org/docket/files/92/7375.pdf

40 *Case Concerning Pulp Mills on the River Uruguay* (*Argentina v. Uruguay*) Judgment of 20 April 2010, at the ICJ's website at http://www.icj-cij.org/docket/files/135/15877.pdf

41 *Aerial Herbicide Spraying* (*Ecuador v. Columbia*); see the latest developments at the ICJ's website at http://www.icj-cij.org/docket/index.php?p1=3&p2=3&code=ecol&case=138&k=ee

42 This case was decided by the ICJ on 13 July 2009: *Dispute Regarding Navigational and Related Rights* (*Costa Rica v. Nicaragua*), judgment at http://www.icj-cij.org/docket/files/133/15321.pdf/

43 *Certain Activities carried out by Nicaragua in the Border Area* (*Costa Rica v. Nicaragua*), instituted in 2010, still pending. See the history of the case from the ICJ's homepage, at http://www.icj-cij.org/docket/index.php?p1=3&p2=3&k=ec&case=150&code=crn&p3=3

44 Nicaragua's application can be found from the ICJ's homepage at http://www.icj-cij.org/docket/files/152/16917.pdf

45 *The Future We Want*, http://www.uncsd2012.org/content/documents/727The%20Future%20We%20Want%2019%20June%201230pm.pdf

46 See further Chapter 3.

Further reading

Berkhout, F., Leach, M. and Scoones, I. (eds), *Negotiating Environmental Change: New Perspectives from Social Science*, Cheltenham: Edward Elgar, 2003.

Birnie, P., *The International Regulation of Whaling: From Conservation of Whaling to the Conservation of Whales and Whale-Watching*, New York: Oceana, 1985.

Bowman, M. and Redgwell, C. (eds), *International Law and the Conservation of Biological Diversity*, The Hague: Kluwer Law International, 1996.

Boyle, A. and Freestone, D. (eds), *International Law and Sustainable Development: Past Achievements and Future Challenges*, Oxford: Oxford University Press, 1999.

Brown Weiss, E., *Environmental Change and International Law: New Challenges and Dimensions*, Tokyo: United Nations University Press, 1992.

Freestone, D., 'The Road from Rio: International Environmental Law after the Earth Summit', *Journal of Environmental Law*, 6, 1994, pp. 193–218.

Hurrell, A. and Kingsbury, B., *The International Politics of the Environment: Actors, Interests and Institutions*, Oxford: Clarendon Press, 1992.

Kiss, A., 'The International Protection of the Environment: The Structure and Process of International Law', in R.St J. Macdonald and D.M. Johnston (eds), *Essays in Legal Philosophy Doctrine and Theory*, pp. 1069–94, The Hague: Nijhoff, 1983.

Kuokkanen, T., *International Law and the Environment: Variations on a Theme*, The Hague: Kluwer Law International, 2002.

Onuma, Y., *A Transcivilizational Perspective on International Law*, The Hague: Nijhoff, 2010.

Pallemaerts, M., 'International Environmental Law from Stockholm to Rio: Back to the Future?', *Review of European Community and International Environmental Law*, 1(3), 1992, pp. 254–66.

Robinson, N.A. (ed.), *Agenda 21 and the UNCED Proceedings*, New York: Oceana, 1992.

Sohn, L.B., 'The Stockholm Declaration on the Human Environment', *Harvard International Law Journal*, 14, 1973, pp. 423–515.

Weeramantry, C., 'Separate Opinion'. Case Gabčíkovo-Nagymaros project in UN International Court of Justice, at http://www.icj-cij.org/docket/files/92/7383.pdf.

Websites

Commission on Sustainable Development: www.sustainabledevelopment.un.org/csd.html

Earth Negotiations Bulletin, United Nations Conference on Environment and Development, UNCED 1992: http://www.iisd.ca/vol02/0200000e.html

Earth Summit Watch: http://www.earthsummitwatch.org/

International Environmental Agreements (IEA) Database Project: http://iea.uoregon.edu/page.php?file=home.htm&query=static

United Nations Economic Commission for Europe (UNECE): www.unece.org

3 Enacting and developing international environmental law

The Vuotos reservoir was a project of national importance in Finland. It had been under consideration in various guises by the people of Finnish Lapland since the 1960s. I happened to be writing my doctoral dissertation just as the Vuotos application by hydropower company, Kemijoki, was being processed, in accordance with the Finnish Water Act. Kemijoki filed its application in 1992 before the Water Court of Northern Finland and the matter was expected to proceed without any problem: inspectors would first survey the environmental impact of the Vuotos reservoir project and then the Water Court would decide whether to grant or withhold permission.

Unexpectedly, the Finnish Environment Ministry announced in 1995 that Finland would apply the provisions of the Convention on Environmental Impact Assessment in a Transboundary Context (the Espoo Convention) to the Vuotos reservoir project. The Convention had been signed in Espoo in 1991 but was not due to enter into force until 1997. The Ministry considered that Vuotos would probably have environmental impact on the Gulf of Bothnia including areas under Swedish jurisdiction; therefore Sweden ought to be notified. This came as a surprise to the Kemijoki company, to the inspectors, and to the Water Court. There was good reason for this surprise. It had been expected that the Water Act would govern the application process; should any transboundary impacts be found by the inspectors, it would be up to the Water Court to decide, on the basis of the valid international treaty (the Nordic Environmental Protection Convention), whether Sweden need be notified or not.

I enquired of the Environment Ministry as to their reasons for insisting that Sweden be notified about the matter before the inspection procedure had been completed and before the NEPC would require Finland to act. The Ministry answered that when the Espoo Convention was signed, the parties agreed to implement its provisions as soon as possible, even before it formally came into force. They considered the Espoo Convention, signed but not yet in force, as a soft-law obligation that bound Finland.[1]

The case is a good example of how complex it can be in this day and age to define precisely the obligations on states at any given time.

This chapter reviews the ways in which international environmental law is created and developed. Before looking at the actual sources of law, it is important to consider who is able to participate in the making of international environmental law and politics, as well as the role of science in the development of international environmental law.

International environmental law develops and it is regulated according to rules that are defined in the sources of general international law. The key ways that international law develops are explicit consent (treaties) and implicit consent (customary international law). General principles are also a recognized source of law. States have concluded an enormous number of environmental treaties, so it is important to consider the essential features of these treaty regimes. Subsidiary sources of law include the decisions of the international courts and research by associations of international lawyers. The task of these sources is mainly to clarify and specify the contents of international law produced by states.

Yet, international environmental law also allows states to protect the environment with so-called soft-law instruments, which have challenged those who practise international law to reassess at a more general level their assumptions about how international law can be created.

Who is responsible for the creation and development of international environmental law?

General international law defines who can participate in international politics and in the development of international law: that is, who can be actors in the international community. States are the original subjects of international law and hold original personality. As sovereigns, they are entitled to conclude agreements, or in some cases to take another state to a court of arbitration. Intergovernmental organizations (IGOs) can also be subjects of international law. Their authority, however, comes from agreements between states, so their competence in international politics and in the creation of law is controlled and limited.[2] This is known as derivative personality.

Actors in international environmental law and politics are much more diverse than in other branches of international law and politics. There are two main reasons for this.

First, preventing environmental pollution and contamination is in the interests of all possible actors. This has become obvious at the UN conferences where indigenous peoples, farmers and local administrations have expressly been accepted as groups of actors.

Many different groups participate in the making and shaping of environmental treaties. Today's climate regime, for instance, includes not only the parties, but also observing states, intergovernmental organizations and several non-governmental organization actor groups based on the Agenda 21 groups: indigenous people's organizations (IPOs), business and industry non-governmental organizations (BINGOs), environmental NGOs (ENGOs), local government and municipal authorities (LGMAs), research and independent NGOs (RINGOs), trade union NGOs (TUNGOs), farmers' NGOs, women and gender NGOs, and children and youth NGOs.

Second, environmental protection is increasingly considered a human rights issue. This trend has entitled individuals, civil groups and environmental organizations to actively contribute towards environmental protection. This was seen best in the implementation of Principle 10 of the Rio Declaration, which led to wider promotion of environmental democracy. In Principle 10, states undertook politically to increase their citizens' access to information about environmental hazards, and their opportunities to influence decision-making that concerns the environment.

The principle also states that public have access to redress and remedies through judicial and administrative proceedings. This principle is implemented by the Aarhus Convention, a regional convention within the UN Economic Commission for Europe. The UN and regional human rights systems have also started to obligate states more and more explicitly to consider these groups as participants who are affected by environmental decisions. In other words, the inhabitants of an affected area must be actively informed, and given the opportunity to influence environmental decision-making.

When climate change or persistent organic pollutants harm the environment and health in a certain area, it is natural that various actor groups want to influence international as well as local decision-making. Article 3(7) in the Aarhus Convention encourages its parties to promote the application of its principles in the international environmental regimes (i.e. creating better opportunities for individuals and non-governmental organizations to participate in international decision-making processes) and in international organizations in matters relating to the environment. By virtue of this non-legally binding article, the Almaty Guidelines[3] were developed and have since been observed and expounded by a dedicated task force.

The role of science in international environmental law

Science has a particularly significant role to play in international environmental law. Environmental problems are generally observed and verified through scientific research; the objects of regulation are therefore constantly shifting environmental problems. International environmental problems are not solved by mere ordinary rules and actors influencing international politics because before they can take any effective decisions, actors must first understand the science behind any environmental problem and this understanding is based on the research shared by scientists and scientific institutions.

It is not merely a question of defining environmental problems according to scientific research; the progress in natural sciences leads us to understand the problems and solutions better. While previously we might have seen a river as an object of regulation that we could perceive straightforwardly as being, for example, within the boundaries of a state, modern science has complicated this simplistic approach: water system areas usually consist of an intricate network of surface and ground waters, a drainage area that generally spreads over several states' territories, and waters that flow on to the seas. In this way, our increased scientific knowledge has turned a problem that was once considered national into a complex international one.

Although science plays a very central role in defining environmental problems and providing research data about their evolution, we should remember that international environmental politics is still inherently political: a recommendation by a scientific institution alone would seldom define how international environmental regimes react to environmental problems. International environmental regimes have for various reasons selected different methods of incorporating science into their regimes. There is increasing recognition that science cannot provide decision-makers with fully objective and complete information. The scientific approach is still the best way to find out how an environmental problem originates, how it evolves and how it interacts with other environmental problems, but there will very often be gaps in the knowledge it provides owing to incomplete data or incomplete or unproven theories regarding, *inter alia*, causation of complex, intertwined phenomena.

The key scientific syntheses, such as, for example, those produced by the Intergovernmental Panel on Climate Change (IPCC)[4] do not report results from a single research project. Instead, a huge number of scientists compile the essential trends from a vast number of peer-reviewed, high-quality research results: that is, they compile the reflected general image of the change. As politicians and diplomats are continually required to navigate their way through a deluge of information, there is a tendency to popularize scientific assessments for them in brief, simplified reports translated into standard language. This is how politicians and the general public are able to observe the progress of an environmental problem.[5]

In the development of international environmental regulation, the most common response to an aggravating environmental problem is to establish a task force whose aim is to keep key decision-makers updated about the progress of the environmental problem. For example, the ozone regime created a scientific assessment system in the Montreal Protocol and the assessment panels have fairly independently managed to produce scientific information about the progress of ozone depletion so that the parties have been able to tighten and accelerate the schedules to reduce CFC emissions.

The introduction of new scientific research into the climate regime takes place more slowly, because the IPCC is not part of the climate regime. The Subsidiary Body for Scientific and Technological Advice (SBSTA) filters the IPCC's scientific assessments into the climate regime. The IPCC assessments – and, more importantly, the summaries that are produced from them for political decision-makers – are also subject to intergovernmental political play.

The scientists who contribute to the IPCC assessments often complain that the wording of their summary reports is compromised by international negotiators, and in the process loses some of its objectivity. Governments focus on negotiating the tone and emphasis, with some governments even trying to water down the agreed scientific consensus by softening the way it is expressed when preparing the summaries for decision-makers. The summary reports are of paramount importance, because the more detailed scientific assessments are highly technical and beyond the comprehension of most non-experts.

Since 2007, the international community developed the idea of establishing a scientific panel to assess the third essential global environmental problem, the loss of biodiversity. The Intergovernmental Science-Policy Platform on Biodiversity and Ecosystem Services (IPBES)[6] finally commenced in April 2012.

The panel addresses marine and inland water ecosystems and terrestrial ecosystems. It observes the changes in them, especially from the perspective of human well-being. The Millennium Ecosystem Assessment, published in 2005,[7] initiated a process intended to create a permanent mechanism for bringing science and politics together in relation to biodiversity issues. The model for the IPBES is the IPCC and its mode of functioning.

Increasingly, ways of expanding scientific influence in decision-making are being explored. One good way of doing this is for research to be conducted in close collaboration with those who are actually going to be affected. The use of environmental impact assessments (EIAs), for example, has shown that it is beneficial to establish the EIA procedure for a large planned factory in a way that would enable the people living in the affected area to actively contribute to decision-making (what should be examined, by whom and how). This increases their confidence in the scientific data and in the entire decision-making process.

The gradual evolution of the principle of precaution has been important in making sure that scientific evidence is taken into account in decision-making, even before it can prove anything close to certainty. According to this principle, if the consequences of human action are likely to be severe or irreversible, action must be taken even before scientific certainty has been proven.

An even more effective way of involving the public is to allow residents to compile and submit data directly. For example, the indigenous peoples of the Arctic participated in the Arctic Climate Impact Assessment (ACIA). Indigenous peoples, especially those who maintain traditional indigenous lifestyles, spend a great deal of their lives observing the environment; there is no other way to hunt successfully or manage animal or fish stocks. Constant observation has given them unique information about the changes in the Arctic over the course of their lifetime. Having actively participated in ACIA as researchers alongside Western scientists, the final research report also contained a section discussing the impact of climate change on the Arctic indigenous peoples both now and in future.

Traditional ecological knowledge

Traditional ecological knowledge (TEK) of indigenous peoples has gained ground in Western science and environmental decision-making. TEK refers to knowledge drawn from centuries of continuous interaction with the environment, generally handed down orally through generations. The knowledge of indigenous peoples is practical as it is based on continuous observation of the environment in practising a traditional livelihood, and this knowledge has afforded them the ability to preserve game stocks for thousands of years. The belief systems of indigenous peoples are also often central to sustainable development, emphasizing the status of humans as part of the natural system instead of human supremacy over nature.

Soft and hard law

A special characteristic of international environmental law is that many environmental problems (such as land-based marine pollution, which is the greatest cause of marine environmental problems) are regulated by non-binding soft-law instruments which allow for quicker responses to international environmental problems. Governments tend, for various reasons, to avoid legally binding treaty regulation but they are often more willing to accept a written plan of action or declaration, at least expressing a political will to solve a problem.

When making international agreements, the different constitutional requirements of multiple countries must be met: for example, the way in which the national parliament will accept and implement a treaty. Such issues need not be considered when using soft-law instruments. In many cases, governments use soft-law instruments to test how they should relate to a new environmental problem or how a new environmental policy should be promoted before proceeding to treaty negotiations.

The following example is a case in point. Under the auspices of the UN Economic Commission for Europe, the various state actors considered how the access of citizens and environmental organizations to decision-making related to environmental matters could be promoted. In the Environment for Europe Meeting in 1995, the ministers accepted the Sofia Guidelines which paved the way for the Aarhus 1998 Convention regarding access to information, public participation and the right to appeal against environmental decisions.

In roughly the same way, a legally binding agreement was made on access to genetic material and the fair distribution of the gains from it; ('genetic material' refers to genetic material that is or can be valuable[8]). Article 15 of the 1992 Biodiversity Convention outlined the general principles of the conditions for exploiting genetic material in the country of origin and distributing the gains. The sixth meeting of the parties of the biodiversity regime accepted the Bonn Guidelines, which defined more specifically how Article 15 should function. They were, though, non-binding, and so the negotiations continued to bring about a protocol on the basis of the Bonn Guidelines. This was finally accomplished in Nagoya, Japan, in the tenth meeting of the parties of the treaty system, when a legally binding protocol[9] was accepted on 29 October 2010.

Soft-law instruments are not always just predecessors to an actual treaty employed by states to test their readiness to commit themselves to a legally binding treaty. Many scholars consider the programme of action against marine pollution from land-based sources[10] adopted in Washington in 1995 to be a good example of how global environmental regulation can be based on a non-binding soft-law instrument. The practical implementation is linked with the UN Environment Programme (UNEP) Regional Seas Programme.

Another case of efficient use of a soft-law instrument is the UN General Assembly resolution of 1991 to prohibit driftnet fishing on the high seas. A General Assembly resolution, even if not legally binding, was well observed by those states whose vessels had carried on fishing with wide driftnets, which are destructive to the ecosystem.

Similarly, many of the instruments through which international environmental law is enacted are actually non-legally binding instruments. Even if the instrument itself is not legally binding, this does not mean that the adoption of the instrument would be without legal relevance. In fact, many important developments in international environmental law have been effected via non-legally binding instruments. Some good examples are presented by the 1972 Stockholm and 1992 Rio Declarations, the latter of which is widely considered to be the most authoritative codification of international environmental law principles. UNCED also produced Agenda 21, which, even if non-binding in international law, has influenced the development of international environmental law. Decisions taken during meetings of the parties to multilateral environmental agreements have also been particularly significant in international environmental law. Even if they are not legally binding, these decisions are normally adopted via consensus and thus exercise influence on the extent to which states develop and implement the treaty regime.

Although soft-law instruments may be influential in changing the behaviour of states and other stakeholders, it is important to remember that from a strictly legal point of view they are not legally binding. They may be politically or morally binding on states and their leaders, but not legally. Instruments endorsed by private actors, such as the Equator Principles adopted by private banks (see Chapter 1, p. 26) are sometimes characterized as soft-law instruments, but they do not create any obligations (not even political or moral) on states.[11] Even if international treaties include very soft obligations, such as Article 8(j) of the Convention on Biological Diversity (which we considered previously), these remain legal obligations, the content of which may be open-ended but needs to be determined in any case. (There are, of course, also provisions in international treaties that are worded in such a way that does not create a legal obligation, through the use of modal verbs such as 'should', for example.)

It is important to keep in mind that soft-law instruments are not as such legally binding, as opposed to hard-law sources, such as international treaties, customary international law or decisions of those intergovernmental organizations that have the power to enact legally binding decisions. Legal consequences can only result from violating hard-law rules, which are defined in the sources of international law.

The sources of international law

The doctrine of the sources of law defines, *inter alia*, how legal rules and principles are enacted and developed in any given legal system.[12] In the legal systems of many nation-states, the law that is enacted by their respective parliaments generates collectively binding legal rules and principles ('norms') that guide the behaviour of individuals and businesses. On another level, the process remains similar: European Union member states are legally bound by the directives adopted by the ordinary legislative procedure of the European Parliament and the Council of the European Union. The closest process to this within the international legal system would be if the Security Council of the UN takes legally binding measures on the basis of Chapter VII of the Charter of the United Nations in order to counter a threat to international peace and security.

The doctrine of sources of law exists in every legal system, including international law. The sources of general international law apply in all branches of international law – including international environmental law. However, it can be argued that, in a way, international environmental law has challenged international lawyers to reconsider the classical doctrines of the sources of international law.

Article 38 of the Statute of the International Court of Justice lists the generally accepted sources of international law. Although this article is directed only at the International Court of Justice, it has over the years evolved into a generally accepted definition of what the sources are in international law. It also expresses how states can develop and enact new international law.

The primary sources, according to the article, are customary international law (primarily legally binding on all states in the world), international conventions (binding on the parties only), and general principles of law. Secondary sources are judicial decisions and the opinions of highly qualified experts of international law. This division is based on the fact that states principally have the monopoly on enacting and developing international law. The secondary sources (judicial decisions and expert opinion) can, therefore, only be applied to define the contents of the primary source rules, not to create international law.

Different actors view the sources of international law in diverse ways. States' foreign ministries frequently follow other states' environmentally relevant foreign policies and take stances on them; in this way the reaction (or non-reaction) can influence the development of a new rule in customary international law. When an international organization makes plans for new international environmental regulation, it has to consider whether a soft-law instrument or an international convention should be selected. A soft-law instrument allows the regulation to be implemented sooner as it does not require ratification by states; ratification always delays the entry into force of a convention. On the other hand, soft-law instruments are not legally binding and seldom engage states in any really ambitious environmental protection, whereas international conventions are binding. The judges in international courts make their decisions on the basis of the sources of general international law. They seek to resolve conflicts between states by considering all the international legal regulations, not just the environmental regulations.

Problems with the sources of international law

Although Article 38 of the Statute of the International Court of Justice provides a solid basis for sources of international law, it leaves many questions unanswered. Are the listed sources of equal weight, or is there some degree of hierarchy? In principle, customary international law, conventions and general principles of law are of equal weighting: all are considered formal sources of law and authoritative in their own right. In practice, some are more equal than others, although there are a few exceptions to this basic rule.

The Charter of the United Nations can be seen as the 'constitution of the international community'; it overrides other international agreements. This is expressed in Article 103 of the Charter which states: 'In the event of a conflict between the obligations of the Members of the United Nations under the present Charter and their obligations under any other international agreement, their obligations under the present Charter shall prevail.' This means that provisions of the Charter (a treaty) should take precedence over other international treaties.

Another exception from the basic rule is that the so-called *jus cogens* norms override all other sources of international law. These universal principles reflect the basic values of the international community, and they shall be accepted by the community of states as *jus cogens* norms; no derogation from them is possible by international treaties (Vienna Convention on the Law of Treaties, Article 53). The most important *jus cogens* norms are those that prohibit genocide, slavery or torture.

There is also a debate as to whether any of the principles of international environmental law has the status of *jus cogens* – being of such importance that states cannot override it by mutual agreement. In the dispute between Hungary and Slovakia concerning their mutual dam project, the International Court of Justice only stated in its 1997 judgment that neither one of the parties claimed that *jus cogens* norms invalidated their agreement of 1977. It is not easy to prove that the principles of international environmental law are *jus cogens* norms which cannot be overridden by an agreement.

International agreements

Since the Second World War, the predominant source of international law has been international treaty law, because a great volume of conventions have been negotiated by states. This was a significant change for the international community, which had previously been governed largely by customary international law. States are now able to read in written treaties the rules that govern their conduct. The earlier vague and unwritten customary law rules were far from ideal, as the precise obligations of states were often unclear.

The UN International Law Commission (ILC) played an important role in codifying customary international law. The principal objective of the ILC is the progressive development of international law and its codification. The ILC consists of 34 recognized world experts in international law who work in an individual capacity (i.e. they are not representing any state); however, they engage in an ongoing dialogue with states' representatives to determine the content of international law as well as likely directions for its progressive development. The ILC performed the preparatory work for the negotiations of many important treaties including those related to international environmental law.

It is notable that in international environmental law states have negotiated an enormous number of bilateral, regional and global environmental agreements – more than in many other branches of international law. The International Environmental Agreements Database Project has compiled more than 1,000 multilateral and 1,500 bilateral environmental treaties.

The role of customary international law remains supplementary, as governments have reacted to increasing environmental problems through treaties or by establishing international organizations. Sometimes states react to environmental problems with non-binding soft-law instruments (see above, 'Soft and hard law', p. 58) but these are generally baby steps on the road to fully fledged environmental agreements.

The stages of an agreement

International written multilateral agreements have many names: covenant, treaty, convention, agreement, protocol. All of them are regulated by customary international law which applies to all treaties (and is mainly codified by the Vienna Convention on the Law of Treaties[13]); these rules apply in cases where the parties do not otherwise specifically regulate a matter in an agreement (in other words, they are the default rules of treaty law).

The Vienna Convention regulates adoption, amendment, interpretation, and many other issues related to all written treaties. As of January 2013, there are 113 parties to the Convention; the International Court of Justice has in several decisions emphasized that many of its articles codify customary international law.

When states sign a treaty, they undertake, by virtue of Article 18 of the Vienna Convention, 'not to defeat the object and purpose of a treaty prior to its entry into force'. This is an important point to understand. Newspapers and journals sometimes refer to the parties of a treaty as its signatories, which is actually an incorrect term. Signing a treaty is not synonymous to becoming a party, although states do sometimes agree that an agreement becomes valid by virtue of signature alone. (In practice, this is never the case with environmental treaties.) Usually, a procedure is followed by which an agreement is first signed by states to indicate their goodwill and intention to become a party in the near future.

After signature, the agreement enters the national legislative process of each state according to its domestic constitutional law. When the state is ready to be bound by the treaty, it is deposited with the body defined in the agreement (for example, the Secretary-General of the United Nations).

However, even ratification of an environmental treaty may not necessarily result in a state or states being immediately bound. A treaty must also enter into force internationally. Most treaties will specify a minimum number of states that must become party to the agreement before it can enter into force. For example, to date, 29 states[14] have ratified the UN 1997 Convention on the Law of the Non-Navigational Uses of International Watercourses, but the Convention will not enter into force until 90 days after the 35th party accepts and deposits it with the UN Secretary-General.

A multilateral environmental treaty generally proceeds as follows:

1 **At the negotiation stage**: besides drafting the substantive obligations, states also discuss how the final text in the treaty will be adopted, how the will to become a party is expressed, when the treaty becomes binding on a state, and the conditions under which it will enter into force internationally. There is often a specific article defining how states become full party to a treaty. If a state signs a treaty, even before it comes into force, it must abstain from actions that would defeat the object and purpose of that agreement. Since a state does not become a party to a treaty simply by signing it, the treaty does not fully become legally binding on that state as yet.

2 **After signature**: many states must submit the treaty to their own domestic parliament for approval. Thereafter, the state signals its consent to be bound by the treaty depositing the ratification instrument with the depositary defined in the treaty (under the terms of the treaty). The treaty often specifies a short period of time between deposit of the instrument of ratification and recognition of the state as a party. In the case of global environmental treaties especially, it is possible for states to become parties directly, bypassing both the negotiating stage and the act of signature. This process is usually referred to as accession.

3 **Coming into force**: many treaties also specify a minimum number of ratifying states required for the treaty to enter into force internationally. This is mainly because it is futile to implement the treaty before a sufficient number of states have engaged to combat the international environmental problem in question.

Wording of agreements

Parties to modern environmental treaties tend to specify in increasingly specific detail how the terms are to be understood, thus decreasing states' power to interpret them in such a narrow way as to minimize their obligations. For the same reason, most environmental treaties do not accept reservations.[15]

On the other hand, most environmental treaties are relatively weak; they do not prescribe an obligation to compensate for environmental damage or require compulsory dispute settlement between the parties in the event of disagreement. Many of the articles were negotiated to be so vague that they only constituted a very open-ended obligation.

Institutional framework

Up until the 1970s, it was considered sufficient to establish substantive obligations in international legal agreements without any follow-up or enforcement mechanisms. The representative of a state would negotiate a treaty and return to their country to have it ratified, and the expectation was that states would dutifully observe the treaty according to the principle *pacta sunt servanda* ('agreements must be honoured'). An example of such an agreement was and remains the 1974 Nordic Convention on the Protection of the Environment (NEPC) between Denmark, Finland, Norway and Sweden. Under this convention, these four Nordic countries guaranteed that the authorities and citizens in each other's states would be able to participate in any administrative and judicial proceedings related to a proposed project, if that project should have transboundary environmental impact. No meetings of the parties were established to monitor the implementation and application of the convention.

During the 1970s, this kind of attitude to environmental treaties was gradually abandoned as ineffective. In its place, a new model became the main standard:

1   At the negotiation stage, an article is created establishing a regular 'meeting of the parties' (sometimes called the 'conference of the parties', which represents all the states' parties), which has the authority to develop a treaty regime. A funding model for the operation of the treaty regime is also designed at this stage.

2   These meetings of the parties, consisting of representatives of each state, define how the treaty regime is to be developed and what, if any, treaty bodies should be established. At the meetings of the parties all the decisions in the agreement system are generally made by consensus (i.e. no state should be specifically in opposition).[16]

3   The meeting of the parties establishes a mechanism for monitoring compliance with the treaty (the implementation committee or compliance committee), usually consisting of a small number of delegates representing

the parties. Generally the duty of the committee is limited to providing assistance to any violating parties (such as financing, education) to
improve compliance rather than applying any sanctions, although certain
penalties can be used (from naming and shaming to temporary suspension
from the treaty regime).

4   In this way, the parties can be said to have established a permanent
    management mechanism in order to react effectively to a changing envi-
    ronmental problem. This is only possible if updated scientific information
    about the environmental problem and potential solutions continue to be
    filtered into the regime (for instance through advances in technology).
5   The regime should also be able to monitor and confirm that the parties
    are developing their own domestic policies effectively and implementing
    what has already been decided by the meetings of the parties and other
    sub-bodies of the regime.
6   The meeting of the parties should also continue to develop the treaty
    regime in various ways, via soft-law and hard-law measures, depending on
    the new challenges that are presented.

States can also conclude agreements to establish standing organizations for the
promotion of environmental protection. By entitling these organizations to
take legally binding decisions, states are thereby able to enact international
environmental law. The European Union is an extreme example of this
progress but it is today considered a *sui generis* (unique) legal system. Bodies
such as the Commission of the Convention for the Protection of the Marine
Environment of the North-East Atlantic (OSPAR) are also able to make decisions that will bind their member states.

Most environmental agreements do not establish a formal international
organization but a kind of a mini organization (outlined above) focused
around the agreement. The mini organization can then be linked to existing
international organizations; the environmental treaties negotiated within the
UN Economic Commission of Europe (UNECE) are a good example.

States generally select the meetings of the parties as the main decision-
making forum. The meetings define how the treaty system is developed and
whether it will be necessary to establish any treaty bodies. The meetings also
generally make consensus decisions relating to the treaty regime. Frequently,
sub-committees are established to ensure that the treaty regime is regularly
developed in order to meet new challenges and to ensure that new scientific/
technical research is filtered into the regime.

Another important mechanism that must be established is the funding
mechanism. The funding model is often subject to much political wrangling.
In the 1992 Rio Environment Conference, the developing countries pushed
through a decision about the financing of international environmental protection which was of great importance to them. The World Bank, UNEP and
United Nations Development Programme (UNDP) established the Global
Environment Facility (GEF) in 1991 which the Rio Conference designated

the core funding mechanism for averting climate change, preventing the loss of biodiversity and implementing Agenda 21. It is intended to secure additional funding for developing countries to implement Agenda 21 and to achieve further objectives in resolving the main threats to the global environment. The developing nations succeeded in negotiating favourable voting rules within the GEF. The decision-making body in the GEF is the Council, which is made up of 32 members, half of whom represent the developing nations.

Within the context of global environmental treaties and agreements, developing nations have frequently demanded financial assistance and technological know-how from their more industrial counterparts as a prerequisite for full participation in resolving or controlling an environmental threat. They argue that these rich industrial countries have contributed significantly to pollution as they developed; therefore, in creating their wealth, they have been responsible for causing global environmental problems.

Although the reality is not this simple, this position is quite common in global environmental treaties and agreements. The biodiversity regime, for example, considers technical and financial assistance to developing nations to be a vital trade-off for allowing the industrial countries and their businesses to exploit their diverse biological resources. Relocating technology into developing countries has been too much for the USA, which is not a party to the Convention on Biological Diversity or its Protocol on Biosafety.

International environmental agreements as regimes

The regime theory evolved within international relations research, as scholars increasingly came to understand that rules do count in international politics. Perhaps the best-known definition of 'regime' is that of Stephen Krasner, expressed in 1982. He defines regimes as 'implicit or explicit principles, norms, rules, and decision-making procedures around which actors' expectations converge in a specific issue-area'.

International lawyers have, naturally, always considered the norms defined by Krasner to be significant to international politics. The significance of the regime theory in international environmental law is, however, that lawyers were better equipped to understand international agreements which were, in fact, constantly changing processes by which both soft and hard-law measures could function as an integral whole.

This is how most environmental treaties work. Some environmental regimes start by adopting a highly general framework agreement whose obligations are not particularly onerous. This process guarantees the earliest possible actions among the maximum possible number of states. The loose rules of the framework agreement can be gradually specified and made tighter by protocols negotiated under the original framework agreement.

A good example is provided by a convention we will study later. The Convention on Long-range Transboundary Air Pollution (LRTAP) was negotiated under the auspices of the UN Economic Commission for Europe; it contains several protocols that regulate various harmful substances (see Chapter 4, 'Long-range transboundary air pollution', pp. 116).

Another example is an agreement with loose clauses that comprehensively regulate an environmental threat. The Convention on Biological Diversity actually only provides a basis for closer regulation. It has therefore been supplemented by soft-law decisions of the meetings of the parties, and, in the case of crucial issues, by protocols constituting separate agreements that are linked in many ways with the parent agreement.

The regime theory helped scholars of international environmental law understand and sustain the image of environmental treaties as constantly changing bodies of rules. This was significant because as environmental problems change and scientific discovery becomes more sophisticated, so too the management regime must evolve. Classical international law did not provide the tools for this kind of evolution. It categorizes international agreements as rules as fixed and immutable as they were when they were agreed and adopted by the negotiating states; they are to be interpreted primarily according to their wording at the time of the conclusion of the treaty.[17]

Innovative environmental regimes

International environmental regimes have gradually developed their own ways of reacting to regional and global environmental problems. Earlier regulatory errors have contributed to our experience and understanding, and international environmental law has been able to create innovative environmental regimes that embrace the significance of environmental scientific research.

An essential problem in international environmental regulation – and in regulation generally – is that often measures are only taken after a catastrophe has occurred, commanding the attention of decision-makers. One of the best-known examples is that of the sinking of the *Titanic* when it collided with an iceberg in the North Atlantic Ocean on 14 April 1912. The disaster resulted in an international negotiation process and the adoption of the SOLAS Convention (Safety of Life at Sea, predecessor of the current IMO Convention) in 1914. Oil tanker disasters are also classic examples that have provided a great incentive to regulate, in many cases having been quickly followed by a related environmental treaty. The Chernobyl nuclear plant disaster was followed almost immediately by two treaties establishing ways in which states can cooperate with each other and with the International Atomic Energy Authority (IAEA) to reduce damage from nuclear power plant disasters.

Most of the modern challenges in environmental protection are not posed by dramatic, isolated events but are related to environmental problems that have evolved gradually over time. In these cases, it is much more difficult to build the necessary momentum to regulate than in the aftermath of a catastrophe. One reaction to gradually aggravating environmental threats is for the environmental regimes to assign a more important role to scientific research in controlling international environmental problems. Scientists can inform politicians and the public via popularized assessments to show how rapidly and dramatically a problem is likely to escalate if no action is taken.

Existing international environmental regimes have created regulatory models that allow the scientific knowledge of the environmental problem to influence the way the regime responds to it. In this capacity, the LRTAP is the pioneering convention. In the first instance, a framework agreement was adopted containing general obligations. The establishment of the scientific monitoring programme EMEP made it possible to access precise information about the emissions of various harmful substances: where they originate and where they end up. This made it possible for the parties to negotiate the reduction of harmful substances by means of additional subsequent protocols.

This framework agreement model has since then been applied to almost all the key international environmental regimes; indeed, some regimes go further still, with the creation of accelerated amendment methods. For example, amendments can be made to the Montreal Protocol by a qualified majority.

The framework agreement model helps address some of the challenges in international environmental protection. Regulation can start at an early stage, as the agreement obligations do not require much from the parties. This also encourages a greater number of participants in decisions relating to a global or regional environmental threat, because the obligations are not very onerous.

Legally binding protocols can usually be negotiated into a framework agreement to specify and operationalize the general obligations. The parties to a framework agreement can participate in the protocols but they are not required to do so. This can be problematic: a regime can split into different groups, for example when the first protocol is ratified by only half of the state parties, whereas the majority participates in the second protocol. Such problems are frequently resolved over time, as the states gradually bind themselves to the various protocols in the framework agreement.

A framework agreement creates a legal connection between agreements that have been adopted at different times. As protocols are negotiated into a framework agreement and between its parties, the general regulations in the parent agreement typically apply to its protocols. The Biosafety Protocol Article 32 states that except otherwise provided, the Convention on Biodiversity applies to any subsequent protocol.

If the secretariat of a framework agreement is part of an existing international organization, it also maintains institutional continuity. It is frequently the only body in an international regime that is expected solely to implement the objectives of the agreement and its protocols; other regime bodies are composed of state representatives who may well also be inclined to advance the interests of their states.

Monitoring verification and compliance with obligations

International environmental law differs from traditional international law in the manner in which it obligates parties to an international environmental agreement to actually observe their obligations. The main rule in general international law is that if state A violates its obligation the injured state B can take the following measures:

1   State B can first attempt to settle the dispute politically: that is, by negotiation, or through mediation by a third party.
2   If still unsatisfied, state B can take the dispute to a court of arbitration or an international court of justice, with the consent of the parties to the dispute; (consent is not necessary in certain legal procedures such as WTO dispute settlement procedures). In most cases, states will try to settle the dispute themselves through negotiation rather than submitting it to legal procedures.
3   In many cases, the injured state can only react to a treaty violation by countermeasures. Countermeasures are measures taken by the injured state that would normally be contrary to international law; they are rendered lawful because they are a justified response to state A's earlier breach. The obvious result in many cases is a vicious spiral: state A denies having violated its obligations towards state B, and in turn takes its own countermeasures in response to the measure taken by state B.

Such processes will hardly advance international environmental regulation. The objective is to combat or even eliminate an international environmental threat (which is harmful for all treaty parties). It is therefore vital, as far as possible, to avoid mutual disputes related to non-observance of treaty regulations. Most environmental treaties do include an article relating to dispute settlement. Yet normally this just encourages states to settle their disputes via the means they themselves deem appropriate. In other words, by becoming parties to international environmental treaties, states do not necessarily commit to legally binding third-party dispute settlement, such as arbitration or submission of the dispute to the ICJ.

Environmental treaties take a different approach and aim at settling violations through collective implementation committees. A meeting of the parties generally establishes the reporting procedures and nominates an implementation committee tasked with creating ways of processing violations so that they cause as little damage as possible to the overall functioning of the agreement system.

The implementation of a treaty (and possible violations) is reviewed by the implementation committee and/or at meetings of the parties. These committees can only function if they are advised as to how states are observing their obligations. The information they receive should be as objective as possible. This is a difficult arrangement, but environmental treaties have gradually managed to create procedures that at the very least yield better information about how states implement and apply treaties.

The first task is to ensure that regular reporting on implementation to the meeting of the parties or the implementation committee must be a legal obligation. The duty to report has sometimes been omitted from a treaty and so the parties have not considered it a legal obligation. An example of this is the Espoo Convention.

The Espoo Convention on Environmental Impact Assessment in a Transboundary Context was adopted in 1991. There was no agreement on e.g. the duty to report. The second amendment in 2004 attempted to rectify the matter by making reporting compulsory. However, since an insufficient number of states have ratified the second amendment, it has still not entered into force. The meeting of the parties of the Espoo Convention resolved this problem with the establishment of an implementation committee which made a synthesis report on its most important decisions.

The implementation committee came up with an interesting solution relating to the duty to report: it stated that although the second amendment has not entered into force, the states are obliged to issue reports; otherwise, they can be taken to the implementation committee for non-observance. The implementation committee refers here to the fact that the second amendment was clearly accepted in the meeting of the parties, and the obligation to report should therefore be considered comparable to a legal obligation.

It is essential to ensure that states are legally obliged to report. How can we ensure that the regular reports that the states write about themselves remain objective, however?

Human rights treaties have solved this by establishing a separate monitoring committee of independent human rights experts to which the country reports are submitted. At the same time that a state submits its own report, the committee also receives reports from other sources, including human rights NGOs. This gives the committee the opportunity to ask difficult questions when the representatives of the states explain how they are complying with the human rights treaty in question.

A similar idea is being implemented in environmental treaties, although it is less well developed. The state reports go to either the meeting of the parties, the treaty secretariat, or directly to the implementation committee. They are generally inspected by representatives of states – not independent experts in international environmental law. Some environmental treaty regimes have started to receive information from NGOs but to a much lesser degree than the human rights bodies. States usually report on their own implementation of the treaty obligations. This, of course, is not the most desirable development as many countries are tempted to issue good reports even in problem situations.

Figure 3.1 The fourth meeting of the parties to the Espoo Convention took place in Bucharest, Romania, 19–21 May 2008. At the meetings of the parties, the member states met to make key decisions on the development of the treaty regime. (Photo © UNECE)

The most ambitious environmental treaties can use expert panels. In the climate regime, for instance, the greenhouse gas emission and sink inventories by the Annex I states are first certified by the secretariat and then by the expert panel. If the expert panel is dissatisfied with a state's inventory, it will forward questions to the compliance committee.

Implementation committees have become the trademark of environmental treaties, in the same way that monitoring committees are for human rights treaties. The implementation committees of environmental treaties are different from the monitoring committees of human rights treaties in one essential point: the members of a human rights treaty monitoring body are independent human rights experts, whereas the members of the environmental treaties are representatives of states (the unique Aarhus Convention's compliance committee members serve in their personal capacity, and nominations for election can also be proposed by NGOs). The outcome is that the monitoring bodies for human rights agreements are generally more outspoken in their criticism of states. Both committee types share the same objective: to protect the common good independent of states – human rights and the condition of the environment.

Since the ozone regime, the implementation committees of environmental agreements have functioned as follows:

1   The implementation committee solves a problem (for example, a member state will not or cannot comply with the treaty) preferably through financial and technical assistance (or education), especially in the case of a developing country.
2   In the case of an obvious deliberate violation the implementation committee attempts to avoid punitive measures and reverts to subtle pressure such as 'naming and shaming': the meeting of the parties (by consent of the implementation committee) names the non-observant country as being in breach of the treaty. The meeting of the parties also asks the country for a well-founded account of what measures it is taking to resume observation of the treaty obligations.
3   As a last resort, especially if a state is in deliberate violation of the treaty, repeatedly or over a long duration, the implementation committee can also take stronger measures such as temporary suspension of treaty rights.

The establishment of implementation (or compliance) committees has frequently proved problematic, unless the committee was specifically established in the treaty itself. The most notable example was that of the compliance committee of the climate regime.

The climate regime compliance committee's enforcement branch has been empowered to take strong decisions against non-compliant parties, such as, for example, excluding states from carbon trading. According to Article 18 of the Kyoto Protocol, when the Protocol enters into force the meeting of the parties shall approve procedures to address cases of non-compliance. However, it expressly states: 'Any procedures and mechanisms under this Article entailing binding consequences shall be adopted by means of an amendment to this Protocol.'

Nevertheless, this compliance committee was established by a decision of the meeting of the parties instead of an amendment; it would have been simply too time-consuming for all parties to process the amendment via their national systems. It would also probably have split the parties into those who accepted the amendment and those who did not. Such a result would have been unfortunate for a compliance committee whose objective was to apply penalties equally to all Annex I states that had bound themselves to emission reductions.

The enforcement branch of the climate regime's compliance committee therefore has real powers. Unless a state fulfils its obligation of emission reduction, the enforcement branch can, for example, suspend its right to apply the flexible mechanisms in emission reduction: that is, terminate its right to trade in emission reduction credits.

The fact that, as with all other decisions, the conclusions of the implementation committee are submitted to the meeting of the parties for acceptance can pose practical problems. These decisions are considered legally binding only in academic literature. States have clearly stated that they do not consider these decisions to be legally binding.

Amendments

In international environmental regulation, a model has been developed to amend an agreement flexibly so that it is consistent with updated scientific research about a particular threat and its severity. The model was first developed with the LRTAP framework convention; it initially accepted general principles and rules, which were then supplemented as knowledge increased by the negotiation of new protocols into the treaty regime.

The main problem is that according to classical international law, as sovereigns, states must accept each amendment. As we have seen above, this has often resulted in untenable situations: an amendment to an international environmental agreement is urgently needed but the only way to accomplish it is to create a protocol or to make a formal amendment. There are two drawbacks:

1 If an amendment requires a certain number of states to ratify it, it may take a long time to enter into force, even though it has been urgently needed for some time (or it may never enter into force).
2 Even if an amendment enters into force, certain states may be party to one amendment but not to others. This fragments the treaty system by establishing different obligations for each party. Such a situation is untenable from the point of view of the unity of the treaty regime.

This is why environmental treaties have started to create accelerated amendment procedures which can react to new information about an environmental threat quickly if necessary. These regimes tend to differentiate between regular obligations and technical amendments, the latter of which can be amended in an accelerated manner.

A prime example is the ozone regime, which can perform technical amendments by qualified majority. As a result, a state can become legally bound to a technical amendment without its consent. The ozone regime has managed to accelerate schedules for the reduction of CFC compounds. Another good example is the amendment procedure of the MARPOL Convention (on ocean pollution). Unless an amendment is objected to by one-third of all parties, or the parties controlling 50 per cent of merchant fleet tonnage, the annex amendment is automatically accepted. In practice, amendments are generally made by consensus so that there are no objections; under the MARPOL Annex, states are given a specified time period in order to register their objection to a proposed amendment.

Another way of accelerating and simplifying amendments is by taking important decisions at the meetings of the parties. This is an interesting procedure because the decisions are generally made by consensus. Although these decisions are not in themselves considered legally binding, they can sometimes have distinct legal consequences. The implementation rules of the Kyoto Protocol (the Marrakesh Accords), for instance, were internally implemented in Finland by the President's decree in the same way as many other treaties, although in real terms they represent decisions taken by the treaty parties (and specifications of the general rules in the Kyoto Protocol).

It seems clear that international environmental regimes must find ways of reacting to rapidly changing environmental problems. With decisions being made in the meetings of the parties and parties' representatives sitting in the compliance committee, this decision process – although formally non-binding – seems increasingly frequently to be the mode by which parties develop their regimes.

The trend in the implementation committees is also interesting. These committees seem to have imitated the monitoring committees of human rights treaties, at least to some extent. An increasing number of compliance committees work in a manner analogous to courts of justice to the extent that they consistently continue to observe their own earlier interpretations of the treaty. The bodies monitoring human rights treaties give, on the basis of individual country reports, general statements of how a certain treaty provision should be interpreted. The implementation committees of environmental treaties do not give official general statements but some of them have started to publish synthesis reports of the most important findings in their earlier decisions as a guideline for how the treaty should be interpreted.

The decisions of these compliance committees are generally submitted to the meetings of parties for acceptance, which gives them a high legitimacy for the parties since they have themselves contributed to the decision. Irrespective of how their legal status is assessed – whether they are legally or politically binding in any way – the parties generally comply with their conditions. These meetings of the parties are the only way of making quick decisions in the international community, as the agreement system will in every case have to react to updated information about the environmental threat on the basis of scientific research.

Questions to be considered at the various stages of an environmental treaty (based on the biodiversity regime as the main example)

1   Do the negotiators from the individual states start with a blank sheet, or has a particular body already prepared a draft for a new treaty?
     In the example of the Biodiversity Convention, the first draft was prepared by the International Union for Conservation of Nature (IUCN).
2   Are the official negotiations in a regime connected to an existing international organization?

The negotiations for the biodiversity regime and for many other regimes were arranged and led by UNEP.

3   How is a regime financed?

The financing mechanism for the biodiversity regime is GEF.

4   How does a regime function between signature and entry into force?

The biodiversity regime entered into force so promptly that no intermediate solutions were necessary. By contrast, the Espoo Convention was signed in 1991 and did not enter into force until 1997; in this case, the parties decided to arrange signatories' meetings of the parties to prepare for entry into force.

5   What bodies can be established by a meeting of the parties in a treaty in order to promote the objectives of the agreement regime?

The biodiversity regime did not establish an implementation committee but the meeting of the parties does review the regular reports from each country; the regime has also established the Subsidiary Body for Scientific, Technical and Technological Advice (SBSTTA), and various other working groups and programmes to implement the obligations vaguely expressed in the Biodiversity Convention.

6   How often does a meeting of the parties take place, and when does it make the essential decisions?

The meeting of the parties of the biodiversity regime meets every second year, while that of the climate regime, for instance, meets every year, and that of the Espoo Convention, about once in three years.

7   How does a treaty regime specify the general obligations?

The biodiversity regime has adopted both non-binding guidelines and two legally binding protocols.

8   How does an agreement regime secure compliance with its obligations?

The biodiversity regime does not have a separate body to review compliance, whereas the Espoo Convention has a specific implementation committee for this purpose.

9   How are amendments made to the treaty regime?

The parties to the Convention on Biological Diversity and its protocols are encouraged to adopt amendments via consensus, but if this proves impossible, an amendment can be adopted by a two-thirds majority vote. The depositary will then submit the amendment to all parties for ratification, acceptance or approval. Such an amendment will enter into force for those who have ratified it on the 90th day after the deposit of instruments of ratification, acceptance or approval by at least two thirds of the parties.

Customary international law

The rules of customary international law have evolved gradually to reflect the changing international community. Before the Second World War – and before the international law was explicitly recorded as written international agreements after the war – customary law was considered to evolve slowly and to require genuine action by the majority of states. The notion was that as a certain international practice is found legally binding (*opinio juris*) by the majority of states, it gradually evolves into a legally binding rule. Such a practice shall be widespread and virtually uniform and it shall have prevailed for a certain time. States should also feel that they are observing a practice because they are obliged to do so by a legal rule. In contrast, other customs and ceremonies are observed in many areas of international cooperation, although not because states consider them legally binding.[18]

The development of customary law

The rights of coastal states to the continental shelf provide a good example of the development of customary law.

When the United States, as one of the victors of the Second World War, issued the Truman Proclamation in 1945 stating that it had control of the natural resources of the seabed in areas adjacent to its coastline, other coastal states progressively followed the example. In time, this resulted in all coastal states having the continental shelf as a customary law entitlement. The right of coastal states to the natural resources of their continental shelves was recorded in the 1958 Convention on the Continental Shelf,[19] although the outermost limits of the continental shelf were not defined until 1982 when the UN Convention on the Law of the Sea[20] was adopted.

A similar 'traditional' progress of customary international law resulted from the USA's provocation of Canada in 1969.

The United States considered (and still does) the Northwest Passage to be an international strait free for all the world's ships to cross. In 1969, the USA sent an ice-strengthened oil tanker, the *SS Manhattan*, to cross the Northwest Passage, which created an enormous stir in Canada. As Canada did not consider the Northwest Passage to be an international strait, but Canadian internal waters, the action of the US was considered to be a violation of Canadian sovereignty.

Canada reacted by enacting the Arctic Waters Pollution Prevention Act in 1970,[21] according to which it assumed the right to control all vessels entering the ice-covered Northwest Passage, ostensibly to protect the vulnerable Arctic environment. Canada went so far as to justify its action based on its purported responsibility to humanity. This policy contradicted the international law of the sea, which at the time only allowed very limited intervention in seafaring beyond territorial waters.

Sometimes customary international law can only progress through violation of an existing customary law rule. Canada was active during the negotiations for the UN Convention on the Law of the Sea (UNCLOS) in 1973–82, and gained the acceptance of the international community for its action. Article 234 was written into the UNCLOS text, which guarantees all coastal states adjacent to ice-covered waters the right to control the movements of vessels more closely than anywhere else within their exclusive economic zones (a radius of 370 kilometres, or 200 nautical miles from the coast). Because of the interplay between treaty law and the evolution of customary international law, the codification of this provision in the UNCLOS has resulted in the evolution of Article 234 into a rule of customary international law.

The Arctic coastal states now have wider rights to regulate and control the movements of vessels in their ice-covered sea areas. The situation, however, is altering, as climate change is causing the ice of the Arctic Ocean to melt at an accelerating rate: as states' exclusive economic zones in the Arctic Ocean gradually become ice-free, the application of Article 234 will be increasingly questioned.

Interplay between customary international law and international treaties

Even when an international convention expresses a valid rule of customary international law, as Article 234 does, the two sources of law should be considered distinctly. Customary international law is binding across the entire world, whereas a convention is only binding for the parties to it.

Today, the development of customary international law is different, not least because of the speed at which the international community has evolved since the Second World War and the Cold War. Now, the main focus is on the content of an agreement. If states negotiate a global convention that is legally binding, they are in fact signalling their willingness to be bound by certain rules. Within international organizations and in other forums, states are constantly expressing their opinions of how other states should behave. How states 'talk' and the formal commitments that they make are increasingly important to the development of customary international law. International rules are being created at an accelerating pace, both by treaties and via other international instruments.

The principle of no-harm provides a good example. There is not enough evidence that states in practice – in a uniform manner and all over the world – pay attention to the potential impact in the environment of other states of their own planned projects. Nevertheless, this principle is included in nearly all globally binding international environmental conventions. Since expressed willingness to apply this principle has been expressed in treaty form, it is inadequate and simply wrong to consider it as merely a treaty rule. If a state has already, through committing to several conventions, signalled that a principle is legally binding, is this not a sufficient indication that the principle has developed into a norm of customary international law? It has become difficult to know why states behave according to the principle of no-harm, as it is not easy to say whether a state is observing a convention it has ratified (and the principle of no-harm recorded in it) or the principle of no-harm in customary international law.

International environmental conventions regulate almost all aspects of contemporary environmental law, while customary law plays a supplementary role. The principle of no-harm, for example, applies as a general principle in contamination cases where international environmental conventions do not necessarily apply: most international environmental conventions apply to certain defined cases or actions, excluding other cases outside their scope.

States endeavour to control and prevent most environmental threats by international treaties. It is natural that states should want to expressly record the rules and obligations they are prepared to undertake in order to control a given environmental problem.

Customary international law is not an adequate tool for reacting to environmental threats because it is often open to interpretation.[22] Environmental threats should be addressed at the earliest possible stage and managed in a way that is flexible and able to adapt to the latest scientific research.

One advantage of customary international law is that it binds every nation in the world, whereas conventions bind only the parties to them: so, for example, if 150 states are parties to a global convention, more than 40 states remain outside the regime. If it can be proven and verified that most of the convention rules have evolved into customary international law, the rules will be legally binding to all the states of the world. Even if a state withdrew from the treaty in question, it would still remain legally bound by the customary international law.[23]

This difference remains highly relevant, particularly because the USA, for example, has deliberately remained outside of many global and regional international environmental agreements. It is not a party to the UNCLOS, and therefore not directly bound by the provisions of Part XII of the Convention regulating the protection of the marine environment. Nevertheless, since 1982, Part XII has become accepted as customary international law, and its provisions therefore are binding worldwide. The USA has endorsed these rules as legally binding as a matter of customary international law.

On the other hand, some states have consistently objected to the status of such principles as the precautionary principle as customary international law and they are fully entitled to do so. If a state consistently objects to the evolution of a principle or rule into a principle of customary international law, the principle does not apply to that state, even if the principle evolves into a customary law principle that is binding to all other states. This is known as the persistent objector doctrine.

The greatest problem in the development of customary law is often the fact that it is difficult to say when a customary international law rule came into being or 'crystallized' in the language of international lawyers. The legal status of the principle of no-harm, for instance, has been unclear ever since an international arbitration tribunal was established to settle a dispute between the USA and Canada concerning sulphur oxide emissions from a zinc and lead smelter on the Canadian side, which had caused environmental damage in the state of Washington, on the US west coast. In its decision in 1941, the arbitration tribunal stated that no country is entitled to use its territory, or permit it to be used, in a way that causes damage to the territory of another country, its inhabitants or their property.

It seems, then, that a rule of this type was established as early as 1941. The problem remained that the arbitration tribunal did not, in fact, consider the praxis between sovereign states in transboundary pollution cases (as no such practice existed at the time between sovereign states), but based its decision on the praxis between units of federal states (such as US states or Swiss cantons). This is one reason why heated discussions on the legal status of the principle of no-harm continued among academics for decades, until the UN International Court of Justice confirmed in 1996 that the principle of no-harm is legally binding on every state in the world.

General principles of law

Aside from treaty and custom, Article 38 provides for 'general principles of law recognized by civilized nations' as a formal source of international law.[24] It is, however, obvious that in practice conventions and customary international law are actually the most common routes by which states can develop international law. An indication of this is that even the International Court of Justice has not once in its decisions referred to the general principles of law recognized by civilized nations.[25]

Another difficulty in referring to the general principles of law is that there are several views of how these principles evolve, and what they are. Perhaps the most widely accepted view is that general principles develop when national legal systems worldwide adhere to certain principles. Their function is frequently seen to be to close a gap that might remain uncovered by the main sources of international law – treaties and customary law – even if international tribunals do not expressly use general principles of law in their reasoning.

There is no further explanation of what constitutes the 'civilized nations' whose recognition decides the development of the general principles of law. It may appear odd to contemporary readers that the Statute of the International Court of Justice still refers to 'civilized nations'. The simple explanation is that the predecessor of the International Court of Justice – the Permanent Court of International Justice, established in 1922 – was strongly dominated by European colonial powers and its own statute was the template on which the Statute of the International Court of Justice was based in 1945 (still very much a period of colonialism). The reference in the Statute to 'the general principles of law recognized by civilized nations' was much criticized when African and Asian nations achieved their independence through decolonization: the former European colonial powers had justified the repression of other nations largely by a need to 'civilize' them. The most widely accepted view today is that principles of law can evolve from principles of domestic legal systems which are widely recognized across different kinds of legal systems (such as common law, civil law, religious law) in multiple continents.

There is much debate over what the International Court of Justice meant to express in its 2010 *Pulp Mills* judgment regarding the integration of the environmental impact assessment (EIA) into general international law. The Court defines international EIAs as 'a practice, which in recent years has gained so much acceptance among States that it may now be considered a requirement under general international law to undertake an environmental impact assessment where there is a risk that the proposed industrial activity may have a significant adverse impact in a transboundary context'.[26]

Although the Court fails to expressly state that the transboundary EIA is a general principle of law in the sense of Article 38(c), it does seem to actually consider it so. In the interpretation of most academics, however, the International Court of Justice confirmed that the transboundary EIA has evolved into a principle of customary law. In any case, whether it is a general principle or a norm of customary law, there is no doubt after this decision that states are obliged to perform transboundary EIAs in cases where planned activities pose a threat to the environment of other states or international spaces.

There is a reason why the International Court of Justice is reluctant to apply general principles of law and to discuss and define them: the international community of states is ready to observe the rules which it has created. In concluding agreements states deliberately bind themselves legally to observe their provisions. In this way, states are also contributing to the development of international customary law, albeit tacitly. When the International Court of Justice is called upon to resolve a dispute between states, it should be able to convey that it is only applying the rules and principles to which the states themselves have consented. Otherwise, it is much more likely that states would fail to observe the Court's decisions in cases they lose, or that they might become less willing to submit their disputes to the International Court of Justice in the first place. If the International Court of Justice were to appeal expressly to general principles of law, it is likely that the states might fear that the Court is taking too progressive an attitude to the development of international law, rather than carrying out its basic duties, namely resolving discrete disputes that threaten international relations. From the states' point of view, the general principles of law are too general and indeterminate to constitute a useful source of law that could be applied to settle real world disputes: in theory, these general principles could allow the International Court of Justice to apply norms to states that have given neither express (treaty) nor implied (customary law) consent.

Secondary sources of law

International law can only be developed by states. Secondary sources of law, such as the decisions of international courts of justice or committee reports of international law associations, do not create international law but can clarify and specify the legal status and content of rules developed by states. These are called material sources because they provide supplementary evidence of what the law is without actually being formal sources themselves. Judicial decisions are by far the most important secondary source of law. Although the decisions of the International Court of Justice are formally binding on the parties of a dispute only (and in each dispute only), the UN International Court of Justice plays a crucial role in the development of international law (including international environmental law).

In earlier periods of history, the research findings of individual, prominent international academics were significant in the specification of international law. Today, the influence of academics is mostly channelled through the work of committees of international organizations such as the International Law Association (ILA).

Courts of arbitration used to be more significant, as before the Second World War the Permanent Court of International Justice (PCIJ), established in 1922, was the only one of its kind. During the past 20 years, the decisions by permanent international courts of justice have become more important – especially the decisions of the International Court of Justice – even though the use of arbitration to resolve international commercial disputes has increased enormously.[27] Today there are numerous global standing courts (for example, the International Criminal Court and International Tribunal for the Law of the Sea) and they are called upon to make significant decisions much more frequently than before. The essential difference between a court of arbitration and a permanent court of justice is that the parties can appoint the judges in courts of arbitration, while courts of justice have permanent (though sometimes rotating) posts for judges.

International courts of justice

International courts of justice, unlike courts of arbitration, are permanent (the exceptions are the *ad hoc* criminal tribunals for Yugoslavia and Rwanda, for example) and settle disputes between states on the basis of international law. The first such international court was the Permanent Court of International Justice founded in 1922.

Today, there is one general international court that processes all kinds of legal disputes between states: the UN International Court of Justice; and one court that processes marine law disputes between states: the International Tribunal for the Law of the Sea (although in disputes relating to seabed mineral operations the International Seabed Authority (ISA) and the company that applied for permission to exploit seabed minerals can participate). The members of the WTO can also take their trade disputes to the organization's dispute settlement which includes both a panel process and the right to appeal against a panel decision.

The UN Convention on the Law of the Sea (Part XV) applies both judicial and arbitration procedures: the Convention obliges its parties to settle most of their disputes that cannot be resolved through negotiation (with certain exceptions, for example relating to fishing or marine border disputes) in one of the judicial or arbitration procedures identified in the Convention in order to result in a legally binding outcome. States can also take disputes related to the pollution of the marine environment to judicial settlement.

For instance, Ireland claimed that the United Kingdom had violated several rules of the Convention on the Law of the Sea by approving the Mox Plant which processed nuclear waste; Ireland considered the environmental impact assessment deficient. It claimed that the Mox Plant caused, among other things, radioactive contamination of the Irish Sea marine environment. In 2001, Ireland commenced arbitration proceedings related to the Mox Plant in the Arbitral Tribunal constituted under Annex VII of the UNCLOS. (This was only part of the legal strategy of Ireland that resulted in the EU Commission taking Ireland to the EU judiciary. In 2006, the then European Court of Justice of the European Communities confirmed that Ireland had violated EU regulations by taking a dispute within EU law to arbitration proceedings outside the EU legal system.)

Regional courts of human rights are also considered international courts of justice, such as the European Court of Human Rights or the Inter-American Court of Human Rights, as well as courts of justice that are based on regional integration, such as the Court of Justice of the European Union. During the operation of the *ad hoc* criminal tribunals for the former Yugoslavia and Rwanda, the permanent International Criminal Court (ICC) was established to address massive atrocities such as genocide, crimes against humanity and war crimes; it commenced in 2002. In human rights courts, individuals are litigants in cases of state violation of human rights, whereas individuals stand accused in international criminal courts.

So many new international courts of justice and other international dispute settlement procedures have been created after the Cold War but some academics find this problematic. One of the problems is that states can effectively commence dispute settlement with a strategy to find the most favourable international court of justice or court of arbitration proceedings for their specific dispute (the so-called forum shopping phenomenon, an example of which can be seen in the Mox Plant case above). A case could be considered to be an environmental protection dispute by state B, but state A could instead interpret it as a free trade dispute and take it to the WTO Dispute Settlement Panel.

The decisions of international courts of justice bind the disputing parties only, but in practice can actually influence the development of international law greatly as courts pay a good deal of deference to their own prior decisions and those of one another.

It is in the permanent international courts of justice and courts of arbitration that international law plays the most prominent role. National legal systems do make decisions on the basis of international law as well, but in that context it is just one source of law, to be taken into account alongside domestic constitutions and national regulations. Although states do consider international law in their foreign policies, their national interests are also crucial to decision-making. In the UN International Court of Justice, a dispute between states is resolved on the basis of international law only.[28]

Increasing numbers of international courts of justice and courts of arbitration have intentionally developed international law while resolving disputes between states. The International Court of Justice has also in many cases clarified the criteria according to which we can identify customary international law; we could say that it has updated the principles by which international law is created in the modern international law system.

International courts of justice are doing important work by signalling to the international community when a principle or rule has reached the status of customary international law and becomes legally binding to all world nations. The status of the principle of no-harm in international environmental law (see Chapter 4, 'No-harm principle', p. 109), for instance, was unclear for decades, until the UN International Court of Justice in 1996 stated that it was legally binding worldwide. Since then, international and national courts of justice, foreign ministries and the academic community have been able to concentrate on defining more precisely the content of this principle.

Disputes relating to the exploitation and pollution of the environment are being submitted increasingly to the UN International Court of Justice. However, states have never resorted to the UN ICJ's Chamber for Environmental Matters, established in 1993, which would have special expertise in the settlement of international environmental disputes. This is presumably because states fear that the judges in the Chamber could interpret international law much more strictly in terms of environmental protection. Since 2006, the ICJ has no longer elected members to the Chamber, since it had turned out to be redundant.

From the perspective of environmental protection, the decisions of the International Court of Justice have thus far not been very favourable, but nonetheless have developed and specified international environmental law. This might seem paradoxical and hence merits closer examination.

In its decision on the dam dispute between Hungary and Slovakia (the *Gabčíkovo-Nagymaros* case), the Court simply stated that the parties shall continue to cooperate by virtue of the bilateral treaty of 1977, but when interpreting it, take into account all the rules and principles of the developing international environmental law. Since the Court's judgment in 1997, Slovakia has built a dam on its side of the Danube and initiated another lawsuit against Hungary, claiming that Hungary was not willing to implement the 1977 treaty in good faith.

The Danube environment did not benefit from the Court decision but the Court did give significant statements of sustainable development as the 'concept' (objective) guiding industrial projects. Its implementation should take developing international environmental law into account. The Court also corroborated once again that the no-harm principle is legally binding on all the states in the world and added that it included the obligation of states to undertake environmental impact assessments (EIAs) prior to authorizing projects that could harm the environments of other states.

On the other hand, the court expressly avoided committing itself on the legal status of certain principles. Even when Hungary claimed that the Danube dam project violated the precautionary principle, the UN International Court of Justice did not make any clear determination one way or another.

While the International Court of Justice did not protect the Danube environment, it confirmed the current legal status of the no-harm principle and the duty to conduct an EIA. In the light of this case, foreign ministries around the world have begun to take the principle of no-harm more seriously.

Questions and research tasks

1   Select a prominent case of environmental protection which has been decided by the ICJ, and comment on how the judgment has clarified the content and status of an international environmental law principle, such as the precautionary principle or the obligation to undertake environmental impact assessment of activities with the potential for significant effects on the environment.

2   Customary law develops as a result of the practices of states. Reflect how civic organizations and other non-governmental actors can influence the development of customary law.

3   Find the home page of an international environmental agreement's implementation/compliance committee, and one of its decisions. Has it attempted to assist a party state or to punish it for violation of the agreement? Try and find one article or book that criticizes the implementation committees for not punishing states more actively.

Notes

1   From the legal perspective, the Ministry could have argued that they were only acting on the basis of customary law of treaties as codified by the Vienna Convention, Article 18(2). A state is obliged to refrain from acts that would defeat the object and purpose of a treaty which it has signed. But the Ministry did not invoke this legal argument since Article 18(2) very likely does not require a signatory to the Espoo Convention to commence a procedure on the basis of the Espoo Convention.

2   There has been discussion about whether and how individuals, indigenous peoples, liberation movements, corporations or non-governmental organizations could be considered to have the status of legal subject.

3   Almaty Guidelines on Promoting the Application of the Principles of the Aarhus Convention in International Forums, http://www.unece.org/fileadmin/DAM/env/documents/2005/pp/ece/ece.mp.pp.2005.2.add.5.e.pdf

4   http://www.ipcc.ch/

5   Many people wonder how such scientific institutions as the IPCC are able to give 'weather forecasts' reaching into the future; they speculate about the uncertainties of such forecasts openly admitted by scientists. However, scientists no longer argue about whether or not climate change is caused by humans, or whether or not it causes the changes observed in the climate system; the uncertainties pertain instead in predicting the future behaviour of the global climate system. This is very difficult, not only because the climate system is highly complex, but also because we cannot predict future human behaviour and whether there will be a plethora of climate friendly or climate unfriendly activities. Can our dependence on fossil fuels be severed and on what timescale? How can the tropical forests, 'the lungs of our planet', be preserved? How is land use in general changing? Human behaviour is very difficult to predict and scientists have no other opportunity than to simulate different potential futures on the basis of different assumptions.

6   Intergovernmental Science-Policy Platform on Biodiversity and Ecosystem Services (IPBES), www.ipbes.net

7   Millennium Ecosystem Assessment, 2005, http://www.unep.org/maweb/en/index.aspx

8   The second Article in the Convention on Biological Diversity defines genetic material as 'any material or plant, animal, microbial or other origin containing functional units of heredity'.

9   The Nagoya Protocol on Access to Genetic Resources and the Fair and Equitable Sharing of Benefits Arising from their Utilization to the Convention on Biological Diversity, http://www.cbd.int/abs/doc/protocol/nagoya-protocol-en.pdf

10   Global Programme of Action for the Protection of the Marine Environment from Land-based Activities (GPA), http://www.unep.ch/regionalseas/partners/unep_gpa.htm

11   This is why these types of instruments are increasingly studied as instruments of transnational environmental law.

12   The doctrine of the sources of law defines how governments develop international law, but it has other functions as well. Legal literature generally understands the sources doctrine in terms of defining what sources can be applied in legal decision-making and what the weight and mutual hierarchy of the sources are. The judges in the International Court of Justice or other international courts are bound to resolve a case on the basis of the sources of international law. International law is also studied on the basis of the sources of law.

13   Vienna Convention on the Law of Treaties, http://untreaty.un.org/ilc/texts/instruments/english/conventions/1_1_1969.pdf

14   As at 18 January 2013.

15   Article 2(d) of the Vienna Convention on the Law of Treaties defines what reservation is. It means 'a unilateral statement, however phrased or named, made by a State, when signing, ratifying, accepting, approving or acceding to a treaty, whereby it purports to exclude or to modify the legal effect of certain provisions of the treaty in their application to that State'.

16   This does not imply that every state will positively endorse the final result. Consensus often means that states are able to tolerate the decision of the meeting of the parties.

17   On numerous occasions, international courts and arbitral bodies have also emphasized that treaties should be interpreted in a dynamic fashion: i.e. that they should be interpreted in accordance with the changes in society. Yet only very rarely will

international treaties (especially in international environmental law) be given content via judicial procedures.

18   See the ICJ's guidance on this matter at the North Sea Continental Shelf Cases (Federal Republic of Germany/Denmark; Federal Republic of Germany/Netherlands), (para. 74), at the ICJ's website at http://www.icj-cij.org/docket/files/52/5561.pdf

19   Convention on the Continental Shelf, 1958, http://untreaty.un.org/ilc/texts/instruments/english/conventions/8_1_1958_continental_shelf.pdf

20   UN Convention on the Law of the Sea, http://www.un.org/Depts/los/convention_agreements/convention_overview_convention.htm

21   Arctic Waters Pollution Prevention Act (AWPPA), http://www.tc.gc.ca/eng/marinesafety/debs-arctic-acts-regulations-awppa-494.htm

22   For example, academics in the field often regard most principles of international environmental law as principles of customary international law, but many states (and their foreign ministries) disagree.

23   Even if customary law rules were incorporated into treaties, they still continue to operate in customary law as well. As the ICJ put it in the Nicaragua case, they 'continue to be binding as part of customary international law, despite the operation of provisions of conventional law in which they have been incorporated' (para. 73); see the ICJ's homepage at http://www.icj-cij.org/docket/files/70/6485.pdf

24   General principles of law is a source of law, and should not be confused with principles of international environmental law, which normally develop on the basis of the rules stipulating how customary international law evolves.

25   It is, however, true that the ICJ has decided many maritime border disputes between states on the basis of equitable principles. Even if this is the case, the Court is not asked by the disputing states to decide on the basis of equity, but on the basis of relevant rules of international law (which include equitable considerations).

26   *Case Concerning Pulp Mills on the River Uruguay* (*Argentina v. Uruguay*), para. 204, at http://www.icj-cij.org/docket/files/135/15877.pdf

27   International arbitration on the basis of the European Energy Charter and a large number of bilateral investment treaties has greatly increased over time.

28   The International Court of Justice is entitled, upon the request of the parties to a dispute, to make a decision according to what they deem to be fair and just, even going beyond the formally binding rules of international law (*ex aequo et bono*). No states have to date requested that it do so.

Further reading

Ahmad, A., *Cosmopolitan Orientation of the Process of International Environmental Lawmaking; An Islamic Law Genre*, Lanham, MD: University Press of America, 2001.

Bodansky, D., 'Customary (and Not So Customary) International Environmental Law', *Indiana Global Legal Studies Journal*, 3, 1995, s. 105–15.

Boyle, A., 'Some Reflections on the Relationship of Treaties and Soft Law', *International and Comparative Law Quarterly*, 48, 1999, pp. 901–13.

Brownlie, I., *Principles of Public International Law*, 7th edn, Oxford: Oxford University Press, 2008.

Brunnée, J., 'Reweaving the Fabric of International Law? Patterns of Consent in Environmental Framework Agreements', in R. Wolfrum and V. Röben (eds), *Developments of International Law in Treaty-Making?*, pp. 101–26, Berlin: Springer Verlag, 2005.

Fitzmaurice, M. and Elias, O., *Contemporary Issues in the Law of Treaties*, The Hague: Eleven International Publishing, 2005.

Fitzmaurice, M., Elias, O. and Merkouris, P. (eds), *Treaty Interpretation and the Vienna Convention on the Law of Treaties: 30 Years on*, Leiden: Nijhoff, 2010.

Klabbers, J., 'The Redundancy of Soft Law', *Nordic Journal of International Law*, 65, 1996, pp. 167–82.

Lausche, Barbara, J., *Weaving a Web of Environmental Law*, Berlin: Schmidt, 2008.

Sands, P., 'Treaty, Custom and the Cross-fertilization of International Law', http://www.law.yale.edu/documents/pdf/LawJournals/Philippe_Sands_YHRDLJ.pdf

Stephens, T., *International Courts and Environmental Protection*, Cambridge: Cambridge University Press, 2009.

Trindade, C., 'Separate Opinion', The Pulp Mills case in International Court of Justice, http://www.icj-cij.org/docket/files/135/15885.pdf

Websites

American Society of International Law, Electronic Information System for International Law (EISIL): http://www.eisil.org; international environmental law section: http://www.eisil.org/index.php?sid=606131475&t=sub_pages&cat=18

ECOLEX (information service on environmental law): http://www.ecolex.org/start.php

Environmental Treaties and Resource Indicators (ENTRI): http://sedac.ciesin.columbia.edu/entri/guides/guide-hp.html

International Court of Justice: http://www.icj-cij.org/homepage/

International Tribunal for the Law of the Sea: http://www.itlos.org/

New York University School of Law, Hauser Global Law School Program ('Update: A Basic Guide to International Environmental Legal Research'): http://www.nyulawglobal.org/Globalex/International_Environmental_Legal_Research1.htm

WTO, intergovernmental disputes: http://www.wto.org/english/tratop_e/dispu_e/dispu_e.htm#disputes

4 Principles of international environmental protection

As a student reading international law textbooks, I became conscious of the fact that international law justified many concepts which I had taken for granted – such as the sovereignty of a state in its own territory. I came to appreciate that this was not just a fact but a principle protected and upheld by international law.

I realized then how important the rules of international law are in regulating the legal status of the place where we live. These principles precede the actions of present and future governments. We, our leaders and our governors assume the principles as a matter of course when we confront the complex reality of international politics. The ownership of a territory defines who can protect its environment.

Newcomers to international environmental law are often enchanted by its principles: 'common heritage of humanity', 'common concerns of human-kind' and the 'precautionary principle' sound like magic words with the power to make environmental problems disappear. While this kind of idealism is psychologically important for anyone specializing in international environ-mental law, it will fade over time, while these principles remain as ideals and objectives to spend our lives working towards.

Their legal status and content can seem a little vague, so they do require frequent discussion and clarification. This can cause a bit of a headache as it is difficult even for an expert on the matter to state anything about them with certainty. On the other hand, they encompass such a wealth of rules and principles that they can help us to bring coherence into international environmental law.

This chapter discusses the role of principles in international environmental protection. We will begin by taking a look at the rules of international law which define the legal status of the different parts of the world: that is, who or what body has the power to decide over polluting economic operations in a given area and how the environmental impacts of these operations should be controlled and minimized. The primary principle is the sovereignty of states over their own territories, since states have territorial sovereignty over most of the land mass of our planet, with the exception of Antarctica. Increasingly, indigenous peoples – and their emerging rights – are beginning to challenge the authority of states in their native areas. We also look at deviating arrangements in terms of sovereignty and above all the authority to implement measures for environmental protection: namely, the Spitsbergen treaty system created in 1920 and the impact of EU law on member states' rights and responsibilities pertaining to environmental protection. Areas beyond national jurisdiction – like the high seas or the deep seabed – have their own rules about who can pursue economic activity and under what rules and whose supervision. A unique regime was developed for Antarctica and the Southern Ocean, which should be examined in the context of the international political history of the area.

The second part of this chapter discusses the international environmental legal principles that have developed strictly under the state-centric principles of general international law. These principles frequently set the limitations on how international environmental protection can be promoted. A state's territorial sovereignty can have a significant effect on the promotion of international environmental protection in the current international community. Those principles of international environmental law that are based on widely recognized principles of international law are more likely to gain acceptance as they are framed in a language that states can recognize and understand. Our goal of solving global environmental problems is guided by the 'common concern of humankind' principle. This principle implies only that every state must contribute to the common effort for the environment, although not necessarily by participating in international treaty systems. We discuss the most developed regulation, concerning transboundary pollution between states, and then move on to principles that govern the management of regional and global environmental problems. Next, we review the principles that guide the activities of states where actions within their authority and control have caused harm to the international environment.

Our third focus will be on international environmental legal principles of disputed status but with significant influence on both regional and global environmental protection. We consider the difference between a rule and a principle, the difference between material and procedural principles, and the functions a principle performs in international environmental protection. New approaches to environmental protection will also be introduced as well as methods of influencing environmental protection, many of which have evolved in a national context.

Ownership of land, sea and space

It seems slightly odd to talk about ownership of land, sea or space. How can one 'own' what cannot be tangibly 'possessed'? Our day-to-day life, however, tells us that land can be owned: one can purchase real estate and officially own part of our planet – in domestic legal terms, anyway. Companies exist that sell properties on the Moon or on the other closest planets in our solar system, despite the fact that under international law, sovereign states cannot take these areas into their possession.

But who can own any meaningful area of the planet or atmosphere according to international law? Are any areas classified as a kind of common area of the global community? Questions such as these can be answered according to the principles of international law. It is important to be familiar with these principles, because they specify the environmental protection rules that are applicable in any given area and who has the right to enact and implement these rules.

State jurisdiction

Even scholars of international relations can find it strange that the international community developed rules as to the ownership of each part of our planet. However, this is the case. The greatest part of Earth's land is 'owned', administered and managed by sovereign states. International law does not refer to ownership by states, but to 'sovereignty', although the word is in many ways synonymous with the ownership rights a private individual might have to an area of land.

Within the limits of international law, a state is entitled to form its own rules for administering its territory and to decide on how these rules are to be implemented and enforced. Other states are obliged to respect its territorial sovereignty and they are not free to intervene in matters that take place within its territory. States are, then, not allowed to enact laws that apply to the territories of other states and they are definitely not allowed to send their officials (e.g. police forces) to enforce such laws.

Figure 4.1 A private beach at Lake Michigan in the USA. The landowners planted the sign in order to prevent others from accessing their beach areas although the public trust doctrine states that these are common areas. (Photo © Melissa K. Scanlan)

From an environmental law perspective, this means above all that the nearly 200 states in the world are sovereign in the regulation of the use and protection of the environment and in the implementation of related legislation in their own territories, within the limits of international law. However, decisions by the WTO dispute settlement bodies have further defined that states can, on certain conditions, act to protect the environment beyond their sovereignty – as, for example, in the *Shrimp/Turtle* case when the USA sought to protect turtles outside its territory (see Chapter 5, p. 145).

Which areas are then considered to be under the 'ownership' of states? First of all, states are sovereign in their land areas. Nearly all land areas belong to states; the most prominent exception being Antarctica, where sovereignty claims are frozen (but not renounced) (see below, 'Antarctica and the Arctic regions', p. 101).[1] Ownership of a territory – that is, a state being sovereign in a territory – also includes sovereign rights to certain adjacent maritime spaces and superjacent airspace. A state is sovereign up to the outer edge of its territorial waters (12 nautical miles), which is also the outer edge of a state's airspace.[2]

In many cases, territorial sovereignty is, in reality, a mere illusion. Intergovernmental treaties have opened the world's airspace to all airlines. On the territorial sea, foreign vessels have been legally guaranteed 'innocent passage'.[3] Multinational companies operate across many countries and in a fully global market in terms of goods and services.

Today, coastal states enjoy sovereign rights to the natural resources of their exclusive economic zone and the continental shelf. The exclusive economic zone may extend to a maximum of 200 nautical miles (370 kilometres) from the baseline,[4] and the continental shelf may extend even further, up to a maximum of 350 nautical miles (and even beyond that in some cases). States have the exclusive right to control the use of the natural resources (for example, fish stocks) within their exclusive economic zones. If a state decides to establish an exclusive fishing or economic zone (which must be publicly declared if the state wants to enjoy exclusive rights), it is also obligated to protect the marine environment in the same area.

The continental shelf is considered a natural extension of the land territory, so it is not necessary for a state to make a specific claim to it. A state has the exclusive right to exploit seabed and sub-seabed resources, including oil and gas resources, minerals and certain seabed fauna. As the continental shelf can extend to over 200 nautical miles, it is pertinent to consider whether a state has the right or, indeed, the obligation to protect the environment of the so-called outer continental shelf. We will consider this question below in connection with the international law principle of no-harm. A state is obligated to prevent and minimize the probability of environmental harm from any operations it permits in its jurisdiction and control. Since a coastal state can permit oil drilling in its continental shelf, say, 400 kilometres from the coast, it is also liable to arrange for an appropriate environmental impact assessment to be performed before deciding to grant the permission.

Development of the rights of indigenous peoples

A state is above all a creation of international law. International law defines the criteria a state must meet and how they can be established. Many schools of thought present the state as a natural political unit: we speak, for instance, about the 'nation-state'. The state is hence justified by being the organization model of a natural political community – the 'nation'. In reality, a state often comprises several peoples, as in Nigeria or Belgium.

One of the challenges for the international community is to consider how natural resources should be administered; one of the major developments we have seen in recent years is the gradually increased legal status of indigenous peoples. Already it can be argued that they have rights to territory and natural resources and the related obligations of environmental protection.

The Charter of the UN already contains many references to peoples. It starts dramatically by stating what 'We the peoples of the United Nations' undertake for the sake of world peace and a better world. However, only recognized states can be members of the UN. A similar paradox is contained in two of the main principles in international law. First, the customary international law principle of no-harm begins: 'States have the sovereign right to exploit their natural resources according to their environmental and developmental policies ...'.[5] The two most important global human rights agreements, the International Covenant on Civil and Political Rights (ICCPR) and the International Covenant on Economic, Social and Cultural Rights (ICESCR), state in their common Article 1 (items 1 and 2):

1   All peoples have the right of self-determination. By virtue of that right they freely determine their political status and freely pursue their economic, social and cultural development.
2   All peoples may, for their own ends, freely dispose of their natural wealth and resources without prejudice to any obligations arising out of international economic co-operation, based upon the principle of mutual benefit, and international law. In no case may a people be deprived of its own means of subsistence.

'States', then, have the sovereign right to exploit their natural resources according to their own environmental and developmental policies, while at the same time 'peoples' may freely dispose of their natural wealth and resources for their own ends. This contradiction can be eliminated by interpretation: one can argue that 'state' and 'people' are roughly the same thing in this largely post-colonial age. International law guarantees the right of self-determination, developed specifically to help former colonies achieve independence; one by one, African and Asian countries won their independence by demanding self-determination.

However, the issue is not quite that simple. The international bodies that monitor human rights treaties have gradually started to signal to the global community that the indigenous peoples living in their territories are the 'peoples' referred to in the common Article 1. There is no universally accepted definition of indigenous peoples, but these basic elements are agreed: they are peoples who lived in the area before the settlers came, have maintained their traditional livelihoods, wish to continue their cultural existence through their own institutions, and are normally in a non-dominant position within mainstream society.

Article 1 is applied to indigenous peoples by both of the major committees that monitor the main human rights treaties: the Human Rights Committee monitoring the ICCPR and the committee monitoring the ICESCR. Although this is a fairly recent development (since 1999), the work of the committees is relevant when assessing which of the rights of the indigenous peoples can be matched with the sovereign rights of a state.

Negotiations regarding what constitutes the self-determination of indigenous peoples have been ongoing for some time. The UN Declaration on the Rights of Indigenous Peoples took over 20 years to negotiate. One of the most challenging issues was self-determination. A draft declaration on indigenous peoples was accepted in the UN as the basis for further negotiations in 1994. It recorded the full self-determination of indigenous peoples in a very ambitious way, comparable to common Article 1 of the ICCPR and ICESCR: indigenous peoples have full freedom to decide on their political status, including the option of full independence (sometimes called 'external self-determination'). After this, negotiations in the UN between states and indigenous peoples became difficult. Initially, the indigenous peoples were not prepared to back down from external self-determination and so the states involved refused even to enter negotiations starting from this premise.

A compromise was eventually reached in 2006 and the UN's principal human rights body, the Human Rights Council (UNHRC), accepted the declaration, although it significantly watered down the right of indigenous peoples to self-determination. Although Article 3 still states that indigenous peoples have the right to freely determine their political status, Article 4 defines the content of this right: autonomy or self-government in matters relating to their internal and local affairs. Even this was not sufficient for some African states, which feared that the indigenous peoples in their territories would demand their own independent state. The final declaration accepted by the UN General Assembly in 2007 states that the self-determination rights of indigenous peoples may not threaten the territorial integrity or political unity of states, precluding any right to secession (the creation of a new state out of part of a larger one).

The Declaration on the Rights of Indigenous Peoples is a declaration by the UN General Assembly and hence not legally binding as such. It is, however, the result of a lengthy negotiation process, in which states and indigenous peoples reached, through compromise, an understanding of what group and individual rights indigenous peoples actually have. The declaration partly records existing customary international law. Moreover, as a declaration by the UN General Assembly (where almost all the world's states are represented) it

Figure 4.2 Protest by indigenous people living in the Peruvian Amazon rainforest in
   Iquitos, May 2009. The reason for this protest was the permissions to drill
   for oil and gas in their traditional common land. The permissions had been
   granted without the sufficient consultation required by the International
   Labour Organization's ILO Indigenous and Tribal Populations Convention.
   (Photo © Ellen Desmet)

carries weight in the development of customary international law; as the UN
International Court of Justice articulated in its *Nicaragua* judgment in 1986.[6]

   The legal weight of the UN General Assembly declaration also depends on
how well it has been endorsed by the society of states. The declaration was
adopted by an overwhelming majority of 143 states in favour, with four states
against; 11 abstained from voting. Moreover, those four important states (the
USA, Canada, Australia and New Zealand), which have indigenous peoples
living in their territory, have one by one come to endorse the declaration,
which increases the weight of the declaration in influencing the development
of customary international law.

   It is likely that in the near future states will have to decide in one way or
another exactly what is included by the right of indigenous peoples to

self-determination. These states are under increasing pressure not only to acknowledge the self-determination of indigenous peoples but also to decide how indigenous peoples can have legal affirmation and protection for their traditional lands and waters. This implies that environmental protection, too, will become more and more an integral part of the self-determination of indigenous peoples in their traditional areas. Indigenous peoples have often suggested at international forums that they can be a model for other peoples in a world plagued by global environmental challenges: they have lived in harmony with nature for thousands of years. The declaration, in many of its provisions, confirms this close and multi-dimensional relationship between indigenous peoples and their traditional territories as well as providing explicitly that 'Indigenous peoples have the right to the conservation and protection of the environment and the productive capacity of their lands or territories and resources …' (Article 29[7]).

Limits of territorial sovereignty: Svalbard Islands and the EU as case examples

The usual state rights relating to territorial sovereignty are not valid everywhere. Let us now look at two cases in which territorial sovereignty was restricted by an international treaty, which also influence environmental protection by the sovereign states. The first case is the Svalbard Islands archipelago, the sovereignty of which was established by treaty in 1920. The other case we will examine in this section is the EU, which significantly affects the sovereignty and environmental protection of its member states.

Svalbard Islands

After lengthy negotiations, an agreement was reached in 1920 submitting the Svalbard Islands archipelago to Norwegian sovereignty.[8] The original parties to the treaty (today there are over 40 parties) very clearly acknowledge Norwegian territorial sovereignty, but Article 1 distinctly renders this 'absolute sovereignty' limited. From an international environmental law perspective, it is interesting to note that as far back as 1920, there were expectations of Norway to protect the environment; see under Article 2 (2):

> Norway shall be free to maintain, take or decree suitable measures to ensure the preservation and, if necessary, the reconstitution of the fauna and flora of the said regions, and their territorial waters; it being clearly understood that these measures shall always be applicable equally to the nationals of all the High Contracting Parties without any exemption, privilege or favour whatsoever, direct or indirect to the advantage of any one of them.

A comprehensive environmental protection act tailored by Norway for Svalbard Islands entered into force in 2002. To date, a total of 1,195 conservation areas protect the various vulnerable ecosystems in the area and Svalbard Islands is a centre for climate change research.

All parties to the treaty, their citizens and companies are entitled to carry on economic activities in Svalbard Islands on equal terms with the Norwegians (non-discrimination principle). The Russians and Norwegians have continued their coal mining practices in the area but this activity is reducing. The demilitarization and political neutrality of the area is also secured by the treaty (Article 9). Due to its unique administrative system, Svalbard Islands were not included in the European Economic Area (EEA).

The Svalbard Islands arrangement has functioned successfully. The only controversy concerns the legal status of the surrounding waters and seabed. The Svalbard Islands treaty is expressly applied up to the outer limit of the territorial waters only (12 nautical miles today) by virtue of Article 2(1), as longer-reaching marine zones did not exist in 1920. Norway considers the matter clear: the Norwegian position is that the Svalbard Islands treaty applies only to the maximum extent of the territorial sea, as is provided in Article 2; it has exclusive rights (excluding the rights of other parties and their nationals) to establish an exclusive economic zone around Svalbard and is hence free to allow oil drilling and fishing around Svalbard Islands outside of its territorial sea. Other parties disagree. Some, like the USA, object to Norway's claim but fail to express why.

Some parties, like Russia or Iceland, consider that Norway has no right to establish an exclusive economic zone around Svalbard Islands or to claim title to the natural resources on the Svalbard Islands continental shelf. While most states accept that Norway can establish an exclusive economic zone and administer the natural resources in the continental shelf, they consider that the Svalbard Islands treaty should also apply to these marine areas. Their view is that the rights of other states and their citizens would have been extended to these areas if the exclusive economic zone or the continental shelf had been part of the Law of the Sea in the 1920s. They consider that the Svalbard Islands treaty should be interpreted in the context of the evolution of the international law of the sea.

This is a difficult dispute to settle. Meanwhile, Norway established an exclusive economic zone around Svalbard, which it provisionally transformed to a fisheries protection zone, due to resistance from other parties. This protection zone is consistent with the treaty: it treats the citizens and companies of all parties equally. Real pressure to resolve the stalemate will be created if Norway should allow oil drilling in the Svalbard Islands continental shelf, for instance. The fisheries protection zone will probably remain the basis for the administration of the marine areas, because the parties cannot come to an agreement on any other solution. So far, the environment is very well protected: a strict comprehensive environmental protection act is applied to the land areas and there is a fisheries conservation area covering the marine areas.

European Union

The member states of the European Union have voluntarily surrendered their sovereignty to the EU to such an extent that it can no longer be considered an intergovernmental organization (although it is, in principle, and although a member state can leave it if it so desires). The Court of Justice of the European Union (CJEU) specifies that the EU is a legal system of its own, separate from the legal systems of its member states and distinct from international law.

The member states have gradually surrendered significant authority to the EU on environmental issues. The status of a member state in environmental law and policy has changed during its membership, as a good deal of relevant authority has been assigned to the EU over the years. The freedom of action of a member state in environmental policy and law is limited by EU environmental law as well as international environmental law.

The Treaty of Rome of 1957, which founded the EU's predecessor, the European Economic Community (EEC), contained no reference to environmental protection; it was finally included in the Single European Act in 1986. The original motivation of EU environmental regulation was primarily the functioning of the internal market – securing equal opportunities of competition through unified regulations and eliminating unfair competition. The first 'pure' environmental policy (Environmental Action Programme) was adopted in 1973, when the Directorate-General for the Environment in the Commission was established. These action programmes are the policies that still govern EU environmental policy, the most recent of which (the sixth Environment Action Programme) began in 2002 and ended in 2012.

Environmental regulation in the EU is extremely comprehensive. EU environmental law has developed over decades; today, it comprises hundreds of laws, usually in the form of directives and regulations. Environmental law consists predominantly of directives. Member states must implement directives in their domestic legal systems within a certain timeframe and inform the Commission of the measures that they have taken to do so. The directives are binding in terms of their objectives but the forms and means of implementation are for the member states to decide. If a member state fails to implement a directive fully within the time limit, the directive will become legally binding on it anyway (this is called 'direct effect'). Regulations are immediately legally binding when they are enacted throughout the EU, and no further national implementation measures are required by member states.

The Commission ensures that EU law is implemented and applied by the member countries. If the Commission suspects, on the basis of its findings, that a member state has not met its obligations, it initiates a two-stage pre-litigation procedure called the infringement procedure (the letter of formal notice and the reasoned opinion), after which it can take the member state to the EU judiciary.

It should be pointed out that both the EU and its member states are parties to most international environmental treaties (so-called mixed treaties). The EU incorporates environmental treaties as part of its legal system. As the CJEU has stated, environmental treaties are considered hierarchically to be higher than the EU's secondary legislation – that is, directives and regulations – although there have been dissenting opinions on this. Highest in the EU environmental law hierarchy are the founding treaties and the general legal principles as they are now recorded in the Treaty on the Functioning of the European Union, Article 191(2): 'The Union's environmental policy is based on the precautionary, preventive action, correction at source and "polluter pays" principles.'

EU environmental law, comprising the EU principles, laws and environmental treaties, covers most of the major areas of environmental protection. It is constantly changing. International environmental treaties are constantly being amended to meet new challenges, and the EU (and often its member states) is required to adopt these amendments in its legal system. The EU's own environmental actions are altered and extended, which has over time reduced the scope of the member states' environmental law and policy.

When the EU decides whether to participate in the negotiations of a new environmental treaty or whether it enacts a new environmental protection directive, it is imperative to know what kind of competence it has vis-à-vis the member states: exclusive, shared or supporting. The EU competence is always 'derived competence': the member states must submit their competence to it through founding treaties.

The EU legal order relies on the Treaty on the European Union, and the Treaty on the Functioning of the European Union, which are the highest legal norms of the EU, equivalent to domestic constitutions.[9] These two treaties constitute the consolidated version of the founding treaties which have, over time, been amended by successive treaties such as Maastricht (1992), Amsterdam (1997) and Lisbon (2009). With the 2009 Lisbon treaty amendments, the division of competence between the EU and its member states is, for the first time, recorded in a treaty, the Treaty on the Functioning of the European Union.

Environmental law and policy in the EU is generally an area of shared competence: both the EU and its member states have competence here. The EU has exclusive competence on certain aspects of environmental politics such as the conservation of marine biological resources under the common fisheries policy and the common commercial policy. Member states can still apply stricter regulation than the environmental protection directives require, and they can regulate certain segments of environmental law independently. The internal (in relation to member states) and external (in relation to the rest of the world) competence of the EU largely overlap with regard to environmental protection.

An interesting example of the intricacies of EU competence is the forestry policy.

In 2009, researcher Sébastien Duyck, Professor Kai Kokko and I conducted a study ordered by Forest Europe (earlier the Ministerial Conference on the Protection of Forests in Europe, MCPFE). Among other things, our goal was to analyse the competence of the EU to participate in a planned pan-European international forest management treaty. The Finnish position at the time was that the EU has no competence in forest matters, and that EU forestry policy had long been guided by policy-type instruments (such as the forestry strategy on sustainable management of forestry, accepted by the Council of the EU in 1998).

The Forest Europe process was sufficiently well advanced down the route of developing a legally binding treaty that we were able to analyse whether or not the EU has competence on the basis of two draft treaties which the Forest Europe secretariat had prepared. I will not describe this complex study in detail, but it was interesting that the Finnish view was very clear: the EU has no legal competence in forestry policy. This is now confirmed by the Treaty on the Functioning of the European Union. However, civil servants – even Finns – argued that the definition of legal competence by and large depends on what your perspective is.

The two draft treaties presented the most diverse viewpoints to sustainable forest management. Sustainable forest management, naturally, implies protecting the biological diversity, the significance of the forest in rural culture, and the essential role of forests in combating climate change. It can also mean extensively integrating the forest ecosystem services in policy-making, or concentrating in the optimization of wood production, or turning forest reserves into biofuel. Another important consideration is the relationship to the rest of the world. How can a pan-European treaty guarantee that unsustainably felled forests from the other side of the world do not end up as wood in the European market? Can import bans or restrictions be applied, and if so, how?

Although there are different perspectives to forest usage and management, the EU does have competence in forestry policy. Both draft treaties clearly proved that it does: although forestry policy is not expressly mentioned in the lists of competence even now – after the Lisbon amendments – this does not negate the EU's competence through its other competences: environmental policy, common commercial policy, energy policy, and so on. During all its years of regulation, the EU has accumulated such significant competence that it has at least some competence in virtually every field of policy.

It is interesting to note that Forest Europe initiated the negotiations for an international forest management treaty in 2011.

Common areas

Certain areas outside the territory of any particular state are deemed common, meaning that they can be enjoyed freely by any state or individual. All states and the ships registered in them can operate fairly freely on the high seas. The high seas area includes all seas and oceans beyond the exclusive economic zones of states – amounting to approximately two-thirds of all marine areas. Free navigation is even more extensive, as ships are permitted to navigate through coastal states' territorial seas and exclusive economic zones largely in the same way as on the high sea; they have the right of innocent passage, although there are a number of conditions applicable to this form of passage. No state can subject the high seas to their sovereignty and everyone has equal rights to use the natural resources found there. Similar international 'freedom areas' include international airspace, which extends to the skies superjacent to the outer limit of states' territorial seas, and outer space.

States, their ships, businesses and citizens have extensive freedom to operate in international common areas. The only limitation is that the area must be used without causing unreasonable harm to the interests and rights of other states and their ships. This has made it difficult to protect the high seas.

The greatest concerns relating to the high seas today include the overharvesting of discrete high seas' fish stocks – such as certain mackerel species – and the depletion of biological diversity. Few states have any motivation to limit overfishing, and the weakening of fish stocks has been discussed in the UN General Assembly many times with little progress.

Another kind of arrangement for common areas was negotiated in Chapter XI of the Convention on the Law of the Sea and amended by a special implementation agreement in 1994. Non-living resources (mostly minerals) in or on the seabed in the area beyond the outer continental shelves of states were declared the 'common heritage of humanity'. The International Seabed Authority (ISA) was established to administer these resources and to be in charge of environmental protection of this area. To date, there has been no commercial exploitation of these resources, largely because of economic factors, though some preparatory activities have taken place.

The 1979 Moon Treaty had a similar objective when exploitation of resources became topical: the Moon was similarly declared the common heritage of humanity. The Moon Treaty entered into force in 1984, but it has no practical relevance as few states ratified it and the major states engaged in space exploration have not become party to it.

Tragedy of the commons

Garrett Hardin launched the term 'tragedy of the commons' in *Science* magazine in 1968. The term 'commons' referred to those areas freely used by everyone (the use of which cannot be limited). It is particularly applicable to the high seas.

Hardin used the example of a pasture where herders graze their cattle. As long as there are few grazers, there is no problem. The capacity of the pasture or the common resource decreases when new herders enter it.

Hardin showed that in such a case, it is reasonable for one herder to use the pasture as much as possible: to take all that he or she can and not to consider the impact on other users. When every herder tries to exploit the pasture as fully as possible, the quality of that pasture will at some point deteriorate. The end result is that the pasture is no longer fit for anyone to use. In this way, reasonable decisions taken by an individual can lead to a miserable end for the community.

Antarctica and the Arctic regions

The legal status of Antarctica is unique. Before the 1959 international treaty, seven states (Norway, France, New Zealand, Australia, Great Britain, Chile and Argentina) had claimed sovereignty over parts of the continent. The Cold War parties, the USA and the Soviet Union, had also established scientific research stations in the area. Neither of them staked their own claim to sovereignty over any of Antarctica, nor did they recognize the claims made by the seven aforementioned states.

The United States took the initiative to begin treaty negotiations in an attempt to settle the difficult situation, resulting in the Antarctic Treaty, by which the sovereignty claims of the states were 'frozen': under the terms of the treaty, nothing the states did or said would be considered relevant to either substantiating a claim or renouncing it. This 'agreement to disagree' made it possible to administer Antarctica and the surrounding Southern Ocean internationally through the Antarctic Treaty[10] and the Antarctic Treaty Consultative Meetings (ATCM). The key aims of this administrative system are to demilitarize the area and to declare it as a zone of peace and science.

> I became familiar with the Antarctic Treaty and the administrative system that had evolved around it for the first time when I was working on my doctoral dissertation. It seemed amazing that the seven states that had claimed segments of Antarctica were prepared to suspend their claim (most states do not recognize any of these claims).
>
> Without this treaty, at least seven different states would have had the power to decide what could be done in each part of Antarctica and under what rules. Moreover, being coastal states, they would also potentially have a claim to 200 nautical miles of exclusive economic zones and rights to explore and exploit their Antarctic continental shelves. The treaty has granted the world an incredible ice-covered continent dedicated to science and nature conservation, where mining is also now prohibited.

The Antarctic Treaty System is continually expanding. Any state that conducts a full research operation in the region can be admitted as a consultative party of the Antarctic Treaty.[11] Related agreements include the conventions regulating seal hunting and fisheries resources in the Southern Ocean[12] and the 1991 Protocol on Environmental Protection to the Antarctic Treaty (Madrid Protocol).[13] All these agreements and the international bodies that administer them constitute the Antarctic Treaty System (ATS).

One of the notable successes of the system of governance in Antarctica is that the full consultative members of the Antarctic Treaty Consultative

Meetings have acted very responsibly to protect the vulnerable environment in the region. A good example is the prohibition of mining for 50 years. When the issue was discussed in the 1970s, the parties decided to ban mining until an international treaty on controlling and minimizing the environmental impacts of mining could be agreed.

This treaty containing very strict regulations on environmental protection was tentatively agreed in 1988 – the Convention on the Regulation of Antarctic Mineral Resource Activities (CRAMRA); however, this proved insufficient for France and Australia who refused to ratify the Convention and thus prevented it from ever coming into effect. Fortunately, the stalemate was quickly resolved by the 1991 Madrid Protocol on Environmental Protection to the Antarctic Treaty, which came into force in 1998. The Madrid Protocol, *inter alia*, banned mining altogether for 50 years (until 2048), set strict regulations for environmental impact assessments of all human activities in the area and established a system to create dedicated protected areas for conservation.

The greatest challenges for environmental protection in Antarctica today are climate change, increasing tourism and the commercial exploitation of the unique biota, ('bioprospecting', or biological prospecting) under the pretext of scientific work.

The ATS system has been proposed as the model for the environmental protection of the other polar area, the Arctic. This was proposed by the European Parliament in October 2008.[14] The proposal is unrealistic. The ATS system is based on freezing contentious sovereignty claims, some of which overlap. It is an international area that has been dedicated to science and the protection of its unique environment. This state of affairs is completely different from the Arctic region, where eight states (Russia, Canada, the USA and five Nordic countries) enjoy full sovereignty to all the land areas and sovereign rights over their exclusive economic zones and continental shelves over a great part of the Arctic Ocean. The two polar areas are therefore polar opposites in terms of political and legal characteristics.[15]

As a result of climate change, the Arctic Ocean's ice cover is rapidly melting. Sooner or later, the Arctic Ocean will no longer be ice-covered, at least during the summer months. A new sea will gradually be revealed where once there was a permanent thick sea-ice. The central part of the Arctic Ocean is beyond 200 nautical miles from the nearest coast and therefore constitutes the high seas, where any country in the world and their vessels can enjoy freedom of navigation as well as fishing rights. International law of the sea grants extensive navigation rights for various purposes (tourism, transport of goods and oil, for example) in the area. In addition, foreign ships have the right of innocent passage, even on territorial waters near the coast.

Figure 4.3 Demonstrators dressed as penguins outside a meeting related to the Antarctic Treaty in Bonn in April 1991. It was not clear before this preparatory meeting whether the parties would allow or ban mining in Antarctica. It was, in fact, banned. (Photo © Andrew Jackson)

Perhaps the pressure to protect the sensitive Arctic environment will magnify to the extent that one day the environmental threats to it might be addressed by an administrative model established by an international treaty. Efforts to protect the vulnerable environment are now being made by the Arctic Council. It is a cooperating forum of eight Arctic states, which cannot make binding decisions but has conducted valuable work especially in researching Arctic environmental threats.

My Dutch colleague Erik Molenaar and I carried out a three-stage research report for the WWF to consider how the Arctic governance system might be strengthened.[16] At first, we conducted an overview of all the international treaties and other regulations that could be considered to be valid and applicable to the new emerging Arctic Ocean. We then considered how the adjacent states could best meet the enormous challenges posed by climate change and the emerging commercial activities that it makes possible (such as seafaring, oil drilling). Finally, we established the basic elements of an outline for one possible governance solution for the area: how the existing soft-law organization, the Arctic Council, could gradually be developed by an international treaty into an organization that could promote sustainable development in the area.

As we began to present our ideas at international conferences, to political decision-makers or to international organizations, we understood that this was not the right time for a discussion about an Arctic treaty. We faced a vast amount of misunderstanding, because the very term 'Arctic Treaty' is often associated with the Antarctic Treaty. From one meeting to another, we tried to explain that we certainly did not think that the Antarctic Treaty System could be applied in the Arctic but we encountered the same opposition at the next conference. In effect, the European Parliament had committed a disservice in having expressly promoted an Antarctic Treaty-type administrative model in the area.

We concluded that at the very least, we had made a contribution to the discussion. We had suggested something new to those who understood that what we proposed was not just a transplant of the Antarctic Treaty System into a completely different political and legal environment. When the time is ripe for the discussion, I trust that our ideas will provide some basis for more sustainable governance of the Arctic area.

Principles of international law and the environment

The difference between 'rules' and 'principles' has been discussed extensively, especially within the realm of legal theory. Rules give clear instructions for behaviour, while principles provide looser direction to act in a particular way. Rules are either valid or not valid, applied or not applied. Principles are valid to a lesser or greater degree and multiple principles can be used to regulate a single situation, often in competition with one another: their mutual weight in resolving a matter depends on their relevance to a given situation. Together, principles and rules are referred to as 'norms'.

From the perspective of government, rules are clearer, as they distinctly state the conduct that is required. For example, the London 1972 Convention related to marine dumping of waste from vessels and aircraft prohibits the dumping of any of the substances listed in its Annex I – that is, it provides rules. Principles, on the other hand, give reasons for a decision to follow a particular course of action but leave a government much more discretion in the implementation.

How should governments address the import of genetically modified material, for instance, if they are taking the precautionary principle seriously?

This chapter is discussing the general principles of international law as they apply to international environmental protection. This is an important point to understand, because international environmental law is not a self-sustained legal system. International environmental law scholars often attach a great premium on the principles of international environmental law, as if forgetting that they form only one part of the very extensive system of international law.

Many of these principles – for example, the territorial integrity of states – have evolved over a very long time so it would be unwise to consider international environmental protection without a basic knowledge of what these principles are. With a thorough understanding of international law principles, it is easier to understand the thinking behind the most important principles of international environmental law.

The principles of international law are the starting point for the development of international environmental law. These principles have been centuries in the making and facilitate continuity in the rapidly changing world of international relations. For instance, the decision by the *Trail Smelter* arbitration tribunal in 1941 continues to be consulted in contemporary disputes related to transboundary pollution.

Territorial sovereignty of states

One of the fundamental principles in international law is the territorial sovereignty of states. The primary focus of this principle is the independence of states: that is, a sovereign state cannot be under the command of another state (and states are equal from this point of view).

From the standpoint of environmental protection, it is essential that each state is entitled to establish a social system of its own and hence to pursue its own environmental protection policy and law. The international community cannot interfere in the domestic environmental protection within another state. For example, at the Rio 1992 Conference the host country, Brazil, was criticized for not having been able to stop the accelerating destruction of the rainforests. The host country's representatives were offended by the accusations, arguing that the rainforests are within sovereign Brazilian territory and hence an exclusively Brazilian responsibility.

The collective responsibility of the international community to intervene in the internal matters of a state has been debated in cases where a state oppresses an ethnic or other group (responsibility to protect, or R2P). The status and contents of this principle are still not fully defined and it remains controversial, not having yet been adopted by the international community against any state that is destroying the environment within its own territory. Such actions certainly violate the principle of sustainable development but it is unclear what weight the principle of sustainable development has in international law. Is it a norm or just a concept or even an objective for the international community? When environmental disasters occur, intervention from the international community is more likely to come in terms of humanitarian assistance.

The territorial sovereignty of states is the single most influential principle governing international environmental protection, and under this principle, the world is divided into nearly 200 separate states. The point of departure, according to international law, is that states are entitled to pursue their own environmental law and policy in their own territories. Even if they have bound themselves to international environmental treaties and are liable to observe customary international law, they are (1) free to decide by virtue of their constitutions how (or if) the regulations of an international environmental treaty are given legal status in their national legal systems and what hierarchic level these international rules have; and (2) they can then decide how the regulations are implemented so that the appropriate authorities are made aware of the new regulations and are able to apply them routinely. It is essential to ensure that violations of international environmental treaties result in legal sanctions and that adherence to the rules is regularly monitored.

With the exception of Antarctica, all of the world's land mass falls under the jurisdiction of states (even if some areas are contested by more than one state, especially in border areas). Sovereignty over land areas also entitles a coastal state to exercise its sovereign rights over its continental shelf and its exclusive economic zone. These areas, however, are not part of that state, but, as we considered above, the state has exclusive rights to exploit the natural resources contained therein. Moreover, those coastal states have both the authority and the obligation to protect the environment in their exclusive economic zones and continental shelves.

A significant division occurs between the areas within a state's authority and those outside it. A state has, in its territory, the authority to protect the environment and the responsibility for the environment according to (a) what international environmental treaties it has bound itself to; and (b) what rules of customary international law bind it in environmental law and policy.

Marine environmental protection is more complex. The oceans have always been international and the jurisdiction of coastal states at sea has only started to expand after the Second World War. There are a huge number of international rules that must be observed in marine environmental protection; examples include regulation by the Convention on the Law of the Sea and the IMO agreements related to seafaring (see Chapter 5, 'Marine environmental protection', p. 149).

Transboundary pollution

Territorial sovereignty, then, entitles a state to develop its social and legal systems independently within its territory. A state can, for example, permit polluting activities according to its industrial policy. An activity permitted by one state can, however, cause or be at risk of causing environmental harm in the territory of another.

In relation to environmental protection, there are two main rights under state sovereignty: a state can invoke territorial sovereignty to justify its irresponsible environmental policy, or to defend itself against environmental harm from another state. Paradoxically, the same principle justifies pollution and allows a state to fight against it. State A may not interfere with the environmental protection of state B. On the other hand, if state B causes pollution in state A, state A is entitled to invoke its territorial sovereignty: it can send a 'diplomatic note' to state B, stating that B is not at liberty to use the territory of state A as its 'dumping ground'.

Two well-known cases of transboundary pollution come from the USA:

The Rio Grande flows from the state of Colorado and becomes the boundary river between the USA (Texas) and Mexico before emptying into the Gulf of Mexico. In 1894, Mexico sent a diplomatic note to the US Secretary of State about a problem in the Mexican border towns: farmers on the US side had diverted water from the river for irrigation, reducing the amount of water on the Mexican side and severely impacting on farming.

Mexico sent another notification to the US Secretary of State at the end of 1895. The State Department did not have a lawyer of its own at that time, so the Secretary of State requested legal advice from the Attorney General as Mexico had relied on its rights under international law.

Attorney General Judson Harmon's legal advice to the Secretary of State was clear: every state enjoys absolute territorial sovereignty, in this case implying that the USA may administer the river on its side of the border just as it wants to. This legal advice became known as the Harmon doctrine: a state can operate in its own territory just as it wants to, without regard for the interests (and alleged rights) of other states.

Paradoxically, despite becoming an established doctrine, this piece of legal advice did not in any way affect US actions when settling the dispute with Mexico. Instead of relying on it in the negotiations, the USA referred to the principles of equity.

In the 1920s, the USA was affected by transboundary pollution in the so-called *Trail Smelter* case: a zinc smelter in Trail, Canada, 10 miles from the border (between British Columbia and the state of Washington) was emitting sulphur dioxide which was being carried to the US side, causing damage to the crops and property.

US private entrepreneurs and citizens tried to sue the smelter company (the Consolidated Mining and Smelting Company of Canada Ltd) under the US legal system but the legal systems of the USA and Canada at the time made this impossible. They therefore referred the matter to the USA to exercise diplomatic protection on behalf of its citizens by making it an international dispute against Canada.

An interesting point is that both countries at first relied on their own sovereignty: Canada on its sovereign right to permit legal activity taking place within its territory, and the USA on its right to territorial integrity to argue that it should not have to tolerate harmful interference from Canada.

Initially, the countries first referred the dispute to the boundary water treaty between the USA and Canada and to its Commission, which in 1931 decreed that Canada pay US$350,000. The parties refused to accept this and decided by agreement (*compromise*) to establish an arbitration tribunal to resolve the dispute. The arbitration tribunal gave its interim decision in 1938 and its final decision in 1941.

The arbitrators working to resolve the *Trail Smelter* dispute realized that international law as it currently stood could not resolve the case. Of course, sovereignty both protects a state's right to pursue legal activities in its territory and its territorial integrity against pollution from other states. Sovereign states cannot be arranged in 'rank order' since they are equal in international law, and in this example both states were relying on the same principle of sovereignty. Evidently, the state of origin cannot permit any legal activity irrespective of its impact on other states, but at the same time, an affected state has no veto over legal activities conducted by or in another state. The tribunal therefore developed a new set of principles practically 'from scratch' (at least from an international law point of view) by which to resolve the dispute. Both Canada and the USA pleaded their sovereignty, but the arbitrators applied an old Roman principle, *sic tuo utere*, which they considered applicable in intergovernmental disputes as well: 'So use your own as not to injure another's property.'

It was essential to find a principle according to which the tribunal could roughly define what kinds of pollution impacts from one state to another were permissible. As the tribunal could not find help in the international legal arena, it based its decision largely on the practice of federal states in corresponding cases – especially on the way in which similar environmental disputes between US states had been resolved.

The tribunal stated in its decision of 1941:

> The Tribunal, therefore, finds that the above decisions, taken as a whole, constitute an adequate basis for its conclusions, namely, that, under the principles of international law, as well as of the law of the United States, no State has the right to use or permit the use of its territory in such a manner as to cause injury by fumes in or to the territory of another or the properties or persons therein, when the case is of serious consequence and the injury is established by clear and convincing evidence.[17]

So, the tribunal was able to find criteria according to which the territorial sovereignty of neither state was absolute; only considerable transboundary environmental damage is illegal.

The *Trail Smelter* case only became widely known during the 1970s when international environmental protection first reached the agenda of the international community. The *sic tuo utere* principle applied by the tribunal was reflected in the 1972 Stockholm Conference Declaration Principle 21, which the UN International Court of Justice has endorsed as part of international law since 1996.

The positive influence of the *Trail Smelter* case in the development of international environmental law is, unfortunately, not reflected in a prevention of the transboundary environmental impact of the smelter itself (now run by the Teck Cominco company). In 1999, the Colville Indian Tribes petitioned the US Environmental Protection Agency (EPA) to examine the contamination of the Columbia river that flows from Canada through the United States to the Pacific Ocean. In 2003, the EPA found that there was a significant amount of contamination in the Upper Columbia (including heavy metals such as arsenic, mercury and zinc) and ordered the company at the other side of the border to investigate and determine the nature of the contamination at the site. Both the liability case in the US judicial system and the requested environmental conditions study in the Upper Columbia river are still pending.

Sadly, although we can congratulate the *Trail Smelter* arbitration tribunal on the successful settlement of the 1941 environmental dispute and its consequences for the development of international environmental law, the actual transboundary pollution that was at the heart of the dispute is still not under control. We could also ask whether other intergovernmental environmental dispute decisions have made a positive contribution to environmental protection, or simply resolved a diplomatic argument that threatened intergovernmental relations.

No-harm principle

The *sic tuo utere* principle is wider today: it binds states in general to prevent transboundary pollution (including pollution caused to areas beyond the jurisdiction of any state, which will be discussed later). This principle of no-harm is expressed in several global environmental treaties and in the declarations of the Stockholm (1972) and Rio (1992) UN conferences on the environment, as follows:

> States have, in accordance with the Charter of the United Nations and the principles of international law, the sovereign right to exploit their own resources pursuant to their own environmental (and developmental) policies, and the responsibility to ensure that activities within their jurisdiction or control do not cause damage to the environment of other States or of areas beyond the limits of national jurisdiction.

The legal status of this principle was for a long time unclear, but the UN International Court of Justice has confirmed that it does form part of general international law and is therefore binding on all the states of the world.

It is important to examine the contents of such a general principle more closely. Violation of the no-harm principle is considered to be any activity that fulfils the following criteria:

1   Activities by a state – or by a private enterprise that the state has permitted to operate – thereby causing pollution in another state.
2   Transboundary environmental harm must be 'significant'; that is, minor transboundary pollution is legal.
3   The polluting state has been negligent (that is, has not exercised due diligence). If harm is caused to another state when the state of origin has taken careful precautions to ensure that no transboundary environmental harm should be caused, the state will not be responsible.
4   The affected state is able to demonstrate the connection between the environmental harm and the origin of pollution in the source state: that is, it can demonstrate a causal link.

The no-harm principle is expressed in a general way. It therefore requires both internal action by a state (for example, establishing permit procedures for projects that are known to be potentially polluting and regulating them to minimize impact) and agreements with other states so that no significant transboundary pollution harm occurs. Principle 19 of the Rio 1992 Declaration requires prior notification and information from a state, if significant environmental harm could potentially be caused in the territory of another. The state of origin is further required to consult the affected state at an early stage and in good faith.

In the 2010 *Pulp Mills* case between Argentina and Uruguay (relating to the construction of a pulp mill on the Uruguayan side of the boundary river), the International Court of Justice established that, by virtue of general international law, the states must prepare an environmental impact assessment (EIA), to assess the environmental impact of potentially harmful activities on other states prior to authorizing the activities. However, the Court's judgment does leave considerable scope for interpretation as to what kind of an EIA system the states may wish to establish.

The most important treaty on intergovernmental communication procedures in case of transboundary environmental impact is the Espoo Convention on Environmental Impact Assessment in a Transboundary Context. The Espoo Convention obliges the party of origin of a proposed project to notify the affected party if it is likely that there will be significant environmental impact on the territory of the latter. The affected party and its public are then entitled to participate in the national EIA procedure in the party of origin and to comment on the transboundary environmental impact. The affected party should notify the party of origin of its opinion on the proposed project in consultations between the states. The party of origin (and normally its permit decision-maker) shall take all the comments by the affected party and its public into account when making a decision whether or not to license a project, and it shall submit this decision to the affected party once it has been made. The parties can agree on the monitoring of the impact.

The principle of no-harm applies somewhat differently to international inland watercourses such as rivers, lakes and groundwater within the territories of multiple states. Interestingly, the rules already agreed in 1966 by the International Law Association (ILA) in Helsinki became more widely adopted in customary law between states. This was not due to the status of the ILA but simply because the principles adopted reflected the current practice so well that they could be said to record the existing customary international law. The Helsinki Rules require that states make decisions based on considerations of equity and consider the rights and benefits of both states if disputes arise from the use of a river.

Gradually, questions began to emerge about the procedure in cases where considerable environmental harm is caused from the territory of one riparian state to the territory of another. The UN International Law Commission published a draft of legal principles applied to inland watercourses in 1994. These draft articles were finally adopted as a convention in 1997;[18] they are based on the right of every riparian state to reasonably exploit and use a river. They also establish a separate procedure in cases where considerable transboundary environmental damage is likely. In such cases, one possible way of settling a dispute is the payment of damages. The objective of the convention is to promote management in accordance with the ecosystem approach.

It is not easy to say whether this UN convention reflects customary law, and if so to what extent – particularly because it is not yet in force. It seems to have at least sustained the view that transboundary environmental damage is central to consideration of what constitutes reasonable use of a river or an inland watercourse. The UN Economic Commission for Europe's 1992 Helsinki Convention on the Protection and Use of Transboundary Watercourses and International Lakes[19] has great regional importance. Under this Convention, general principles are drafted for the management of inland waters and parties are encouraged to establish regional cooperation bodies.

Nuclear power and transportation of hazardous substances

The no-harm principle is best applied in situations where a country of origin is able to ensure that there will be no transboundary environmental impact or that it will be minimal. Nuclear power plant disasters, however, can cause significant damage to the environment and people of other countries, even if the country of origin has been extremely diligent. In the case of a nuclear power plant disaster, the country of origin will rarely have violated the no-harm principle of international law (in other words, it has exercised a high standard of care) although it nevertheless has caused significant environmental damage to the environments of other countries.

The 1986 Chernobyl nuclear power plant disaster in the former Ukrainian Soviet Socialist Republic (part of the former USSR) was a rude awakening for the international community. It was not the first nuclear power plant disaster but it was so catastrophic that many countries considered taking legal action against the USSR. In this case, there was a strong likelihood that the USSR had violated the no-harm principle (with its requirement to act diligently) because there were reasonable grounds to doubt the quality of the Soviets' management processes. However, in the end, many countries decided that although they had incurred extensive damage, legal action would have been useless.

As is often the case with international environmental regulation, it took a disaster to motivate the international community to take steps to prepare for such a situation should it ever happen again. A few months after the Chernobyl disaster, two conventions were adopted under the auspices of the International Atomic Energy Agency (IAEA): the Convention on Early Notification of a Nuclear Accident[20] and the Convention on Assistance in Case of a Nuclear Accident or Radiological Emergency.[21] This development was also recorded in Principle 18 of the Rio Declaration: states shall immediately notify other states of any natural disasters or other emergencies that are likely to produce sudden harmful effects on the environment of those states. The notification and assistance rules soon developed into rules of customary international law.

As we have seen above, an affected party – that is, a state under the threat of a significant transboundary environmental impact – has no veto over any legal activities in the territory of the party of origin if they do not result in significant transboundary pollution. The party of origin is therefore free to damage the environment of the affected party, albeit only to a limited extent. In contrast, in order to deliberately transport harmful waste or hazardous substances to the territory of another state, a licence must usually be received from a competent authority in the affected party. In this context, the veto would normally apply, contrary to situations where the hazardous substance enters the territory waterborne or airborne.

Trends in the popularity of nuclear power

The popularity of nuclear power in energy production declined after the Chernobyl plant disaster. It was even anticipated to be a 'sunset industry'.

Paradoxically, increased knowledge about the consequences of climate change resulted in a renaissance in the nuclear power sector in the 1990s. As nuclear power produces low greenhouse gas emissions in comparison with other forms of energy production, its popularity rose when the climate change convention system required governments to cut their greenhouse gas emissions.

The trend was bucked, at least temporarily, when an immense undersea earthquake of magnitude 9.0 about 70 kilometres off the Oshika Peninsula triggered a tsunami on the eastern Japanese coast causing the Fukushima Daiichi power plant nuclear disaster on 11 March 2011.

The impact was at first assessed as low, until the real state of affairs was gradually revealed: the Fukushima disaster is considered to be as severe as the Chernobyl nuclear power plant disaster. The IAEA later confirmed that the cores of three reactors had melted, at least partially. The worldwide consequence has seen the closing down of nuclear power plants and a reassessment of the entire nuclear power policy.

Most states in the world are party to the 1989 Basel Convention on the Control of Transboundary Movements of Hazardous Wastes and their Disposal,[22] which creates the procedures for transporting hazardous waste. Transportation is based on the written consent of competent authorities in both the exporting and importing countries.

In 1991, the then Organization of African Unity reacted to the Basel Convention's global bureaucratic approach to transboundary waste transport. It negotiated the Bamako Convention which banned the import of hazardous waste to Africa. The third meeting of the parties to the Basel Convention in 1995 responded by adopting decision III/1, amending the Basel Convention so that hazardous waste may not be taken from OECD countries to developing countries. The Rotterdam 1998 Convention on the Prior Informed Consent Procedure for Certain Hazardous Chemicals and Pesticides in International Trade[23] states that when chemicals listed in Annex III are exported, the importing country must have sufficient advance information in order to make an informed decision to import.

Customary international law in transboundary pollution cases

Customary international law comprehensively regulates instances of transboundary pollution:

1   in which the source of transboundary environmental impact is traceable to a project – or a proposed project – within the territory of another state; such projects are generally large and located near the international boundary;
2   in which the environment and run-off of the boundary river change due to activities approved by the upstream state;
3   in which intrinsically hazardous activities – for example, nuclear power plants – cause damage to the environment of other states.

Customary international law roughly defines the procedures that states should follow in these cases (notification and EIA procedures, for instance). In case of damage, customary law also defines the activities that constitute a violation of international law. There is also a wealth of bilateral and multilateral treaties related to these situations.

Long-range transboundary air pollution

Some of the most challenging cases in international law are those concerning the transboundary transmission of pollutants in which the origin of the pollutants is difficult to trace to any single, identifiable project. The principle of no-harm and the procedural rules in customary international law technically apply to this kind of diffuse pollution as well. However, as it is difficult, if not impossible, to prove that any particular state has caused any of the pollution, it is impossible to show who is accountable. Diffuse transboundary air pollution requires collective regulation by the international community or a regional group.

One innovative example of such collective regional regulation dates back as far as 1979: the Convention on Long-range Transboundary Air Pollution (LRTAP).[24] The convention was organized in response to scientific research conducted in the 1960s which revealed that the acidification of Scandinavian lakes was being caused by sulphur emissions from industries in continental Europe. The Convention, negotiated under the auspices of the UN Economic Commission for Europe, included the following Article 5:

> Consultations shall be held, upon request, at an early stage between Contracting Parties which are actually affected by or exposed to a significant risk of long-range transboundary air pollution and Contracting Parties within which and subject to whose jurisdiction a significant contribution to long-range transboundary air pollution originates, or could originate, in connection with activities carried on or contemplated therein.

This type of agreement is, however, insufficient where the polluting substances and their origin and final destination are unknown. The need to improve cooperation on the monitoring and evaluation of the long-range transmission of air pollutants (especially sulphur dioxide) in Europe therefore became central to intergovernmental regulation (EMEP, Article 9). Already in 1984, the protocol on long-term financing of the cooperative programme for monitoring and evaluation of the long-range transmission of air pollutants in Europe[25] was adopted by the contracting parties. The following year, the protocol on reducing sulphur emissions and transboundary sulphur flux by 30 per cent[26] was also adopted.

To date, eight protocols have been negotiated to the LRTAP Convention. Their objective is to reduce – besides sulphur emissions – nitrogen oxides, heavy metals and POP compounds, with a view to mitigating environmental problems such as acid rain. For the most hazardous substances, country-specific reduction targets are given. Under the European monitoring and evaluation programme (EMEP) it has proved possible to measure with a considerable degree of precision which substances can be carried and in what amounts, where these substances originated and where they end up. As a result, the implementation committee of the convention system has been able to monitor whether states are adhering to their obligations. Where they have failed to do so, the implementation committee has taken up the problem in the meetings of the parties. Substantive penalties have rarely been imposed; it is generally sufficient that a non-compliant party is 'named and shamed' as having breached its obligations. The most common response of these violating states has been to adjust their activities to meet the obligations in the protocols. In this way, the regional treaty system of the UN Economic Commission for Europe has been able to effectively reduce the long-range transmission of air pollution.

What about long-range transmission of this kind of pollution to the other side of the world? According to the Stockholm Convention,[27] persistent organic pollutant (POP compounds such as aldrin, chlordane, dieldrin, DDT, endrin, heptachlor, mirex, toxaphene), 'possess toxic properties, resist degradation, bioaccumulate and are transported through air, water and migratory species, across international boundaries and deposited far from their place of release, where they accumulate in terrestrial and aquatic ecosystems'.

Persistent organic pollutants behave according to the so-called 'grasshopper effect'. They 'jump' towards the north in line with their grade of volatility. They evaporate in warm conditions and are transmitted by air currents towards colder areas in the north. If rain flushes them down to the soil, they do not degrade but evaporate again to be transmitted by air currents towards the north. They concentrate in the cold environment, ending up in the soil and unable to evaporate again.

In this way, POP compounds have been detected in the Arctic where they are rarely if ever used or produced. Plants and animals absorb POP compounds which gradually reach the predators at the top of the food chain. Many of these top predators are hunted and eaten by Arctic indigenous peoples. This is why Inuit women in Greenland feature exceptionally high polychlorinated biphenyl (PCB) concentrations even though the Inuit neither produce nor use PCBs. Furthermore, because many of the POP compounds are toxic, they could be harmful to the foetus of a pregnant woman.

John Buccini, the chairman of the negotiations leading up to the Stockholm POP Convention, kept a sculpture of an Inuit woman holding a baby on his desk in order to emphasize the importance of reducing these harmful substances for future generations. For these reasons, the Stockholm POPs Convention contains a preambulary paragraph referring to the Arctic: 'The parties to the Convention acknowledge ... that the Arctic ecosystems and indigenous communities are particularly at risk because of the biomagnification of persistent organic pollutants and that contamination of their traditional foods is a public health issue.'

The LRTAP treaty system is one mechanism whereby POP compounds can be controlled regionally: each country is given a reduction quota for each particular harmful substance. A system like this means that precise data is required as to the quantity of trans-border transmission of these harmful substances: that is, it requires a scientific cooperation network like the monitoring and evaluation programme EMEP.

To implement a similar programme on a global scale would be unrealistic. The Stockholm Convention therefore concentrates on prohibiting the production and use of POP compounds and on the control of their import and export in international trade. The objective of the Convention is to end the production and use of deliberately manufactured POP compounds through prohibiting the production and use, and with certain exceptions the import and export, of the chemicals listed in Annex A. The production, use, import and export of chemicals listed in Annex B are limited.

Another objective is to prevent new POP compounds from entering the market. All industrial chemicals and pesticides currently in use must be assessed considering the POP criteria defined in the Convention. By banning the most hazardous compounds and careful examination and restriction of new compounds, POP compounds can be taken out of natural circulation. Since this is a global problem, the Convention enjoins industrial nations to provide technical and financial assistance to developing countries and transition economies.

The Stockholm POP Convention acknowledges the principle of no-harm, but it is clear that the issue is the prevention of a global collective problem rather than a traditional transboundary pollution problem. The introduction to the Convention therefore also mentions such principles as 'Common but Differentiated Responsibilities' and 'Polluter Pays'. The Convention even bases its objective in Article 1 primarily on the precautionary principle[28] reflecting Rio Declaration Principle 15: 'Where there are threats of serious or irreversible damage, lack of full scientific certainty shall not be used as a reason for postponing cost-effective measures to prevent environmental degradation.'

This is quite a long way from an environmental dispute between two states. It is practically a global governance system. The LRTAP regime is also a regional governance system in which a major principle is the precautionary principle.

In 2009, The UN environmental programme decided to begin negotiations on the mercury convention. Mercury is a heavy metal and behaves like POP compounds: it degrades very slowly in the environment, it is transmitted in the atmosphere and sea currents, and it accumulates in the food chain, also ending up in the human body; it has significant health and environmental effects. The text for a global mercury treaty was finally adopted on 19 January 2013 after four years of negotiations. The Minamata Convention is scheduled to be opened for signature in October 2013.

Common concerns: ozone depletion, climate change and loss of biological diversity

Greenhouse gases, CFC compounds and POP compounds cause global environmental damage: depletion of the ozone layer, changes in the climate system, and air pollution, resulting in damage to the environment and to health. The POP, ozone and climate regimes regulate truly global environmental problems arising from diffuse pollution around the world and which are causing harm to all humankind.

The climate system and the ozone layer can only be considered to be sovereign islands divided among states in a very abstract way. Most of the atmosphere and hence the climate is to some extent included in the sovereign airspace of states just like the ozone layer in the stratosphere. While the climate system is protected by the UN Framework Convention on Climate Change,[29] and the ozone layer is protected by the Vienna Convention for the Protection of the Ozone Layer,[30] and its Montreal Protocol on Substances that Deplete the Ozone Layer,[31] they are, in fact, natural systems in which the conduct of individual states or limited regional groups of states have limited impact. The parties to the Climate Change Convention state this pertinently: 'the change in the Earth's climate and its adverse effects are a common concern of humankind'. Ozone depletion, climate change and POP compounds are legally considered 'common concerns of humankind' and problems that need to be addressed politically by the entire international community.

This can also be applied to the loss of biological diversity. The treaty system established to prevent the rapid depletion of biological diversity – the UN Convention on Biological Diversity – affirms that 'the conservation of biological diversity is a common concern of humankind', while also affirming that 'States have sovereign rights over their own biological resources'.

The loss of biological diversity differs from climate change and ozone depletion because biodiversity and genetic material are usually considered to be under the actual physical control of states. Biodiversity should therefore be protected differently: the goal is not merely to protect biological diversity but also to utilize it and divide the yield fairly between states and other parties (indigenous peoples, for example). These four global environmental problems – climate change, damage by POP compounds, ozone depletion and loss of biological diversity – are connected to such an extent that they must all be considered common concerns of humankind, as they cannot be resolved by individual states or any single regional group of states.

Some argue that to use the term 'common concern of humankind' implies that if the existence of a global environmental problem can be proven, participation in global treaties should no longer be optional. States should no longer have the basic right secured in international law: the liberty to decide on participation in international treaties. However, at this time, this view is too far-reaching to be widely accepted. Today, the term 'common concern of humankind' suggests that no state can argue that such matters are solely within its own jurisdiction. Every state has to contribute to the joint action, although not necessarily by participating in international treaty systems.

While we can criticize the USA for opting out of the binding emission reduction obligations in the Kyoto Protocol, it is still a party to the UN Climate Change Convention, at least making some contribution to averting climate change, mostly at state and local levels. Nearly all the states in the world are parties to the ozone regime (196 parties), the climate regime (195), the POP regime (176) and the biodiversity regime (193); however, significantly, the USA (one of the world's largest, most populous and most polluting states) has joined neither the Convention on Biological Diversity, the Stockholm Convention, nor the Kyoto Protocol to the climate regime.

Areas outside the jurisdiction of states

In reality, most of the Earth falls outside the jurisdiction of individual states: the marine areas are beyond the exclusive economic zones and the seabed beyond the continental shelves of coastal states; airspace is measured from the outer limit of the territorial sea (at present, it is unclear how high the sovereignty in the atmosphere reaches, as the lower limit of outer space is disputed); and all of Antarctica, for as long as sovereignty claims remain, is preserved by the 1959 treaty. The space beyond our planet is also outside the jurisdiction of states.

The principle *sic tuo utere* regulates pollution among states. It was extended in 1972, when the Stockholm environmental conference adopted the no-harm principle (italics added):

> *States have,* in accordance with the Charter of the United Nations and the principles of international law, the sovereign right to exploit their own resources pursuant to their own environmental policies, and *the responsibility to ensure that activities within their jurisdiction or control do not cause damage to the environment* of other States or *of areas beyond the limits of national jurisdiction.*

This principle today forms part of customary international law and is therefore binding on all states. It obligates them to control such actions under their jurisdiction or control that can cause harm to the environment beyond their jurisdiction. The requirements of the no-harm principle on states were referred to when New Zealand and Australia sued France in the UN International Court of Justice.

France carried out a series of atmospheric nuclear tests from 1966 to 1972 at its Mururoa atolls in the Pacific Ocean. It also established exclusion zones that extended into the high seas. Australia and New Zealand claimed, *inter alia,* that in so doing, France had restricted the high seas rights secured by the international law of the sea to them and all states, including the right to free seafaring and fishing in the area.

The International Court of Justice did not comment on the merits of the case in its decision in 1974 (whether France was acting lawfully or not); it founded its decision on the unilateral, legally binding promise of France to end its atmospheric nuclear testing. Even though the Court did not make comment on the claimants' legal arguments, the process nevertheless compelled France to end its atmospheric nuclear testing.

International environmental law, then, can be seen to have extended its reach in order to protect areas that are beyond the jurisdiction of states. The following situations would all be covered by international environmental law:

1   Activities within the territory of a state that harm or have the potential to harm the environment beyond its jurisdiction.

    Example 1: A state permits oil drilling in its outer continental shelf; an accident occurs, causing damage to the superjacent water column, surface and their contents: that is, the high seas.

    Example 2: A state permits a large smelter in its territory; its high chimneys transmit sulphur emissions into international airspace. Rain flushes these emissions out to the sea, reducing its acidity, and harming the biota of the high seas.

2   A ship registered in one particular state causes environmental damage to the marine area beyond that state's jurisdiction. *Example: A ship carrying hazardous substances capsizes in a storm on the high seas.*

In recent military testing, China destroyed an unused weather satellite, thereby increasing the amount of space debris[32] already in orbit around the Earth. Space debris can damage other satellites or spacecraft, endangering human life as well; it could eventually even end up on the Earth, causing environmental harm.

On 24 January 1978, The USSR nuclear-powered Kosmos 954 satellite fell onto northern Canada. Fortunately, the satellite fell on an uninhabited area. However, it did cause severe environmental damage and the USSR was required to compensate Canada in financial damages. A similar disaster could as easily have occurred over the high seas or Antarctica.

If a state causes environmental damage in seeking to exploit non-living resources in the deep seabed such as oil, gas and especially minerals, such as polymetallic nodules containing manganese, cobalt, copper or nickel, it is a different situation. This is because the deep seabed is recognized as the common heritage of humanity and it is administered by the International Seabed Authority (ISA).

Exploration licences for these resources have been granted to states, and also recently to private enterprises with state sponsorship, primarily for the Clarion-Clipperton zone (in the seabed of the Central Pacific Ocean, southeast of Hawaii) and the Indian Ocean. The ISA has adopted precise rules for environmental impact assessment in such circumstances. Although the circumstances are different from those we considered earlier, the fundamental question remains the same: what are the no-harm obligations for a state, if it sponsors deep seabed activities detrimental to the deep sea marine environment? The ISA is responsible for granting licences for exploration and eventually exploitation but the state is obligated to guarantee that the marine environment will not be damaged. These obligations were defined in an advisory opinion by the International Tribunal for the Law of the Sea (Seabed Disputes Chamber) in 2011.

The small Pacific island state of Nauru sponsored a private company's application to the ISA for permission to search for polymetallic nodules in the deep seabed. Nauru later withdrew from the project, fearing problems if the company's activities polluted the marine environment. Nauru persuaded the ISA to ask for an advisory opinion from the International Tribunal for the Law of the Sea about what the duties of a sponsoring state should be when the actual actor in the exploration and exploitation of the deep seabed is a private company.

The Seabed Disputes Chamber stated in its advisory legal opinion that all states have an equal responsibility to license and monitor these activities. What was important in this opinion was the statement by the International Tribunal for the Law of the Sea that all states have equal obligations in relation to private exploration of the deep seabed, derived from the principle of due diligence.

The Chamber thus rejected the possibility of setting up the same sort of 'flag of convenience' states – or, in this case, 'convenience mining' states – in deep seabed exploitation as exist in seafaring. After this statement there is less incentive for companies to flag their companies in countries with lax environmental protection standards since all states have the same extensive responsibilities to guarantee that environmental protection is heeded in the exploitation of deep seabed mineral resources.

A difficult question is how to administer activities that operate beyond the jurisdiction of states and pose a threat to biological diversity. An activity that is also on the increase on the high seas and in the deep seabed is bioprospecting, or biological prospecting: searching, processing, patenting and commercial usage of rare biota.

One such example is the discovery of 'hydrothermal vents', which have been discovered in depths down to 5 kilometres. The conditions at such depths (pressure about 350 bar, temperatures ranging from 2 to 400 degrees Celsius, no light) might be expected to exclude the possibility of life. However, alongside the very hot water discharges from these vents, there exists a rich and unique set of species with potential for commercial use; it is vital to use these biota sustainably. Another disturbing new trend on the high seas is that of industrial trawling, during which the entire seabed biota and not just the fish are vacuumed away. The problem is that such activities – fishing, marine research and bioprospecting – fall under the freedom of the high seas, at least according to the Convention on the Law of the Sea, and maritime law permits their practice within the limits of international law.

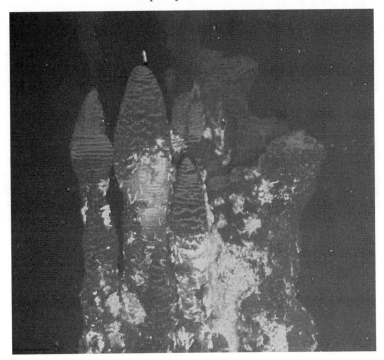

Figure 4.4 The Beebe hydrothermal vent, 5,000 metres deep in the Caribbean Sea near the Cayman Islands. Hydrothermal vents are underwater hot wells. Unique biota live around them, such as a shrimp with a photophore on its back. (Photo © HyBIS RUV, National Oceanography Centre, Southampton)

The European Union adopted its new Integrated Maritime Policy in December 2007 to pursue two administrative models for the high seas: an agreement on high seas biodiversity conservation, and the establishment of marine protected areas on the high seas. The conservation of high seas biodiversity is currently under negotiation in the BBNJ Working Group[33] established under the UN General Assembly.[34]

The BBNJ Working Group has been working on this issue since the mid-2000s. The latest news from the UN in 2011 was that proper consideration would be given to an international agreement on the regulation of biodiversity in areas beyond the jurisdiction of states, perhaps through an implementation agreement under the Convention on the Law of the Sea. The outcome document of 2012 Rio +20, *The Future We Want*, also supports negotiations for such an implementation agreement.

The successful conclusion of a convention is still fraught with many challenges, however. For instance, the principle behind the division of the benefits from commercial utilization of biological diversity is unclear if those benefits have been derived from areas beyond the jurisdiction of states. It is clear that the West is unwilling to accept the jurisdiction of the ISA. The new Nagoya Protocol to the Biodiversity Convention is based on the idea that should a foreign company seek to utilize genetic material within the territory of a state, that state would agree and would negotiate the terms of utilization. However, if the West is unwilling to accept the ISA in this role, who would grant permission when the activity takes place in areas outside the jurisdiction of states?

An added challenge to the negotiations for a new agreement is that many states consider the Convention on the Law of the Sea as a 'package deal'. Marine political issues were negotiated wholesale in the lengthy negotiation process and no exceptions were allowed. Many states fear that even the smallest amendments will open to question the entire compromise package; they are therefore reluctant to question the 'integrity' of the whole agreement and keen to maintain the status quo.

Principles, approaches and regulatory instruments in international environmental law

Unlike most of the principles of international law, many of the international environmental legal principles have not been given a clear legal status in international law. Only the principle of no–harm is unambiguously accepted because it emanates from general international law. Some principles of international environmental law – such as the precautionary principle – are slowly beginning to be recognized as customary international law (crystallizing) but most are in fact not yet widely considered to have crystallized, which is to say that they are not (yet) binding on all states. On the other hand, the principles of international environmental law serve a number of functions beyond simply mandating state conduct in given situations.

Principles of international environmental law are often considered to be generalizations of a large number of individual rules. Sustainable development, or the precautionary principle, can be defined in general terms but lawyers tend to prefer a pragmatic rather than a theoretical approach, asking how the precautionary principle can be interpreted by the application of more detailed rules, such as the requirement of a risk analysis of planned commercial activities, or even by requiring proof that a proposed project will not result in irrevocable or serious damage.

Principles operate below the surface or between the lines of international environmental agreements. If a particular international environmental problem is resolved through the application of certain fundamental principles in negotiations, it is clear that both legal scholarship and any future environmental negotiators will give due consideration to the guiding effects of the principles.

A number of principles could be seen as offering potential solutions to environmental protection problems. Instead of concerning ourselves with their legal status, it is more relevant to establish the basis or justification the principle provides for the administration of a particular environmental problem. Nonetheless, when one particular principle is repeatedly adopted in multiple agreements, it becomes clear that its legal status has changed and it is beginning to emerge as a legally binding principle. If a principle of international environmental law evolves into a principle in international law, it can be the decisive principle in a legal dispute. This is why states – the most powerful ones especially – are careful when reacting to the development of principles in negotiation processes. A good example of this can be seen in the conduct of the United States at the Rio 1992 environment conference.

The USA made a number of interpretative statements to the Rio Declaration, for example in respect of Principle 15, which declared the precautionary approach to be a principle of international environmental governance. The USA declared that it was against the precautionary principle developing into a principle of international law – a position it was justified in taking in line with the persistent objector doctrine.

By the same token, the USA and certain other industrial nations acted to delete Article 3, which defined the principles in the UN Framework Convention on Climate Change. They were concerned that these principles could gain individual application: that they could be applied in dispute settlement or could create obligations for the parties over and above those defined by the objective (Article 2) and the specific climate convention rules.

Although they were unsuccessful in removing or amending Article 3, they did manage to add a definition to the introduction to Article 3: the principles could only guide actions 'to achieve the objective of the Convention and to implement its provisions'. They thereby succeeded in limiting the independent effect of the principles Article 3 enunciates in the interpretation of the climate convention.

Principles of fairness

The most generalized principles of international law seldom have a direct effect on the negotiations of international environmental agreements, not to mention disputes that go into litigation. One such principle is 'sustainable development', which the 1987 Brundtland Report (*Our Common Future*) defines as 'development that meets the needs of the present without compromising the ability of future generations to meet their own needs'. Such a general principle of fairness between present and future generations seldom finds concrete implementation. There are, however, exceptions:

Lawyer and environment activist Juan Antonio Oposa filed a suit against Fulgencio S. Factoran, who was in charge of the Environment and Natural Resources Department of the Philippines. The government had granted a huge number of logging permits in the rainforests. Oposa considered this to be a violation of the constitutional right to a sound environment.

Oposa took legal action on his own behalf and that of his children, the youngest of whom was only nine months old. The action was also taken on behalf of anonymous future children who would not even see the Philippine rainforests at the present rate of felling. To the surprise of many, the Supreme Court deemed in 1994 that minors and children yet unborn could be considered to have the status of party to this case:

> This case, however, has a special and unique element. Minor Petitioners assert that they represent their generation as well as generations yet unborn. We find no difficulty in ruling that they can, for themselves, for others of their generation and for the succeeding generations, file a class suit. Their right to sue on behalf of the succeeding generations can only be based on the concept of intergenerational responsibility insofar as the right to a balanced and healthful ecology is concerned. Such a right, as hereinafter expounded, considers the 'rhythm and harmony of nature'. In this context, Nature means the created world in its entirety. Such rhythm and harmony essentially includes, *inter alia*, the judicious disposition, utilization, management, renewal and conservation of the country's forest, mineral, land, waters, fisheries, wildlife, offshore areas and other natural resources to the end that their exploration, development and utilization be equitably accessible to the present as well as future generations. Needless to say, every generation has a responsibility to the next to preserve that rhythm and harmony for the full enjoyment of a balanced and healthful ecology. Put a little differently, the minors' assertion of their right to a sound environment constitutes the performance of their obligation to ensure the protection of that right for the generations to come.

The petitioners were successful in their case against the Environment and Natural Resources Department.

It should not be forgotten that although intergenerational equity (part of the concept of sustainable development) seldom has distinct concrete manifestations, it provides background guidance for international environmental agreements. The climate and ozone regimes are, of course, intentionally designed to work for the benefit of future generations as well.

The clearest principle of fairness in international environmental law is that of 'common but differentiated responsibilities'. According to general international law, states are equal and this is immediately apparent in the negotiation of international agreements. Each state can decide whether or not to participate in the negotiations, on what terms and in which group, whether or not to accept the outcome from the negotiations, and – in certain countries – whether its parliament is prepared to ratify the agreement.

The 1992 Rio environment conference included the principle of common but differentiated responsibilities in the Rio Declaration. Principle 7 states that industrial nations bear a wider responsibility for the health of the Earth's ecosystem because they have historically contributed significantly more to environmental degradation. The developed countries also acknowledge in Principle 7 that due to their greater technological and financial resources they should take primary responsibility for this joint environmental work. Consequently, the principle of common but differentiated responsibilities appears in nearly all global environmental agreements.

The 'polluter pays' principle is another that is based partly on the same idea as common but differentiated responsibilities. The idea is very reasonable: should not the originator of an environmental problem or damage be liable for compensation, and also for the return of the environment to its previous state where possible? The polluter pays principle has evolved chiefly in Western countries and it has been developed primarily by the Organisation for Economic Co-operation and Development (OECD). The term 'polluter' can refer to a group of states, a state or a private business. The OECD connects the principle with the notion that a company should include all the true costs of a product in its prices, including any expenses that it may incur from polluting the environment (which would otherwise be 'externalized' – that is, the cost is borne by someone other than the company, and not necessarily in monetary terms). The polluter pays principle is often referred to in connection with agreements of strict liability (see Chapter 6, 'Strict-liability agreements', p. 178).

These principles – common but differentiated responsibilities and polluter pays – are also expressed in the introduction to the UN Framework Convention on Climate Change. The principle of fairness is very clear: developed countries have largely caused climate change[35] and are primarily responsible for most of the current emissions; furthermore, they have the greater financial and technical resources in order to cut their greenhouse gas emissions.[36]

The entire UN climate regime was, in fact, constructed upon these principles. In the 1992 convention, the industrial nations undertook to provide financial and technical assistance and to generally take actions to cut greenhouse gas emissions; these nations are listed in Annexes I and II. By the 1997 Kyoto Protocol, the industrial nations committed to undertake legally binding reductions in emissions, while the developing countries have no binding reduction duties; all countries share the responsibility to prevent climate change, by virtue of the climate regime.

The principle acts as the basis of the climate regime, but it is facing increasing criticism now that China has overtaken the United States as the world's greatest emitter of greenhouse gases. The basis of fairness still remains: historically, China has only made a small contribution to climate change, although its greenhouse gas emissions per capita today exceed the levels of many industrial nations. As China, India and many other emerging economic powers are now producing a much higher share of overall greenhouse gas emissions and as their capacity to make reductions has grown considerably, binding emission reductions are now being required of them in order to prevent climate change.

As with all principles, the principle of common but differentiated responsibilities only gives highly general guidance on how, for instance, emission reductions should be divided within the G77 group. At some point, the practical application of the principle is likely to change so that parties obviously affected by climate change (small island states threatened by rising sea levels, for example) continue to be exempt from emission reduction, while certain rapidly progressing 'developing nations' will be required to consent to at least some legally binding emission reduction targets. This move can be seen in the example of the 2011 Durban Climate Change Conference (see Chapter 7, 'Achievements of the Durban Conference', pp. 201–203).

Material and procedural principles

Environmental decision-making is guided by both material and procedural principles. Material (or substantive) principles in environmental law establish the level of environmental quality to be attained, whereas procedural principles establish the process whereby environmental targets are to be achieved (who is in charge of organizing the process, under what measures and with whom). Material principles are significant when conflicts between norms are resolved, for example, gaps in regulation are filled, and open and flexible norms are interpreted. Environmental permit decisions are made on the basis of material principles above all. Procedural principles engage and guide various actors to influence the way environmental decisions are made.

We could argue, for instance, that the environmental impact assessment (EIA) procedure will affect the substance of an environmental permit decision, since the permit decision should be partly based on scientific findings of the likely environmental impacts. If the EIA procedure is completed, it is highly likely that the substantive outcome of the permit decision will change. We can say, then, that the EIA procedure has both a procedural dimension and a content-related dimension which guides decision-making.

As the EIA procedure is not a decision-making procedure in itself, the permit decision-makers should base their decisions on material rules, taking the data from the EIA procedure into account. This implies that although the division into material and procedural principles is a simplification, it is sometimes vital to distinguish between them in order to understand the essential features of each. By and large, the material principles in international law are highly general, whereas the procedural principles can be very detailed. The material principles often remain general, because legal systems at various levels are seeking to strike a balance between promoting economic activities and protecting the environment.

'Sustainable development' is the most common material principle. The definition of the Brundtland Commission is rather too general to function as guidance for practical environmental protection. The International Court of Justice defined sustainable development in a simpler way. In the Danube dam dispute between Hungary and Slovakia, the ICJ stated that sustainable development is meant to reconcile economic development with environmental protection. This does not provide much guidance but it does at least capture the essence that economic activity with no regard for the environmental impact is no longer acceptable. We can argue that the 'human right to a decent or satisfactory environment' has evolved into a material principle which obligates the international community to work to maintain or repair the state of the environment. The material objective in the EU marine strategy directive is the 'good environmental status' of marine areas. Material principles and objectives share a common problem: it is difficult to define exactly what constitutes a 'decent environment' or 'good environmental status', just as it is difficult to define sustainable development. It can be argued that if a state permits the operation of a seriously polluting factory in its territory, it is in violation of the sustainable development principle, the human right to a decent environment and the objective of good environmental status. In his doctoral dissertation, Robert Utter asks the very pertinent question whether all environmental law (international environmental regulation included) is based on a concept of a certain level of environmental quality, even if that precise level cannot be exactly defined.[37]

Some human actions are clearly prohibited by international environmental law. Even if the advisory opinion of the International Court of Justice did not provide a clear answer as to whether nuclear weapons can be used in a situation where the existence of a state is threatened, it did state that the use of nuclear weapons should normally be banned, for example on the basis of principles of international environmental law. Nuclear weapon testing has been permitted for a long time despite its serious environmental impacts. As we saw earlier, New Zealand and Australia sued France in the International Court of Justice because France was performing atmospheric nuclear tests in its Pacific islands; such tests are today prohibited by international law.

The procedural principles aim to guarantee that the material principles are implemented – that such targets as sustainable development or the human right to a decent environment can be achieved. They can be divided into three categories:

1   Principles to guarantee that scientific and other research is considered appropriately in environmental decision-making.
2   Principles to create a framework for environmental decision-making that involves people and organizations in the project area.
3   Principles to obligate companies to implement their production processes in as environment-friendly ways as possible.

Significant material-procedural principles[38] expound the status of scientific knowledge in environmental decision-making. According to the principle of prevention, environmental protection should commence when a high degree of scientific certainty of the environmental problems of a given human activity is achieved. The precautionary principle,[39] in contrast, requires action before full scientific certainty has been achieved if serious or irrevocable consequences may follow.

The precautionary principle exemplifies a new relationship between scientific 'certainty' and environmental decision-making. It cannot easily be classified as either procedural or material as it is often implemented through procedures (reversed burden of proof, or EIA procedure), while it also represents an ideal by which environmental decisions should be made: before scientific certainty, and promptly if the consequences could be serious or irreversible.

Natural science increasingly reminds us that it is impossible to achieve absolute certainty on environmental issues. Moreover, the modern world is fraught with different environmental problems, often mutually interacting, so it is difficult to identify any single issue in which to achieve any degree of scientific certainty.

Economic scholars argue that the precautionary principle is incompatible with modern economic operations even if it actually reflects the way we usually act in our own everyday lives. Most people avoid serious risks; they make decisions with caution and do not risk seriously injuring themselves if they can avoid it. Companies do not make their decisions on the same bases, because in the end neither the company nor even its owners will suffer if environmental problems occur. Even in the case of a massive tort action, the company can shield itself behind bankruptcy laws and the owners will not be obliged to pay compensation. Companies work in a relatively open competitive environment whereby to exclude sectors of their activity based on serious environmental risks could put them at a competitive disadvantage compared with other firms that are prepared to take such risks. This is why environmental law is enacted: legislation levels the playing field by requiring the same environmental measures of all companies.

German sociologist Ulrich Beck[40] says we have created a risk society in which regional and global environmental problems are generated by the decisions of multiple business actors, each of which when taken alone is relatively harmless. Such decisions should be counterbalanced by a powerful government, or intergovernmental treaties and organizations that are able to consider the overall benefit of society.

The precautionary principle is perhaps the most debated and the most controversial principle in international environmental law. This is partly due to the rapid development of its status in international law. The precautionary principle also contains potential for radical environmental regulation, causing the business world and some governments to regard it with suspicion. According to some interpretations, the principle requires an actor to prove that an action will not harm the environment and ecosystems. Such a reversed burden of proof is applied in some treaty regimes but most of them do not apply it.

Dumping waste in the sea was not heavily regulated by the London Dumping Convention of 1972. The Convention only prohibited the dumping of those materials listed in the Annex I blacklist (such as mercury), while materials listed in the Annex II grey list could be dumped with the permission of a competent authority. High-level radioactive waste could not be dumped, while low-level radioactive waste could. In 1985, the meeting of the parties adopted a resolution banning the dumping of all radioactive waste.

When the Soviet Union dissolved, Russia announced that the Soviet Union had dumped both high-level and low-level radioactive waste, primarily in the Barents Sea. This provided the motivation for a further meeting of the parties, which banned the dumping of radioactive waste completely. Annex I was amended accordingly in 1993. The only state to withdraw from the amendment was Russia; it could therefore legally continue to dump low-level radioactive waste.

A protocol was negotiated to the London Dumping Convention in 1996 which reflects the precautionary principle. Annex I now consists of a permissive list: only materials specifically named on the list may be dumped; there is a ban on all other materials. Actors who might want to see a waste material added to Annex I have to perform a risk assessment and prove that the material will not cause any harm to human health or the environment.

Another good example of the application of the precautionary principle can be seen in the Antarctic Treaty Consultative Meeting (ATCM)'s approach to consideration of mining in the continent.

The ATCM decided in the 1970s that mining would be prohibited until a regulating agreement could be negotiated. The negotiations began, and the parties accepted the Convention on the Regulation of Antarctic Mineral Resource Activities (CRAMRA) in 1988. Partly due to powerful pressure from Greenpeace, both Australia and France announced that they would not ratify the CRAMRA. The Convention could not enter into force unless it was ratified by all the original signatory states to the 1959 Antarctic Treaty. The parties soon came to a decision to regulate mining by banning it for 50 years from the entry into force of the environmental protection protocol adopted in 1991.

The precautionary principle is also used in the Framework Convention on Climate Change as a guiding approach for the convention system. Unfortunately, as yet there are hardly any signs of its practical application in the operation of the climate regime. If there is one environmental problem today that seems to be irreversible, it is climate change. Considering the risks for all of mankind, the precautionary principle should be strictly applied. To date, states have continued to evade their responsibilities and the levels of greenhouse gases in the atmosphere continue to increase, despite the completion of the first commitment period of the Kyoto Protocol at the end of 2012. Considering increased scientific consensus about climate change, human involvement in its aggravation, and its effects, we could question whether the precautionary principle is still applicable to climate change at all. Instead, where the negative impacts of activities are widely recognized and proven, the principle of prevention should apply: states must take no action that knowingly harms other states.

A more moderate interpretation of the precautionary principle is that decision-makers should at least be aware of the level and quality of scientific uncertainty. The Espoo EIA Convention, for instance, expressly requires the parties to establish national EIA procedures. These should obligate companies to perform EIAs that explain in plain language what uncertainties might be contained in the assessment. The essential way of implementing the preventive and precautionary principles is the environmental impact assessment. It is applied in almost all the states in the world.

The environmental impact assessment (EIA) procedure

The EIA procedure obligates authorities to ensure that the environmental impact of a project is assessed before the project is commenced (or before granting a licence).

In many EIA systems, the company in charge of a project performs a comprehensive scientific study of the possible environmental impacts of the project. Generally, the company is also required to assess the environmental impacts of alternative options, and possible measures to prevent environmental impacts. These scientific studies are performed under the watchful eye of the civic society and the relevant authorities.

It is especially important that the people in the area affected by a project are informed about their rights to influence which environmental impacts are to be considered. They should also be able to comment as to how the environmental impacts could be mitigated by the different alternative plans to realize the proposed project.

Authorities should consider any comments from the local community as well as the relevant authorities when making their licence decision, as well as, of course, the results of the EIA study.

The Rio Conference initiated a wider trend of promoting 'environmental democracy'. In Principle 10 of the Rio Declaration, states made a political commitment to increase their citizens' access to information about environmental threats and their access to environmental decision-making. The principle also encourages giving communities an opportunity to improve the environmental management system by appealing against the authorities in administrative and judicial processes. The clearest expression of these ideas is recorded in the Aarhus Convention of 1998 and the Pollutant Release and Transfer Registers (PRTR) Protocol.[41] The latter stipulates that authorities should establish a register into which companies regularly submit information about their emissions for the community to access and use.

The environment is also protected by principles that obligate companies to perform the phases of their production process in as environmentally friendly a way as possible. Legislation can guide companies to apply the 'best available technology' (BAT) and the 'best environmental practices' (BEP), which improve the prospects of sustainable development.

New approaches to environmental protection

Increased environmental scientific research gives rise to constant changes in environmental law and politics. It had long been assumed that ecosystems maintain a certain balance as long as there is no human intervention. However, empirical studies of the functioning of ecosystems proved otherwise. Ecosystems often go through changes and reach a new temporary balance independent of human influence. On the other hand, our activities influence the entire biosphere and the functions of its various parts in one way or another; it is therefore difficult to distinguish the natural environment as a separate island, even, for instance, as a natural park.

These observations have resulted in new models for the protection of the environment. The predominant understanding is that environmental protection should preferably take the form of co-management by actors at multiple levels, engaging both those who have authority in environmental protection and those who suffer from the effects of environmental damage. Environmental governance should also be flexible, as it should be able to react quickly when necessary to the latest scientific research.

Modern environmental governance, both international and national, is essentially influenced by the idea of 'ecosystem-based management'. This management model is based on two mutually sustaining ideas: environmental management should take place so that (1) the plans and decisions over activities in a certain area are coordinated, and (2) the ecosystems in the area remain functional. This approach has broken through in international environmental law.

A good example is the management of two neighbouring seas, the Baltic Sea and the North-East Atlantic, using the ecosystem-based management system; (the treaty regimes of both were renewed in 1992). The 1992 Convention for the Protection of the Marine Environment of the North-East

Atlantic (OSPAR) was created when the Oslo 1972 Dumping Convention and the Paris 1974 Convention on land-based sources of marine pollution were combined. Fifteen states are party to it, three of which are not coastal countries of the North-East Atlantic. Finland is party to it because its northern rivers empty into the Barents Sea and because it was already a party to the Oslo Dumping Convention. Luxembourg and Switzerland are parties because the Rhine flows across their territory and empties into the North Sea.

The main strategy of the convention is ecosystem-based marine management complemented by such principles as the precautionary principle, the polluter pays principle and the principles of best environmental technology and practices. The OSPAR has also established close relations with the North East Atlantic Fisheries Commission (NEAFC), in order to coordinate fishing with other activities in the OSPAR area. The OSPAR has developed innovative ways of protecting the high seas environment in the North-East Atlantic.

The Baltic Sea Convention, which was renewed in 1992, has also gradually assumed the marine ecosystem management system, and the OSPAR and the Helsinki Commission (HELCOM) have given joint declarations about using this management model in the marine ecosystems. Both trends are supported by the intensified EU maritime policy because many parties to the OSPAR and HELCOM are also member states of the EU. Both the Marine Directive and the EU Integrated Maritime Policy increasingly encourage member states to assume ecosystem-based marine management.

Another idea that has increasingly influenced environmental law and politics is the concept of 'ecosystem services'. Ecosystem services are divided into four categories in the scientific UN 2005 Millennium Ecosystem Assessment (MA): provisioning, supporting, regulating, and cultural. Many of us are most familiar with the provisioning services provided by nature: trees and food grow spontaneously, securing the basis for human economy and existence. Nature regulates the composition of the atmosphere and watercourses (regulating services) and provides opportunities for peace and recreation (cultural services). Further services provided by nature are dependent on the supporting services, such as photosynthesis, nutrient circulation and pollination.

The 2005 MA was an important extensive assessment under the auspices of the UN. It demonstrated that most of the ecosystem services have lost their 'serviceability' due to human activity. It also brought to international and national attention the environmental approach that had long been acknowledged by experts. Although the notion of ecosystem services is only just emerging in environmental governance, it has already begun to question the way previous environmental regulation took them for free and granted.

Regulatory instruments in international environmental law

The national and EU environmental legal systems have a versatile selection of regulatory instruments at their disposal in order to promote the objectives of environmental protection. The best-known ones are regulation by 'command and control' and 'economic regulation'.

Examples of the command and control method include the setting of emission limits or structural requirements for products. The government controls the behaviour of individuals and businesses and its administrative bodies supervise compliance with the rules. This method of environmental protection is still prevalent but it is being challenged for several reasons, including the difficulties of exercising control: it requires an enormous amount of bureaucracy and financial resources.

Economic regulation (emissions trading, for example) influences the market so that it becomes more profitable for a company to select environmentally friendly decisions from the available alternatives. Economic regulation is increasing in international environmental law, although the governmental command and control method is clearly more common. This is partly due to the nature of international environmental law: many of the treaties allow national governments to decide how they will implement the obligations.

The MARPOL treaty system, discussed above, is an example of the command and control method – and of how the international community is able to design more efficient methods for environmental protection. Its objective is to reduce contamination of the sea, caused by the routine operations of ships or by accidents. Its Annex I aims to reduce oil emissions from ships; it includes absolute prohibitions (such as that no oil must be discharged near the coast) and limitations and requirements related to the construction of vessels. The focus of regulation is gradually shifting to the structural requirements. This is understandable, since it is very difficult to control whether a certain vessel has discharged oil contrary to Annex I or violated its regulations in other ways.

In 1989, the *Exxon Valdez* oil tanker caused an enormous crude oil discharge of between 260,000 and 750,000 barrels, contaminating about 2,100 kilometres of the Alaskan coast. After the catastrophe, the International Maritime Organization (IMO) pursued the claim that oil tankers should be required to have double hulls to reduce the risk of oil leak. The *Exxon Valdez* did not have a double hull.

There is reason to conclude that regulation requiring double hulls in existing and especially in new oil tankers, would be a more efficient regulation instrument than emission limits: as the vessels are better constructed, oil hazards are efficiently reduced.

Economic regulation is gradually emerging in international environmental law as well. The most prominent example is the Kyoto Protocol to the UN Convention on Climate Change. It obligates the industrial nations listed in Annex I to cut their total emissions by an average of 5 per cent below the levels recorded in 1990 within the time period 2008 to 2012 (the first commitment period); the second commitment period runs from 2013 to 2020.

To achieve this legally binding target, the countries listed in Annex I can apply a flexible mechanism: the 'joint implementation mechanism' (whereby an industrial nation funds projects to cut greenhouse gas emissions, generally in a transition economy), the 'clean development mechanism' (an industrial nation funds emission reduction projects in a developing country), or 'international emissions trading' (an industrial nation that has exceeded its emission limit buys emission credits from another industrial country that has emission credits to spare). An industrial nation receives emission reductions from joint implementation projects and clean development mechanism projects which it can apply towards the fulfilment of its own obligation, or it can buy emission credits from another industrial country. The idea is that acquiring emission credits in industrial nations costs so much more than in transition economies or developing countries that it makes financial sense for an industrial country to get the credits where it is least expensive – or in some cases to buy emission credits from other countries in order to meet its obligations.

Another new trend is the creation of market-based mechanisms based on the same basic idea as in emissions trading in the climate regime: emissions must have a price. In this way, an ecosystem service that everyone uses freely is limited by legal regulation and a market is created.

Many companies barely gave consideration to climate change previously – 'the emissions disperse in thin air'. Now they must change their policies, since limits have been set on the greenhouse gas emissions of, for example, every EU member state. These emission permits are divided by member states internally between those companies accountable for the emissions. Unless they are able to manufacture their products within their own emission quotas, they have to buy permits from other companies that have used fewer permits.

From 2013, the EU has introduced two emissions caps. The emissions trading segment has an EU-wide cap and the national caps and national distribution plans are removed, whereas the segments outside emissions trading (transport, waste management, agriculture, for example) retain the national caps. The EU is gradually moving from distribution plans based on national emission caps to a system of an EU-wide cap where emissions permits are sold to companies by auction.

The same logic applies to ecosystem services.

The salinity of the Hunter river in New South Wales, Australia, is contained by dividing the amount of water in the river theoretically into 365 blocks outside the flood season (when water is low). Each plant along the river is granted emission credits for a certain amount of waste water in a certain block; if a plant runs out of credits, it can buy more in the online trading system maintained by the state environmental protection authority. The system seems to have functioned well. The condition of the river has improved as emissions are matched with the capacity of the river at each time. The environmental quality has improved without the need to limit the total amount of emissions.

Questions and research tasks

Ownership of land, sea and space

1   Although most coastal states now enjoy an exclusive economic zone or exclusive fisheries zone out to the maximum 200 nautical miles (370 kilometres) limit, the majority of the surface of the world's seas and oceans is beyond this limit and hence constitutes the high seas. Do you consider it positive that the international law of the sea has gradually given increasing jurisdiction to the coastal countries over their adjacent waters extending to such a distance? Would it have been better to maintain a larger part of the seas as high seas, open to all? The coastal states have likewise progressively extended their rights to the seabed. Find the Truman Declaration on the internet and consider what its legal effect might have been at the time it was made. Then find out how it has actually influenced the development of the continental shelf rights of coastal states.

2   States have acquired more and more jurisdiction on Earth and in space. Do you think they want to extend their jurisdiction at sea, in the Moon or the space? If this were the case, how could it happen and what would the consequences be for environmental protection in these areas?

3   Do you think that governments will observe the environmental protocol in the Antarctic Treaty and refrain from mining on this ice-covered continent, at least until 2048? What other factors in Antarctica discourage commercial mining? Find the Antarctic Treaty 1959 and the Madrid Protocol 1991 on the internet to check the conditions the protocol gives for starting mining again after 2048.

4   The International Seabed Authority has jurisdiction over the exploration and exploitation for non-living resources in the deep seabed beyond national jurisdiction (the Area). Comment on the benefits and disadvantages of the ISA assuming jurisdiction over marine genetic resources located in the Area.

5   What role could existing regional seas organizations play in protecting the high seas marine environment?

Principles of international law and the environment

1   Considering that states seldom assess the environmental impacts on other states of planned projects within their jurisdiction, how is it possible that this principle has evolved into a principle of customary international law? Try to find the principle of no-harm in various international agreements, looking especially at those covering environmental matters. Note that the phrase 'no-harm' might not be used explicitly. What other expressions are used that you think are equivalent to the no-harm concept? As most states are already legally bound to this principle by international agreements, is it relevant to assess whether it is also a principle of customary

international law? Or is it a general legal principle? Find the homepage of the International Court of Justice and study the *Gabčíkovo-Nagymaros* case and how the principle of no-harm is expressed in that judgment. (Note: it is often helpful to read the Court's own summaries of its judgments before tackling the full texts.) Does the Court define the principle of no-harm in the same manner as the Stockholm and Rio Declarations? If not, does the difference have legal significance and if so, what?

2   Why is it so difficult for states to protect the biological diversity in the areas beyond their own national jurisdiction? This problem is being discussed in a process backed by the UN General Assembly and in the biodiversity system. Find these processes (see the websites list) and consider how the approach to the issue has changed over the past ten years.

3   Find an article about the latest stages in the *Trail Smelter* saga in your database. The fact that a book on the subject has recently been published shows the ongoing importance of the case. The arbitrators stated very emphatically how international law regulates transboundary air pollution. Why then do so many lawyers seem to be unclear about this?

Principles, approaches and regulatory instruments in international environmental law

1   Why did the UN International Court of Justice call sustainable development a 'concept' rather than an objective or a principle? Don't all the states in the world at least claim to be implementing sustainable development? Could sustainable development therefore be considered a general principle of law that binds all states? How would you define sustainable development in more detail? To what types of pollution do you think sustainable development applies? Does it apply to transboundary pollution?

2   What problems, if any, do you see in the precautionary principle from the perspective of businesses? Find the Rio Declaration and see how the precautionary principle is recorded there. How do you think the wording balances the interests of economic activity with environmental protection? Do you think the balance is the right one?

3   Imagine that you are working in a regional environmental agency and you realize that a proposed steelworks that is important for the economy in your area would probably have transboundary environmental impacts. Would you report this to the government department so that the neighbouring country and its citizens could participate in the environmental impact assessment (EIA)? If the EIA legislation gave you an option – if you understood that it would not be necessary to notify anyone if you could not be certain that the steelworks would be likely to cause significant impacts to another state – would you report it? Consider also a scenario in which you would know that the case you are responsible for is also being supervised by the central government.

4   How useful do you think the principle of common but differentiated responsibilities is in resolving global environmental problems?
Are China and India still countries that should be granted differentiated responsibilities along with heavily indebted African countries? Do
you think the principle of common but differentiated responsibilities
could be more closely specified for a heterogeneous group of southern
countries? How might China, India or Brazil be likely to react? Find
environmental agreements that contain the principle of common but
differentiated responsibilities. Read the Durban 2011 Climate Change
Conference end result (Durban Platform) and consider how it discusses
this principle.

5   Comment on the debate going on in the IMO about regulation of greenhouse gas emissions in shipping and whether the common but
differentiated responsibilities principle should apply to the regulation of
these emissions or whether all shipping should be treated in the same way
under the principle of non-discrimination.

Notes

1   Marie Byrd Land in Antarctica has not been included in any state's sovereignty
claims. There are also many areas which several states are contesting, such as the
small Hans Island between Canadian Ellesmere Island and Danish Greenland. Canada and Denmark have taken turns planting their flags on this tiny island.

2   A state's territorial sea is divided into internal and external territorial waters. Foreign vessels are allowed innocent passage through the territorial sea. Internal territorial waters are defined in Article 8 of the Convention on the Law of the Sea:
'Except as provided in Part IV, waters on the landward side of the baseline of the
territorial sea form part of the internal waters of the State.' It is therefore significant
how the baseline is defined, because on the landward side, foreign ships are not
even entitled to innocent passage. See the UN Convention on the Law of the Sea,
Articles 5 and 7.

3   Innocent passage means passage that is not prejudicial to the peace, good order or
security of the coastal state.

4   A state's sea areas are primarily measured from the baseline. The main rule is that
the territorial sea, the contiguous zone, the exclusive economic zone, and in some
cases the continental shelf are measured from the so-called normal baseline – that
is, 'the low-water line along the coast as marked on large-scale charts officially recognized by the coastal State' (Convention on the Law of the Sea, Article 5). A state
can also apply straight baselines in cases where 'the coastline is deeply indented and
cut into, or if there is a fringe of islands along the coast in its immediate vicinity'
(Article 7). The method of straight baselines joining appropriate points can then be
employed in drawing the baseline from which the width of the territorial sea and
other zones is measured.

5   See the 1992 Rio Declaration, Principle 2.

6   *Case Concerning Military and Paramilitary Activities in and against Nicaragua* (*Nicaragua
v. United States of America*), at the ICJ's website at http://www.icj-cij.org/docket/
files/70/6503.pdf

7   See the United Nations Declaration on the Rights of Indigenous Peoples, at http://
www.un.org/esa/socdev/unpfii/documents/DRIPS_en.pdf. See also the only modern
international treaty regulating the rights of indigenous peoples: International Labour

Organization's Convention No. 169 (Indigenous and Tribal Peoples Convention), at http://www.ilo.org/dyn/normlex/en/f?p=1000:12100:0::NO::P12100_ILO_CODE:C169

8 The treaty concerning Spitsbergen, Article 1: 'The High Contracting Parties undertake to recognise, subject to the stipulations of the present Treaty, the full and absolute sovereignty of Norway over the Archipelago of Spitsbergen ...'.

9 There was an attempt to adopt the Treaty establishing a Constitution for Europe (TCE), but this failed because both the Dutch and French rejected this in 2005 in their respective referenda.

10 Antarctic Treaty, 1959, http://www.ats.aq/e/ats.htm

11 A state can join the Antarctic Treaty without assuming the status of consultative party, i.e. as a so-called non-consultative party. The regime now has 28 consultative and 21 non-consultative parties.

12 Convention on the Conservation of Antarctic Marine Living Resources, 1982, http://www.antarctica.ac.uk/about_antarctica/geopolitical/treaty/convention.php

13 Protocol on Environmental Protection to the Antarctic Treaty, 1991, http://www.antarctica.ac.uk/about_antarctica/geopolitical/treaty/update_1991.php

14 The European Parliament, however, accepted a new resolution concerning Arctic policy at the beginning of 2011. It no longer favours a comprehensive international treaty for the region.

15 See T. Koivurova, 'Environmental Protection in the Arctic and Antarctica', in Natalia Loukacheva (ed.), *Polar Law Textbook*, pp. 23–44, Nordic Council of Ministers, 2010.

16 Download the accounts in: http://wwf.panda.org/what_we_do/where_we_work/arctic/publications/?193130/New-Arctic-needs-new-rules-WWF

17 Reports of International Arbitral Awards, *Trail Smelter* case (United States, Canada), 16 April 1938 and 11 March 1941, Vol. III, pp. 1905–82, p. 1965.

18 Convention on the Law of the Non-Navigational Uses of International Watercourses, 1997, http://untreaty.un.org/ilc/texts/instruments/english/conventions/8_3_1997.pdf

19 Convention on the Protection and Use of Transboundary Watercourses and International Lakes, 1992, http://www.unece.org/fileadmin/DAM/env/water/pdf/watercon.pdf

20 Convention on Early Notification of a Nuclear Accident, 1986, http://www.iaea.org/Publications/Documents/Conventions/cenna.html

21 Convention on Assistance in Case of a Nuclear Accident or Radiological Emergency, 1986, http://www.iaea.org/Publications/Documents/Conventions/cacnare.html

22 Basel Convention on the Control of Transboundary Movements of Hazardous Wastes and their Disposal, 1989, http://www.basel.int/portals/4/basel%20convention/docs/text/baselconventiontext-e.pdf

23 Rotterdam Convention on the Prior Informed Consent Procedure for Certain Hazardous Chemicals and Pesticides in International Trade, 1998, http://www.pic.int/

24 Convention on Long-range Transboundary Air Pollution, 1979, http://www.unece.org/env/lrtap

25 Protocol to the 1979 Convention on Long-range Transboundary Air Pollution on Long-term Financing of the Cooperative Programme for Monitoring and Evaluation of the Long-range Transmission of Air Pollutants in Europe (EMEP), http://ec.europa.eu/world/agreements/prepareCreateTreatiesWorkspace/treatiesGeneralData.do?step=0&redirect=true&treatyId=515

26 Protocol to the 1979 Convention on Long-range Transboundary Air Pollution on Further Reduction of Sulphur Emissions, http://ec.europa.eu/world/agreements/prepareCreateTreatiesWorkspace/treatiesGeneralData.do?step=0&redirect=true&treatyId=515

27 Stockholm Convention on Persistent Organic Pollutants, http://chm.pops.int/Home/tabid/2121/mctl/ViewDetails/EventModID/870/EventID/331/xmid/6921/Default.aspx

28 The Rio Declaration uses the term 'precautionary approach'.

29 UN Framework Convention on Climate Change, http://unfccc.int/2860.php

30 Vienna Convention for the Protection of the Ozone Layer, 2002, http://ozone.unep.org/pdfs/viennaconvention2002.pdf

31 Montreal Protocol on Substances that Deplete the Ozone Layer, http://ozone.unep.org/pdfs/Montreal-Protocol2000.pdf

32 Debris and waste from manned spacecraft, tools that astronauts have lost, broken satellites and booster stages, especially in the geostationary earth orbits. A geostationary earth orbit (GEO) is a circular orbit about 35,000 kilometres above the Earth's equator. Communications satellites use them, because their angular speed is equal to the Earth's rotation; a satellite can use directional antennae that need not be turned as the Earth revolves.

33 This is the Ad Hoc Open-ended Informal Working Group to study issues relating to the conservation and sustainable use of marine biological diversity beyond areas of national jurisdiction; see http://www.un.org/Depts/los/biodiversityworkinggroup/biodiversityworkinggroup.htm

34 The biodiversity regime has also been working on this issue but has restricted itself to a technical and advisory role.

35 Their historical responsibility is only referred to in the introduction.

36 This Principle ends with the words: 'in accordance with their common but differentiated responsibilities and respective capabilities and their social and economic conditions'. The expression 'in accordance with their respective capabilities' has caused the industrial nations to appeal to the responsibility of rising developing nations such as China. The industrial nations can no longer prevent climate change alone, and they claim that the responsibility of developing countries to participate in fighting climate change should increase as their economic and other resources improve.

37 Robert Utter, *Normativ miljökvalitet: funktionen av en rättsligt institutionaliserad måttstock beträffande kvaliteten av miljön*, University of Helsinki Faculty of Law, 2007, http://www.doria.fi/bitstream/handle/10024/19239/normativ.pdf?sequence=2

38 It is difficult to classify the precautionary principle as purely procedural or material, since it requires early action if a certain environmental impact is possible; procedures to exercise precaution are often established on its basis.

39 I use the term 'precautionary principle', which seems to be more widely adopted by literature and governmental practice. The terms precautionary principle and principle of preventive action have been given slightly different meanings. The consolidated version of the Treaty on the Functioning of the European Union, Article 191(2), refers to the precautionary principle. The precautionary principle can also be seen as a material principle underlying or justifying procedural principles.

40 U. Beck, *Risk Society: Towards a New Modernity*, London: Sage, 1992.

41 Protocol on Pollutant Release and Transfer Registers, which became legally binding on 8 October 2009, http://www.unece.org/env/pp/prtr.html

Further reading

Ownership of land, sea and space

Anton, D.K. and Shelton, D.L., *Environmental Protection and Human Rights*, Cambridge: Cambridge University Press, 2011.

Duyck, S., Koivurova, T. and Kokko, K., Executive Summary, 'Assessment of possible relations or implications of LBA Content Options 2 and 3 on selected international forest related agreements and on the EU (EC) competence (August 2009)', http://www.foresteurope.org/filestore/foresteurope/Meetings/2009/3rd_WG_LBA_Rome_September_2009/BP5implicationanalysis.pdf

Fitzmaurice, M., *International Legal Problems of the Environmental Protection of the Baltic Sea*, International Environmental Law and Policy Series, Dordrecht: Nijhoff, 1992.

Franckx, E., '200-Mile Limit: Between Creeping Jurisdiction and Creeping Common Heritage – Some Law of the Sea Considerations from Professor Louis Sohn's Former LL.M. Student', *George Washington International Law Review*, 39, 2007, pp. 467–98.

Heinämäki, L., 'The Protection of the Environmental Integrity of Indigenous Peoples in Human Rights Law', *Finnish Yearbook of International Law*, XVII, 2006, pp. 187–232.

Heinämäki, L., 'Protecting the Rights of Indigenous Peoples – Promoting the Sustainability of the Global Environment?', *International Community Law Review*, 11(1), 2009, pp. 3–68.

Heinämäki, L., 'Rethinking the Status of Indigenous Peoples in International Environmental Decision-Making: Pondering the Role of Arctic Indigenous Peoples and the Challenge of Climate Change', in T. Koivurova, E.C.H. Keskitalo and N. Bankes (eds), *Climate Governance in the Arctic*, Vol. 50, pp. 207–62, Berlin: Springer, 2009.

Heinämäki, L., *The Right to Be a Part of Nature: Indigenous Peoples and the Environment*, Acta Universitatis Lapponiensis, 180, University of Lapland, Faculty of Law, 2010, http://www.doria.fi/bitstream/handle/10024/67145/Hein%C3%A4m%C3%A4kiDORIA.pdf?sequence=3

Koivurova, T., *Environmental Impact Assessment in the Arctic: A Study of International Legal Norms*, Aldershot: Ashgate, 2002.

Koivurova, T. and VanderZwaag, D., 'The Arctic Council at 10 Years: Retrospect and Prospects', *University of British Columbia Law Review* 40(1), 2007, pp. 121–94.

Koivurova, T., Kokko, K., Duyck, S., Sellheim, N. and Stepien, A., 'The present and future competence of the European Union in the Arctic', *Polar Record*, Cambridge: Cambridge University Press, CJO 2011, doi:10.1017/S0032247411000295

Marsden, S. and Koivurova, T. (eds), 'Transboundary Environmental Impact Assessment in the European Union: The Espoo Convention and its Kiev Protocol on Strategic Environmental Assessment', London: Earthscan, 2011.

Triggs, G. and Riddell, A. (eds), *Antarctica: Legal and Environmental Challenges for the Future*, British Institute of International and Comparative Law, 2007.

Viikari, L., *The Environmental Element in Space Law: Assessing the Present and Charting the Future*, Leiden: Nijhoff, 2008.

Warner, R. and Marsden, S. (eds), *Transboundary Environmental Governance: Inland, Coastal and Marine Perspectives*, Aldershot: Ashgate, 2012.

Principles, approaches and regulatory instruments in international environmental law

Bastmeijer, C.J. and Koivurova, T. (eds), *Theory and Practice of Transboundary Environmental Impact Assessment*, Leiden: Nijhoff, 2008.

Hossain, K., 'The Realization of the Right to Environment and the Right to Development in respect to the Arctic Indigenous Peoples', *The Yearbook of Polar Law*, 3, 2011, pp. 129–54, Leiden: Brill Academic.

Lowe, V., 'Sustainable Development and Unsustainable Arguments', in A. Boyle and D. Freestone (eds), *International Law and Sustainable Development: Past Achievements and Future Challenges*, pp. 19–37, Oxford: Oxford University Press, 1999.

Lyster, R. and Stephens, T., 'The Rise and Rise of Environmental Markets: Biodiversity Banking in Australia', *Asia Pacific Journal of Environmental Law*, 10, 2007, pp. 1–12.

Rajamani, L., *Differential Treatment in International Environmental Law*, Oxford: Oxford University Press, 2006.

Ruhl, J.B., 'The Law and Policy of Ecosystem Services', Department of Geography and Environmental Resources in the Graduate School Southern Illinois University Carbondale, 2006, http://www.geography.siu.edu/pdfFiles/Graduate/GradPapers/ruhl.pdf

Utter, R., *Normativ miljökvalitet: Funktionen av en rättsligt institutionaliserad måttstock beträffande kvaliteten av miljön. Forum Iuris*, University of Helsinki Faculty of Law 2007, http://www.doria.fi/bitstream/handle/10024/19239/normativ.pdf?sequence=2)

Websites

Ownership of land, sea and space

Antarctic Treaty Secretariat (ATS): http://www.ats.aq/index_e.htm

Arctic Council: http://www.arctic-council.org/index.php/en/

Commission on the Limits of the Continental Shelf (CLCS): http://www.un.org/depts/los/clcs_new/clcs_home.htm

Council of the European Union: consolidated versions of the Treaty on European Union and the Treaty on the Functioning of the European Union, and the Charter of Fundamental Rights of the European Union: http://www.consilium.europa.eu/treaty-of-lisbon.aspx?

International Seabed Authority (ISA): http://www.isa.org.jm/en/home

Principles of international law and the environment

Ad Hoc Open-ended Informal Working Group to study issues relating to the conservation and sustainable use of marine biological diversity beyond areas of national jurisdiction: http://www.un.org/depts/los/biodiversityworkinggroup/biodiversity workinggroup.htm

Marine and Coastal Biodiversity Thematic Programme (under the Biodiversity Convention): http://www.cbd.int/marine/seabed.shtml

UN Declaration on the Rights of Indigenous Peoples: http://social.un.org/index/IndigenousPeoples/DeclarationontheRightsofIndigenousPeoples.aspx

Pew Environment Group Policy Statement on Biodiversity Beyond National Jurisdiction: http://www.pewenvironment.org/news-room/other-resources/policy-statement-biological-diversity-beyond-areas-of-national-jurisdiction-bbnj-85899384181

Principles, approaches and regulatory instruments in international environmental law

IUCN Draft International Covenant on Environment and Development: http://www.i-c-e-l.org/english/EPLP31EN_rev2.pdf

Declaration of the United Nations Conference on the Human Environment (Stockholm Declaration): http://www.unep.org/Documents.Multilingual/Default.asp?documentid=97&articleid=1503

Rio Declaration on Environment and Development: http://www.unep.org/Documents.Multilingual/Default.asp?documentid=78&articleid=1163

International Maritime Organization: http://www.imo.org

5 Branches of international environmental law

Anyone who studies international environmental law must give consideration to its special characteristics. In 1994, Professor Martti Koskenniemi wrote an insightful article in which he questioned whether it is ethically acceptable and strategically wise to read environmental protection values into international law. His article inspired me to contemplate what I was doing as a researcher. Is it not a legal scholar's task to consider the benefit of society as a whole, not just to promote the prioritization of a particular value – in this case environmental protection? Is it strategically reasonable to claim that international law is already quite green, when the same system encourages business activities and promotes the development of free trade law? These remain important questions. If a legal scholar is already familiar with environmental law, is it not his or her duty to criticize the existing system instead of just defending it? Is it not a scholar's duty to understand the reality of international environmental law as part of the broader context of international law and politics?

In 2011, I taught international environmental law as a Visiting Professor at the University of New South Wales in Sydney. I came to know a professor from the United States, who was a specialist in international trade law. In his outspoken way, he stated that he did not even consider international environmental law to be a branch of international law at all, because of its fragmentation. To some extent I had to agree with his view.

International environmental law is essentially an umbrella concept that includes various normative developments related to the usage of the environment and especially its protection. It is clear that international environmental law does not form a coherent branch of law which could, analogously to free trade law, provide governments with clear rules to observe in their environmental policies. On the other hand, international environmental law can be considered a distinct branch of international law, since it has developed its own general doctrines, principles and concepts. Research in the branch is increasing and new textbooks are published at an accelerating rate.

The branches and regimes within international environmental law operate relatively independently so it does not seem reasonable to lump them together artificially. However, there are branches within international environmental law which do clearly feature a kind of unity that needs to be maintained and sustained.

This chapter considers international environmental law with a view to a more coherent understanding of this fragmented and complex body of law. Only in textbooks are the vast numbers of international environmental law regulations organized into a neat whole. Textbook authors have divided the branches of international environmental law in several different ways and on different bases. The legal rules relating to waste, for instance, can be considered a whole, even if the various waste management regimes are, in reality, quite unconnected. The goal of this chapter is to review, by way of examples, some of the branches of international environmental law, such as the protection of the marine environment or biological diversity.

The section on the conservation of the atmosphere analyses the development of the two best-known treaty regimes and their interconnection. Could the most successful regime, the ozone regime, be an example for the development of the climate regime, and how profoundly are these regimes interdependent? This section will not revisit the other regimes related to international atmosphere protection (the LRTAP and POP regimes, for example), discussed earlier in this book.

An interesting regime to start with is the free trade regime, which is highly coherent internally and has important implications for international environmental protection.

The fragmentation of international law

International law has expanded enormously since the Second World War. Almost every conceivable aspect of politics and law is regulated internationally to some extent. International law has grown into such an extensive area that only very few can with justification claim to be in command of the whole. Entire faculties of law could be established around the various sub-disciplines of international law.

As the amount of regulation increases, international law is split into separate branches, such as human rights, free trade rules, and international environmental law. This so-called 'fragmentation' has been identified as a challenge by the UN International Law Commission. The consistency of international law is jeopardized when semi-autonomous systems (the EU and WTO, for example), or branches of international law (international environmental law, human rights law, or law of the sea) interpret international law from their own perspectives. The risk of fragmentation is primarily related to the branches of international law that have their own judicial or arbitration bodies. The risk is that their interpretation of international law can be overly biased in favour of one particular value set, such as free trade, or they can consider themselves so autonomous that they are not willing to apply the principles of general international law at all.

The World Trade Organization (WTO) as an example of a branch of international law

The free trade regulatory system under the World Trade Organization (WTO) is an excellent example of a branch of international law. All states seeking WTO membership are bound to accept the compulsory jurisdiction of the dispute settlement body. Relatively unusually in international law, WTO members are able to take their disputes to a dispute settlement panel even without the other party's consent. If a party is dissatisfied with the panel's decision, it can appeal to the Appellate Body. Although there are a huge number of international environmental treaties, violation rarely results in any kind of legal action. However, if a state acts in the interests of the environment, it may well be accountable for violating the WTO free trade regulation.

The dispute settlement procedures of the WTO's predecessor, the GATT, did not give much consideration to environmental issues, although this would theoretically have been possible according to its rules.

In the *Tuna/Dolphin I* case of 1991 the United States banned the import of Mexican tuna products because the Mexicans used nets that the USA had prohibited on board US-registered vessels or in the US EEZ; US law only permitted fishing nets that would not harm dolphins; and by extension, the US refused to import tuna from states that did not uphold equivalent standards.

Mexico took the USA to the GATT dispute settlement proceedings with the end result that the US ban on import was deemed illegal. According to the GATT Panel, the USA was applying the restrictions of its own domestic law to other member states, which was against the GATT rules. The USA appealed to the exception in GATT Article XX ((b) and (g)): the ban was necessary to protect exhaustible natural resources or animal life. The GATT Panel decided that this exception only justified dolphin protection by the USA in its own EEZ, not in the maritime zones of other member states or on the high seas.

As a result of the GATT Panel's reasoning, it seemed that there was no incentive for a member state to impose a unilateral import ban in order to protect shared natural resources or the environment beyond their own state jurisdiction. Many international environmental law scholars at the time viewed these panels as consisting mainly of international trade lawyers; the panel members regarded the GATT rules as a virtually autonomous regime with its main objective being the defence and development of free trade, with minimal reference to principles from other areas of international law.

Since the foundation of the WTO, environmental considerations have gained ground. Instead of being specialized exclusively in international trade law, the members of the WTO Appellate Body are first and foremost experts in general international law. In its decision in the *US Gasoline Standards* case, the Appellate Body explicitly stated that the WTO rules do form part of international law. This wider perspective to the free trade rules is especially obvious in the *Shrimp/Turtle* case, which has a similar basis to *Tuna/Dolphin*.

The United States prohibited the import of shrimp products from any countries whose shrimp nets did not include a device required by US law to prevent sea turtle deaths. Four Asian states took the issue to the WTO Dispute Settlement Panel, which considered the US import prohibition to be against the WTO rules.

The Appellate Body, however, took a different approach in 1998. It deemed that a member state can impose an import prohibition by virtue of the environmental exception rule if the objective of the prohibition is to conserve common natural resources – including those beyond the territory of the state. The Appellate Body further required the shared natural resource to have a 'sufficient nexus' to the prohibiting state. According to the Body, the sea turtle is clearly a common natural resource: it migrates in the seas of the world, as well as in areas under US jurisdiction. It is also (unlike the dolphin) defined as an endangered species under the Convention on International Trade in Endangered Species of Wild Fauna and Flora (CITES).

However, given the specific facts of this case, the Appellate Body determined that the USA had violated the free trade duties, for instance by not starting negotiations with the exporting states in good faith before it imposed the import prohibition.

Although the end result in both cases was similar (the import prohibition by the USA was deemed to violate free trade rules), the decision in the *Shrimp/Turtle* case in many ways displays a sea change in the attitude of the Appellate Body towards evaluating international trade law in the wider context of other principles of international law, including environmental law. The Appellate Body made reference to several environmental agreements in its decision. Its opinion can be interpreted as follows: if a certain import prohibition can be justified by the implementation of a multilateral environmental treaty, the import prohibition is presumptively in line with the WTO rules. This is an important signal to many environmental treaties that apply restrictions of export and import in pursuing their objectives.

Reasoning of the GATT and WTO dispute settlement process in the *Tuna/Dolphin* and *Shrimp/Turtle* disputes

In the *Tuna/Dolphin* dispute between the United States and Mexico, the GATT did not give sufficient consideration to environmental issues. This caused concern because it considered free trade issues almost exclusively, to the detriment of environmental and animal protection. The reasoning of the WTO Appellate Body in the comparable *Shrimp/Turtle* case was radically different. The message of the Appellate Body can be interpreted that if a particular import prohibition can be justified by the implementation of a multilateral environmental agreement, the import prohibition is presumed to be in line with the WTO rules.

It is interesting to note that although the decisions gave opposite signals as to the interaction of free trade rules with issues of international environmental protection, the cases had quite unexpected end results. The *Tuna/Dolphin* dispute ended temporarily in 1992 with an agreement to avoid endangering dolphins. This agreement very quickly resulted in a reduction of dolphin deaths from fishing. The one-sided action of the USA had violated free trade rules but paradoxically achieved the result that the USA had sought from the outset: tuna fishing now takes the welfare of dolphins into account.

The *Shrimp/Turtle* dispute turned out to be more complex. Having lost the case, the USA attempted to negotiate with the Asian shrimp fishing nations, but Malaysia brought the case to the WTO dispute settlement procedure again. Malaysia held that according to the Appellate Body decision, the USA should have lifted its import prohibition. The USA disagreed. The Appellate Body finally held that the USA need not lift the prohibition because it had observed the Appellate Body's decision and attempted to negotiate in good faith. Today, shrimp can be imported to the USA exclusively by those states that observe the US legislation preventing endangerment of sea turtles through shrimp fishing.

Both cases still continue to be problematic. For a long time, the USA's action in the *Tuna/Dolphin* case seemed to have achieved the best possible result. However, Mexico has once again taken the USA to WTO dispute settlement in the same case. Conversely, the USA's action in the *Shrimp/Turtle* case resulted in victory and in an end result that is not the best possible outcome: the USA now gets to decide according to its own terms who can import shrimp and under what conditions.

From the perspective of the development of free trade rules, however, the *Shrimp/Turtle* case is much more important as it matches the perspectives of free trade and environmental protection in a balanced way: it demonstrates to states that one-sided protective action through import, even beyond one's own jurisdiction, can be acceptable in certain circumstances under free trade rules.

The fragmentation of international environmental law

Fragmentation is a problem of international law generally but also of its branches including international environmental law. International environmental law is made up of a body of a large number of agreements and soft-law instruments and different actors. Legal academics and practitioners are increasingly specializing in the legislation relating to climate change, biodiversity, or another specific branch of international environmental law. This kind of specialization allows a lawyer to keep up to date with the development of the international treaty system and the functioning of the EU and national legal systems.

Compared with the international free trade rules, for example, international environmental law is an incoherent body of international regulation related to the protection and usage of the environment. Free trade rules are made internally coherent by the WTO decision-making bodies and its automatic dispute settlement mechanism which keep the rules fairly coherent and predictable.

International environmental law, for its part, is guided by a vast number of different intergovernmental organizations and global and regional agreements; their bodies and meetings of the parties often produce overlapping and partly contradicting decisions and rules. The International Court of Justice established a division specifically to process environmental disputes but governments were unwilling to rely on it. Perhaps the most important body for the discussion of international environmental problems and the promotion of solutions is the UN Environment Programme (UNEP), but it is merely a UN programme – not even a UN specialized agency – and it lacks the resources and competence to coordinate the fragmented field of international environmental law. Every now and then, the idea of a world environmental organization is proposed; such an organization could unify the diffuse field of international environmental law in the same way that the WTO unifies international trade law. However, there seems to be little political will for the founding of such an organization (see Chapter 7, 'A world environmental organization (WEO)', pp. 195–197).

As we saw earlier, different textbook authors divide international environmental law into branches in different ways. Birnie, Boyle and Redgwell organize the branches of international environmental law by biospheric sections: 'climate change and atmospheric pollution', 'the law of the sea and protection of the marine environment', and 'international watercourses: environmental protection and sustainable use'. They also discuss the conservation of biological diversity generally, in land areas, and separately at sea; 'international regulation of toxic substances', 'nuclear energy and the environment', and 'international trade and environmental protection' are discussed separately. Philippe Sands mostly organizes the branches according to similar lines: atmosphere, seas and fresh water resources have chapters of their own, as do biological diversity and hazardous substances and activities. Unlike Birnie *et al.*, Sands discusses human rights and armed conflicts, rules applied to waste, the polar regions, and the environmental law of the European Union as separate divisions of international environmental law.

Some of the segments of international environmental law are easier to identify as sub-branches than others. The UN Convention on the Law of the Sea forms an excellent basis for a coherent regulatory system related to the pollution of the marine environment, as its Chapter XII covers all sources of marine contamination, albeit on a general level. Similarly, the Biodiversity Convention covers the entire biological diversity, thereby providing at least the potential to consider all the agreements relating to animal and plant species and ecosystems as part of global biodiversity law. Both treaty systems allow the development of improved synergy.

Although international environmental protection is quite uniform in some of its sub-branches, it is impossible to organize into a systematic whole outside of a textbook. This is because international environmental protection depends on the willingness of states to conclude environmental treaties. Environmental protection is just one among many interests for states. States have different priorities in their foreign policies, and the activities of the international community do not often lead to coordinated results in terms of environmental protection.

Most states have prioritized the establishment of free trade rules, with the result of a more coherent regulation. The WTO dispute settlement bodies make decisions that are also highly important for international environmental protection; they are not expected to protect the environment but to guarantee that free trade (and environmental protection as a spin-off) is implemented by the WTO rules.

The extensive legal provisions related to warfare are known as humanitarian law. Humanitarian law also sets limits on the serious and intentional destruction of the natural environment in the course of armed conflicts. Obviously, these provisions have not been developed from the perspective of environmental protection; they are just a by-product of avoiding certain methods in warfare and protecting civilians and the wounded.

States have different levels of jurisdiction in different parts of the world. They are not able to interfere in environmental problems on the high seas in the same way as in the marine areas within their jurisdiction. Economic utilization of the biodiversity of the high seas and exploitative fishing are very difficult issues for the international community to regulate effectively, whereas states do have the means of managing fish stocks within their exclusive economic zones in a sustainable way. The unique status of Antarctica as a non-sovereign and demilitarized continent has allowed the development of an efficient environmental protection regime, while the primary authority in the Arctic lies with each Arctic state.

Even when states do agree that intervention in a particular international environmental problem is necessary, their views of the best possible solutions can be diametrically opposed.

Should waste management, for example, be regulated as a distinct whole, so that industrial nations are required to commit to considerable waste reduction in their own territories by cutting consumption and increasing recycling?

There is no sufficient political will to create such international regulation. We have a fragmented set of rules to control things like dumping and burning waste at sea and reducing the amount of waste drained in inland waterways, and an administrative system that controls the transport of waste for processing abroad. All these means of reducing and controlling waste are regulated by different agreements between various countries. Waste also includes hazardous chemicals which fall under the rules targeted at eliminating the production and use of the most hazardous chemicals and at controlling their export and import.

Although the rules related to waste can be compiled as a separate chapter in a textbook, we cannot say that there has been a systematic attempt to resolve this environmental problem. The chapter on the waste problem in Sands' textbook, for example, exposes the incoherence of waste regulation and reveals the problems in international regulation – hopefully helping future decision-makers unify the means to address the global waste problem.

Marine environmental protection

Marine environmental protection is the branch of international environmental law that can most distinctively be considered as a whole. This is because, first, the entry into force of the UN Convention on the Law of the Sea in 1994 (UNCLOS) established the fundamental rules of who has jurisdiction in different marine areas and how various marine activities should be carried out. Another reason behind the coherence of the marine protection regulation is that the UNCLOS included a whole section, Part XII, devoted to the general rules and principles that apply to the protection of the marine environment.

The sea, on the whole, has always been international. For this reason, international law has played a much stronger role in the regulation of oceans than over land. The marine environment is being rapidly contaminated. The UN 2005 Millennium Ecosystem Assessment (MA) made the following conclusion: 'The ecosystems and biomes that have been most significantly altered globally by human activity include marine and freshwater ecosystems.'[1]

The 'Pacific trash vortex' is a floating area, twice the size of Hawaii (estimates as to its exact size depend on what one considers as trash). It traps floating trash that drifts from the coasts, primarily plastic. Imagine: an enormous area of waste floating in the middle of the Pacific Ocean.

The Baltic Sea has a long history of contamination. The nine coastal states bordering on it are discharging nutrients (nitrates and phosphates) into the Baltic Sea. These nutrients can cause eutrophication: plants and algae have more nutrients, they multiply more rapidly and grow into the vast algal masses we have seen on TV; they cause cloudiness of water, slime build-up on the shores, and depletion of oxygen in the seabed. Nutrients flow into the Baltic Sea from the waste waters of communities and industry and with the nitrogen in the atmosphere but, above all, from agriculture (as nutrients from chemical fertilizers and manure flow from the fields).

As algae and plant-life die and degrade, they consume oxygen, increasing the hypoxic areas in the seabed. Biotoxic hydrogen sulphide accumulates in the hypoxic conditions in the sea floor and nutrients dissolve back into the water, especially phosphorus which also increases marine eutrophication. The nutrients that sink to the bottom accumulate in the sediment and can be released again to be used by the algae. Eutrophication can cause a serious vicious circle that is difficult to break once it has advanced to a certain point.

The history of marine environmental protection

The oceans of the world have been fully international and largely unregulated over the centuries. Before the Second World War, there were only a few rules guiding the ships that sailed on the seas. The central principle was the 'freedom of the seas', upheld by the Dutch 'father of international law' Hugo Grotius in his book of 1609, *Mare Liberum*. Grotius did not stumble upon this principle in an intellectual or economic vacuum: his 'free seas' argument provided the powerful Dutch mercantile fleet the justification to break prevailing trade monopolies and then establish its own monopolies. The freedom of the high seas was the essential principle adopted by states prior to the Second World War. Gradually, for defence purposes, states began to claim sovereignty to a narrow coastal zone that later developed into the territorial sea of a coastal state. Before the war, the zone extended 3–4 nautical miles[2] from the coast.

After the Second World War, coastal states began to claim more jurisdiction in the waters around them. As the war ended and as technology advanced, rights were extended to the sub-sea (continental shelf) adjacent to their coastlines and its oil and gas resources. Gradually, states began to claim more extensive marine areas in which to exercise their exclusive rights to exploit natural resources; in this way the 370-kilometre exclusive economic zone was created.

Protection of the marine environment advanced less rapidly. The first multilateral marine protection treaty was accomplished in 1954 to regulate oil pollution by ships.[3] The first negotiation process aiming at a comprehensive convention on marine issues took place among 86 states in Geneva in 1958. Although the UN International Law Commission that carried out the preparatory work for the negotiations had aimed at producing only one single convention, four separate conventions were agreed: the Convention on the Territorial Sea and Contiguous Zone,[4] the Convention on the High Seas,[5] the Convention on the Continental Shelf,[6] and the Convention on Fishing and Conservation of the Living Resources of the High Seas.[7] However, the protection of the marine environment did not receive much attention in these negotiations.

The Convention on the High Seas, Articles 24 and 25, required states to regulate 'pollution of the seas from the discharge of oil from ships or pipelines or resulting from the exploitation and exploration of the seabed and its subsoil'. It further encouraged states to 'take measures to prevent pollution of the seas from the dumping of radioactive waste'. These 'obligations' had little impact on the protection of the marine environment. They were so limited and vague that they did little to prevent states from continuing to pollute the sea at an accelerating rate. This was not unusual in 1958; international environmental law was still in its infancy and the belief still prevailed that it was impossible to do any real damage to the oceans as they are so vast.

The second UN Conference on the Law of the Sea in 1960 was a failure (the parties were unable even to agree on the breadth of the territorial sea), but the third negotiating conference turned out to be a success. The objective was to agree a single international convention, a package deal, to be applied to all oceans and all maritime issues, and the objective was accomplished. The entire international community continued to negotiate from 1973 until the Convention was signed in 1982. The resulting UN Convention on the Law of the Sea (UNCLOS)[8] recorded the basic rules that generally regulate all activities on all the seas. The UNCLOS permits no reservations: states must ratify it in full.

Part XII of the Convention comprehensively regulates all marine pollution, whether from land, from activities in the seabed, from dumping waste, from vessels and from or by air. It includes provisions related to intervention in marine contamination that are general but comprehensive, such as Article 194(2):

> States shall take all measures necessary to ensure that activities under their jurisdiction or control are so conducted as not to cause damage by pollution to other States and their environment, and that pollution arising from incidents or activities under their jurisdiction or control does not spread beyond the areas where they exercise sovereign rights in accordance with this convention.

It also contains rules to ensure that states 'shall act so as not to transfer, directly or indirectly, damage or hazards from one area to another or transform one type of pollution into another' (Article 195). The obligations are of a very general nature and contain no clear legal guidance. A good example of how general the UNCLOS provisions are can be seen in the way they applied to the oil spill in the Gulf of Mexico in 2010.

The oil rig *Deepwater Horizon*, operated by BP, exploded and started to burn on 20 April 2010, about 70 kilometres off the Louisiana coast, sinking two days later. Several oil-rig workers died in the accident, and the wellhead, about 1,500 metres deep, began to discharge substantial amounts of crude oil. By 2 July, the oil had already contaminated parts of the coasts of the states of Alabama, Mississippi and Louisiana, and representatives of the government estimated that approximately 100,000 cubic metres of oil had been spilled into the sea.

According to UNCLOS Article 192, 'States have the obligation to protect and preserve the marine environment'. This principle applies to the oil disaster in the Gulf of Mexico as well, as it does not limit the protective measures to transboundary pollution at sea. (The USA is not a party to the UN Convention on the Law of the Sea but does accept almost all its rules as binding customary law – including Part XII.)

Article 208 further obligates the parties to take the necessary measures to prevent, reduce and control pollution arising from oil rigs, and requires the national laws and measures to be no less effective than international rules, standards and recommended procedures.

The International Maritime Organization (IMO) does have a guideline for such cases, but it is not legally binding.

The UNCLOS provisions give general legal guidance to coastal states, but if it is to affect the detailed administration of oil rigs, it is clear that states will have to negotiate more specific rules. After the disaster in the Gulf of Mexico, there were even suggestions that a global convention on oil rigs should be negotiated, but as yet no concrete developments in this direction have taken place.

The UNCLOS also regulates how marine environmental rules are to be implemented. The flag state of a vessel still has the primary responsibility, although the Convention increased the rights of intervention of coastal and port states in cases when the flag state does not take measures. However, one problem with the law of the sea is the existence of 'flag of convenience' states, which are paid good money to register vessels and fail to control the observance of international rules.

The UNCLOS also increased the jurisdiction of port states in monitoring and preventing contamination by vessels. This is a good move from the viewpoint of controlling and mitigating vessel pollution, since vessels enter a port within the sovereign territory of a state voluntarily. The jurisdiction of a port state to prevent pollution from vessels is increased by international regulation, such as port state memoranda of understanding which allow for more intense cooperation by port authorities – in the EU, for example, the entry of deficient tankers is limited. The jurisdiction of a port state could, in fact, resolve the problem entirely: if all port states were prepared to prevent deficient vessels from entering their ports (except for emergencies), they would not be able to sail. As yet, however, we have not come this far.

Regional protection of the marine environment: the Baltic Sea regime as an example

While the UN Convention on the Law of the Sea was being negotiated between 1973 and 1982, a number of other regional agreements were also agreed in order to protect the marine environment (for example, the 1974 Baltic Sea Convention and the 1976 Mediterranean Sea Convention); these established more detailed rules for a particular marine area or for preventing contamination from a particular source. Inspired by the 1972 Stockholm Conference, the UN Environment Programme (UNEP) launched its Regional Seas Programme, in which 143 states currently participate. It covers 13 regional seas ranging from the Black Sea to the South-East Pacific and from the Mediterranean to Western Africa. Many of these regional seas are administered by soft-law type programmes but there are some highly advanced treaty regimes within their protocols – such as the Mediterranean regime.

It is important to note that the UNCLOS does not include specific rules as to how states should protect their marine environments; it gives the coastal states considerable discretion. The regional conventions might refer to the UNCLOS in their preambles but they operate largely autonomously to prevent regional marine problems. This is because the UNCLOS only creates the general framework for more detailed regulation, actually encouraging states to implement the general obligations at the regional level. UNCLOS Article 197 declares:

> States shall cooperate ... as appropriate, on a regional basis, directly or through competent international organizations, in formulating and elaborating international rules, standards and recommended practices and procedures consistent with this convention, for the protection and preservation of the marine environment, taking into account characteristic regional features.

The UNCLOS gives only limited instruction of how states should be expected to address the numerous sources of pollution in a regional sea.

In 1974, seven Baltic Sea coastal states (now nine) signed the Helsinki Convention,[9] which entered into force in 1980. Its Article 12 established the Baltic Marine Environment Protection Commission, more commonly referred to as the Helsinki Commission (HELCOM). This was a pioneering convention: it was negotiated and entered into force while the international community was still negotiating the UN Convention on the Law of the Sea. It set a significant example for the UNCLOS negotiations as it was the first convention aimed at preventing marine pollution from all sources.

The Baltic Sea ecosystems are unique (only certain species can live in brackish water) and the sea has faced severe environmental problems (for example, eutrophication, threats to endemic species from foreign invasive species, and reduction in its salt concentration due to climate change). In addition, traffic in the Baltic Sea region has increased considerably in recent years. Intense environmental protection measures are therefore essential. After the Cold War, and as international marine and environmental law changed, the Baltic Sea coastal states, together with the then EC, updated the Convention in 1992. The new Convention[10] entered into force in 2000. One essential difference between the old and new conventions is in the principles guiding their development and application. Article 3 in the 1974 Convention did not actually adopt any of the modern principles of environmental protection, whereas the corresponding new Article ('Fundamental principles and obligations') refers to the precautionary principle, the best environmental practice and best available technology principle, and the polluter pays principle.

The new Convention is also based on the promotion of biological diversity and the ecosystem approach since the early 2000s. The Convention obligates its parties to reduce pollution from all sources, to conserve marine life, and to maintain biological diversity. The Baltic Sea Action Plan (BSAP) within the HELCOM was adopted in November 2007. Its objective is to restore the good ecological status of the Baltic Sea and its ecosystems by 2021.

In April 2004, the Baltic Sea was identified by the International Maritime Organization (IMO) as a 'particularly sensitive sea area' (PSSA). This status allows special measures to be implemented in restricting marine pollution from ships.

The governance of the Baltic Sea has also changed, because one by one its coastal states have become members of the EU. After signing the Convention in 1992, Finland and Sweden were the first to join the EU in 1995; Estonia, Latvia, Lithuania and Poland joined in the following wave in 2004. The Baltic Sea is therefore, in effect, virtually an inland sea of the EU: all its coastal states except for Russia are EU members. As part of its Integrated Maritime Policy, the EU also adopted the Strategy for the Baltic Sea Region, combining EU and local level activities and ensuring cooperation between the countries and regions.

The aim of the EU Marine Strategy Directive is for European seas to achieve good environmental status by 2020. The directive obligates member states to develop a national marine strategy for their marine regions. This strategy must involve an assessment of the status of the marine environment and a programme of measures to be developed by 2016 to improve the status of the marine region. The directive also requires member countries to coordinate their operations and to cooperate with each other and with third parties. To implement cooperation, existing organizations such as the HELCOM have taken an active role.

Regulation of fishing

The regulation of fishing is relatively coherent. It was also unified by the UN Convention on the Law of the Sea. The Convention adopted the emerging right of the coastal states to decide on the harvest and management of the fish resources in their exclusive economic zones of 200 nautical miles. The majority of fish resources were thereby turned from common resources of the high seas (vulnerable to the 'tragedy of the commons') into resources under the jurisdiction, management and responsibility of the coastal states.

The UNCLOS also regulated the general rights and obligations of the states in relation to the following fish species: 'stocks occurring within the exclusive economic zones of two or more coastal states [shared stocks] or both within the exclusive economic zone and in an area beyond and adjacent to it [straddling stocks]', highly migratory species (such as tuna), anadromous stocks (such as salmon that spawn in rivers but live most of their lives in the sea), and catadromous species (such as eel that spawn in the sea but live most of their lives in inland waterways).

The innovative Agreement for the Implementation of the Provisions of the UNCLOS for the Conservation and Management of Straddling Fish Stocks and Highly Migratory Fish Stocks[11] was negotiated and adopted in 1995. It aims at promoting the management of fish species that occur in both exclusive economic zones and in the high seas, according to the precautionary principle and the ecosystem approach. Coastal states and those fishing in the region have a duty to establish regional organizations for fisheries management; a significant number of such organizations have been established. The Commission used to administer the fisheries in the Baltic Sea and the Belts.[12] As the EU has exclusive jurisdiction over the regulation of fishing, this body became redundant when all the Baltic coastal states except Russia became members of the EU.

A great number of regional and bilateral fishing agreements have been concluded, covering most sea areas.

Protection of international watercourses

Rivers have been regulated by international law for some time because they often form the natural boundaries between states and they frequently flow through the territories of several states. Environmental regulation related to rivers developed relatively early; and in 1966 the International Law Association (ILA) adopted the Helsinki Rules which reflected the customary law of the time. The principles of equity in the utilization of a river which the ILA recorded were especially widely accepted by the international community.

Riparian states have over their history faced similar challenges, which have created similar approaches to environmental protection. Experience shows that upstream states do not always consider the interests and rights of downstream states; rivers only flow in one direction, and it can be politically difficult for the upstream states to make concessions in their river policies in the interests of the downstream states if these are seen to create burdens on a state's own population or economic interests.

Most international river agreements apply to single river areas, but regional and even global agreements have also been made to promote the sustainable management of transboundary inland waterways. The UN Economic Commission for Europe and the UN International Law Commission have both played important roles in this work.

The Helsinki Convention of 1992 on the protection of watercourses[13] contains general principles, and obligates the parties to increase cooperation in relation to international waterways. The International Law Commission prepared the Convention on the Law of the Non-navigational Uses of

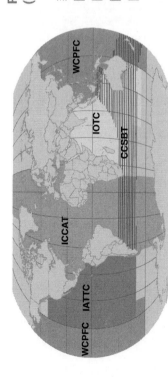

RFMOs for highly migratory fish stocks (tuna and associated species)

	CCSBT	Commission for the Conservation of Southern Bluefin Tuna
	IATTC	Inter-American Tropical Tuna Commission
	ICCAT	International Convention for the Conservation of Atlantic Tunas
	WCPFC	Western and Central Pacific Fisheries Commission
	IOTC	Indian Ocean Tuna Commission

RFMOs for non-tuna species

	CCAMLR	Convention on Conservation of Antarctic marine living resources
	CCBSP	Convention on the Conservation and Management of Pollock Resources in the Central Bering Sea
	GFCM	General Fisheries Commission for the Mediterranean
	NEAFC	North East Atlantic Fisheries Commission
	NASCO	North Atlantic Salmon Conservation Organisation
	NAFO	Northwest Atlantic Fisheries Organisation
	SEAFO	South East Atlantic Fisheries Organisation
	SPRFMO	South Pacific Regional Fisheries Management Organisation (in development)
	SIOFA	South Indian Ocean Fisheries Agreement

Source: European Commission – Eurostat/GISCO. Administrative boundaries: © EuroGeographics, © FAO (UN), © TurkStat.

Figure 5.1 Regional fisheries management organizations for highly migratory fish stocks (tuna and other species) and for non-tuna species

International Watercourses,[14] which was adopted in 1997. Its rules are more detailed and more ambitious, which is probably why it has not yet come into force. Among other measures, it establishes another principle beside the principle of equity in the realm of international watercourses: a state shall not cause significant damage to another watercourse state. To secure this, the convention also provides for communication procedures between the states in order to avoid significant transboundary environmental impacts. Part IV of the convention regulates the ecosystem approach to the entire watercourses.

Rivers, lakes and groundwater are today understood to be an intricate drainage basin: a hydrological unit that also includes the groundwater in connection with the surface waters. In 2008, the UN International Law Commission completed its own draft articles on the Law of Transboundary Aquifers,[15] groundwaters that are not connected with surface waters and can be compared with such legally shared natural resources as transboundary oil and gas wells.

Conservation of biological diversity

Biological diversity is the outcome of 4.5 billion years of evolution. The variety of life has grown more versatile as natural selection has removed the less successful mutations from the genetic stock, while the more successful ones have gradually accumulated. New species specialize and conquer their ecological position; this process can cause the natural extinction of another species. Scientific research has also discovered that since the origination of multicellular organisms, approximately five great waves of extinction have taken place after natural catastrophes.

Scientists now believe that we are at the threshold of the first wave of extinction caused by man. It is estimated that there are about 12 million species, of which only 1.4 million have been scientifically surveyed. Since our actions are resulting in the death of species all the time, we are probably destroying species that were previously unknown. The main reasons why species are dying out are the rapid increase in human population and the changes in the lifestyles of human communities, made possible by economic growth and technological progress.

The depletion of biological diversity is a serious problem: 4.5 billion years of evolution have resulted in a set of species that have, during their histories, adapted to life in highly diverse environments. If some of them perish, we will be less adaptable to the constantly changing conditions on our planet, so long as our actions continue to change conditions at an accelerating rate.

The history of the conservation of biological diversity

In the twentieth century, the international community did little to promote the diversity of species or habitats. After the Second World War, conservation agreements were mainly aimed at protecting big animals, the so-called 'charismatic megafauna'. Many readers will remember Jacques Cousteau and his adventures on board the *Calypso*. He introduced a global TV audience to all kinds of incredible sea life in series such as *The Cousteau Odyssey*. His nature programmes were generally focused on those megafauna that most fascinated the audience.

We are most inclined to protect these charismatic megafauna, although all forms of life (plants, herbivores, predators and decomposing organisms alike) have their own, equally significant roles in the ecosystems. Each ecosystem includes key species: most of the species in a food chain are dependent on their existence. A well-known example is the Baltic Sea blue mussel. Young blue mussels provide food for fish and invertebrates in the seabed and adult blue mussels for eiders. The loss of such a key species would change the structure and functioning of the entire ecosystem.

The international community has negotiated agreements for the protection of some specific animal species, such as the polar bear (1973) and the vicuña (1979). Certain groups of animals have been the focus of attention in, for instance, the 1946 Whaling Treaty, the 1995 Treaty on the Conservation of African-Eurasian Migratory Waterbirds, and the Agreement on the Conservation of Small Cetaceans of the Baltic, North East Atlantic, Irish and North Seas (ASCOBANS).[16] Agreements are also in place to protect multiple species, such as the Bonn Convention on the Conservation of Migratory Species of Wild Animals,[17] (of which ASCOBANS is part). An International Plant Protection Convention has also been agreed.[18]

Certain conservation conventions focus on a particular region. Examples include the 1940 Convention on Nature Protection and Wildlife Preservation in the Western Hemisphere, comprising South and North America (sometimes called a 'sleeping treaty', because it has not been much developed); the pan-European Bern Convention on the conservation of European wildlife; the 1968 African Convention on the Conservation of Nature and Natural Resources; and the 1980 Convention for the Conservation of Antarctic Marine Living Resources (CCAMLR). The EU has an entire programme, Natura 2000, intended to protect both habitats and endangered species.

Some ecosystems are protected by separate universal agreements. The Ramsar Convention[19] protects wetlands important for waterfowl, whereas the World Heritage Convention[20] protects natural heritage sites deemed to be important for humankind. The Desertification Convention[21] aims at combating desertification in countries experiencing serious drought and/or desertification, particularly in Africa. Non-binding instruments such as the UN Forest Principles aim to improve the administration of forest ecosystems. In June 2011, the pan-European cooperation process, Forest Europe, commenced negotiations on a European agreement on sustainable forest management. The Convention on International Trade in Endangered Species of Wild Fauna and Flora, the CITES system,[22] aims at protecting endangered animals and plants by controlling international trade in endangered species.

The body of agreements promoting biological diversity was and still is very fragmented, although synergies are being explored among conventions related to the conservation of biodiversity (see Chapter 7, 'Searching for synergies between regimes', p. 197). It is therefore particularly significant that the Convention on Biodiversity was adopted as part of the Rio 1992 Conference. The objective of the Convention is threefold:

1   The conservation of biological diversity.
2   The sustainable use of its components.
3   The fair and equitable sharing of the benefits arising out of the utilization of genetic resources.

Biological diversity should not be confused with biological resources. Biological diversity is a characteristic of life – a continuing process of change and adaptation according to natural selection – which maintains biological resources: 'genetic resources, organisms or parts thereof, populations, or any other biotic component of ecosystems with actual or potential use or value for humanity' (Convention on Biological Diversity, Article 2).

Svalbard global seed vault

A seedbank was opened in the Norwegian Svalbard archipelago in 2008. Its objective is to safeguard and preserve as many seeds as possible. This secures biological diversity for future generations and diverse cultivated plants, essential for the safeguarding of food safety.

There are numerous genetic banks for seeds in the world but many of them are situated in countries where natural disasters and scarcity of resources threaten their effective conservation. The Svalbard global seed vault is a kind of a 'safety reserve' for existing seed collections. Genetic banks can store their seeds free of charge in the Svalbard rock vault, which is considered perpetual. The seeds are stored in permafrost conditions of minus 18 degrees, and will only be taken out in cases where the original seed collections are destroyed for any reason. The vault has the capacity to hold a total of approximately 2.25 billion seeds.

The scope of the Convention's application is considerable, and the number of parties amounts to 193. The Convention applies to terrestrial, marine and other aquatic biological diversity. Each contracting party is responsible for the obligations related to the various aspects of biodiversity within its national jurisdiction. If a state advances biodiversity relevant processes and activities, its obligations extend to areas both within and beyond its jurisdiction, regardless of where the effects occur. A state must at least identify these activities and monitor them (Article 4), even when the effects are beyond the limits of jurisdiction of the state.

While these obligations operate at a general level, the scope of application is very wide. The Convention therefore has the potential to bring coherence to a fragmented body of different agreements all aiming at aiding the survival of particular species or group of species, or the biodiversity in a particular region. This also suggests a potential contradiction: prioritizing a particular species (such as the polar bear) or ecosystem (such as wetlands) at the expense of other ecosystems or species is not the objective of the Convention; the concept of biological diversity does not rank any species or ecosystems above others.

From the perspective of biodiversity, it is most urgent to protect endangered species. The 'red list' of the International Union for Conservation of Nature (IUCN) plays an important role in verifying the depletion of biodiversity. The list divides species into different categories according to how endangered they are, helping political decision-makers to make conservation decisions.

From the perspective of agreements related to species or ecosystems, the Biodiversity Convention is too general, as it not only includes conservation objectives but also establishes procedures for the use of biological resources. On the other hand, the Convention on Biological Diversity can coexist with other related agreements, because its provisions 'shall not affect the rights and obligations of any Contracting Party deriving from any existing international agreement' (Article 22). Should, however, the exercise of the rights and obligations of an agreement result in serious damage or threat to biological diversity, this would contradict the objective and purpose of the Convention on Biodiversity. In practice, the agreements related to species and ecosystems considered above are generally in line with the objectives of the convention.

Conservation of biological diversity in the marine environment

It is an interesting fact that in some aspects scientists know more about outer space than they do about the oceans; the assumption is that there is an enormous number of marine species that have not yet been discovered.

The Biodiversity Convention contains a separate statement about its application at sea: 'Contracting Parties shall implement this convention with respect to the marine environment consistently with the rights and obligations of States under the law of the sea.' The law of the sea and the UNCLOS must be taken into account when applying the Biodiversity Convention at sea. Yet, it must be noted that maritime agreements are also in contradiction with the Biodiversity Convention if they engender practices that can cause serious damage or threats to biological diversity.

Promoting terrestrial and marine biological diversity are different tasks because the sea is highly international and marine ecosystems are generally more interconnected than terrestrial ecosystems. This has a considerable effect on the promotion of biological diversity and the management of species and ecosystems.

Figure 5.2 Forest destroyed to make way for illegal gold mines in Madre de Dios, Peru. The area that incurred extensive damage is considered a biodiversity hotspot on Earth. (Photo © Andrea Calmet)

Principally, all the land species that require international regulation are subject to the sovereignty of states. When terrestrial animals cross borders between states, they enter another state. To protect terrestrial animals, plants or ecosystems, states have to cooperate and waive their full sovereignty, as is the case with the Bonn Migratory Species Convention, the Ramsar Wetlands Convention or the World Heritage Convention.

The greatest marine challenges are related to the loss of the fish resources in the world. During the negotiation process for the Convention on the Law of the Sea, fish resources were reassigned from a shared high seas resource to the jurisdiction of coastal states within their exclusive economic zones of 200 nautical miles. This was and still is the preferred solution in the opinion of many economists (at least there is a body in charge of managing fish resources), but this extensive amendment in the law of the sea has unfortunately not resulted in an improvement to fish stocks. Instead, the survival capacity of fish populations in large parts of the world has been severely reduced.

The practice of whaling offers a different example. The 1946 Convention aimed to administer whales in much the same way as fish. The original objective of the treaty system was sustainable whaling, but as attitudes changed, the result was a comprehensive ban on whaling.

One result of establishing exclusive economic zones was that coastal states were able to develop their biodiversity conservation rights and policies over a much wider marine area than before. At the moment, states have the right and responsibility to conserve natural diversity over their entire exclusive economic zones, up to 200 nautical miles.[23]

Beyond its jurisdiction – on the high seas or in deep seabed areas (see Chapter 4, 'Common areas', pp. 99–100) – a state is not entitled to promote biodiversity unilaterally, for example by establishing marine conservation areas. The Convention on Biological Diversity (CBD) does encourage states and international organizations to cooperate in conserving the biodiversity of areas beyond their national jurisdiction (Article 5). However, high seas bioprospecting and fishing threaten the biodiversity in these areas, and it is difficult to find political-legal solutions.

The main focus of political disagreement is whether or not genetically valuable organisms found on the high seas can be exploited commercially. The view of developing nations is that such commercial utilization is comparable to the exploitation and utilization of deep seabed oil, gas and minerals, which have been declared the 'common heritage of mankind'. However, the industrial nations refer to the UNCLOS in their position: only inorganic natural resources in the deep seabed are the common heritage of mankind, according to the Convention. They find it an unsustainable argument that a carefully negotiated principle on the usage of the deep sea-bed could suddenly extend to cover the commercial exploitation of marine genetic resources on the high seas. Their opinion is that these more recently discovered resources fall under the freedom of the seas, like fishing or scientific research. The principle of no-harm, on the other hand, expects that activities under the jurisdiction or control of states will not damage the environment in areas beyond their national jurisdiction.

Under customary international law of the sea and the UNCLOS, it seems evident that the industrial nations are right. These conventions limit the utilization of the common heritage of mankind classification very closely to the inorganic natural resources in the deep seabed. The CBD, though, indicates that the biological diversity of the high seas should be regulated in one way or another. The Convention is ratified by nearly all states, and it also applies to processes and activities under the jurisdiction of states that impair biodiversity – even in the case that they impair the biodiversity of international areas.

Development of the biodiversity regime

The biodiversity regime has developed very quickly as a result of the decisions made by the contracting parties, the activities of its sub-divisions, the development of thematic areas, and the contributions of working groups. Two protocols have been negotiated into the Convention.

The Cartagena Protocol on Biosafety[24] was agreed in 2000. The United States participated in the negotiations, although it was not a party to the Biodiversity Convention. The negotiations were difficult. The majority of genetically modified plants in the world (corn, soy and rape, for example) are produced in the USA, so it pushed forward with a treaty that secures the export of these plants.

The participating states disagreed and adopted a treaty based on an advance informed agreement (official). After conducting risk assessment, the importing party can reject the transboundary transportation of genetically modified organisms even when there is no scientific certainty regarding their harmful effects. The Protocol on Biosafety is strongly based on the precautionary principle (Article 10(6)):

> Lack of scientific certainty due to insufficient relevant scientific information and knowledge regarding the extent of the potential adverse effects of a living modified organism on the conservation and sustainable use of biological diversity in the Party of import, taking also into account risks to human health, shall not prevent that Party from taking a decision, as appropriate, with regard to the import of the living modified organism in question as referred to in paragraph 3 above, in order to avoid or minimize such potential adverse effects.

The United States was, of course, dissatisfied with this decision and did not become a party to the Protocol: its view was that the WTO free trade regulation takes priority in respect of the export of genetically modified plants.

The United States had already taken the EC to the WTO dispute settlement in 2003, as the EC had prohibited the import of biotech products. The EC referred to the precautionary principle as part of the WTO Sanitary and Phytosanitary Agreement (SPS) but the dispute settlement found in favour of the USA. The EC also emphasized the importance of the Biosafety Protocol but since the USA was not a party to the agreement, the WTO dispute settlement bodies could not take it into account.

In the recently adopted Nagoya Protocol,[25] the parties created procedures to regulate access to genetic resources and the fair and equitable sharing of benefits arising from their utilization. Genetic resources are defined in Article 2 of the Biodiversity Convention as genetic material that is or can be valuable. Genetic material refers to 'any material of plant, animal, microbial or other origin containing functional units of heredity'.

The Protocol is mainly procedural and requires, *inter alia*, prior informed consent (PIC) of the supplier state of the genetic resources. A competent authority of the state must formally accept the utilization of genetic resources. If the national legislation acknowledges the rights of indigenous peoples and local communities to these genetic resources, the competent authority shall also set the criteria by which the utilizer acquires the prior consent of these peoples and communities and secures their participation in the project.

Atmosphere conservation

Extensive atmospheric conservation began with the Convention on Long-range Transboundary Air Pollution (LRTAP) negotiations under the auspices of the UN Economic Commission for Europe; it was the first treaty regime that addressed air pollution from diffuse sources. Global atmospheric problems were first discovered in the mid-1980s. The ozone layer that protects life on Earth from ultraviolet rays from the Sun was growing thinner and was totally absent in some places due to CFC emissions (chlorofluorocarbons).

It was the ozone depletion that awakened humankind to the realization that our actions do actually impact on enormous natural systems. This awakening also contributed to the acceptance at the end of the 1980s that climate change was possible. It was in the mid-1980s that consideration was first given to combining political-legal actions in order to avert the atmospheric environmental problem.

Meanwhile, the ozone and climate regimes are worlds apart in the minds of specialists. The ozone regime is considered a success story in international environmental law, while the climate regime is considered a failure. It is also good to acknowledge the connection between the treaty regimes, which have mutual influence. Some kind of law to protect the atmosphere could indeed be helpful, if it was able to connect environmental problems with the mechanisms administering them. It is useful to look at how these two, perhaps the most essential of international environmental regimes, evolved, and to consider why one of them succeeded and the other one did not. How could increased cooperation between these regimes help?

The ozone regime

The ozone regime was launched after the adoption of the Vienna Framework Convention in 1985. Although the Convention mainly establishes information exchange programmes and encourages states to increase scientific research on ozone depletion, it is based on the precautionary principle: governments were prepared to work together to solve a global problem even before scientific certainty about ozone depletion and its effects existed. The Montreal Protocol adopted in 1987 was also based on the precautionary principle: although there was more scientific data about the phenomenon of ozone depletion (the wide ozone hole above Antarctica was a proven fact, for example), its effects were largely unknown. The explicit objective of the Protocol was to eliminate substances that caused ozone depletion.

The ozone regime was planned in an innovative way: it was able to evolve as new scientific knowledge emerged about the substances that caused ozone depletion and how rapidly the ozone layer was reducing. New ozone-depleting substances could be added to the ozone system through amendments; these are binding only after ratification by each state.

The schedules and quantities for the reduction of targeted substances can be changed through adjustments to the schedules, without the consent of every state. A majority of two-thirds is sufficient, if it contains the majority of both the developing and the developed nations. This implies that even if a state objects to a certain adjustment, it is legally bound to it if the decision is made in accordance with the majority rules. This has accelerated the schedules for elimination of CFC compounds.

The parties have made some amendments to the regime, for instance, to establish the financing mechanism, the Multilateral Fund – a mechanism separate from the existing financing institutions and directly connected to the motivation of the developing nations to observe the treaty; they receive technological and financial assistance if they have acted according to the rapidly developing ozone regime. The developing nations have been given an option to continue the use of ozone-depleting substances for longer, so that they do not have to have acquired expensive substitutes. The parties also made amendments to secure that they did not import ozone-depleting substances from or export them to states outside the Convention.

The climate regime

The adoption of the climate regime was preceded by the establishment of the Intergovernmental Panel on Climate Change (IPCC) in 1988 by the World Meteorological Organization (WMO) and the UN Environment Programme (UNEP). Although the IPCC preceded the climate regime and is not officially part of it, the four assessment reports it has published to date have been decisive in attaining scientific consensus about climate change, and each one of them has resulted in political action.

Some officials say that the Framework Convention on Climate Change was negotiated too quickly because the negotiation process was integrated as part of the Rio Environment Conference. As the Rio Conference required many 'achievements' by the summer of 1992, the negotiations took place in a hurry and at a stage when there was still not much knowledge about climate change. The first assessment of climate change by the IPCC had only been published two years previously, in 1990.

In any case, the outcome was the 1992 Framework Convention on Climate Change, which did not require much even from the industrial countries: they undertook politically to reduce their greenhouse gas emissions to 1990 levels by 2000. What was important was that the basic elements of the climate regime were agreed on. Every country is obliged to take measures to achieve the main objective – to prevent dangerous human-induced climate change – but only the industrial countries (mainly OECD members) listed in Annex I undertook more detailed obligations. Except for the listed countries, all other countries and transition economies were allowed to continue with lesser obligations. This arrangement closely reflected the Rio compromise between the interests and obligations of the rich North and the poor South; an essential component was the principle of common but differentiated responsibilities.

Soon after the Framework Convention on Climate Change entered into force, it became evident that the treaty system must be made tighter by defining binding emission reduction targets for the industrial countries. The Kyoto Protocol was accepted with strong support from the administration of US President Bill Clinton (his Vice President was Al Gore, who has since focused his career on working against climate change, and has become Nobel Peace Prize laureate). Meanwhile, the US Senate warned the Clinton administration that the USA should not accept binding emission reductions unless developing countries are bound to equivalent obligations.

The Kyoto Protocol was constructed on the Framework Convention on Climate Change: the countries listed in Annex I committed to legally binding emission reductions. The parties did not have to implement all the reductions in their own countries; flexibility mechanisms gave them the opportunity to implement emission reductions where it was least expensive. The idea was that industrial activities in many developed countries were highly energy-efficient and caused comparatively low greenhouse gas emissions, so that it would be less expensive to implement the reductions in developing countries or in Eastern European transition economies, while the impact on climate change would be at least as great.

The 'clean development mechanism' (CDM) allowed an industrial country the opportunity to implement a project in a developing country, as long as it could prove that the project actually reduced greenhouse gases and promoted sustainable development. Joint implementation (JI) was a model by which a country was able to implement a project in a country listed in Annex I (generally Eastern European transient economies) so that the project actually reduced greenhouse gas emissions. Emissions trading for its part allowed countries to sell and buy emission reductions if their own quotas were used up or if they had something to sell.

The detailed rules to define the general rules in the Kyoto Protocol were adopted by non-binding decisions of the meeting of the parties in Marrakesh – the Marrakesh Accords. The Kyoto Protocol provided the authorization to adopt these decisions.

For a long time, it seemed that the Kyoto Protocol would never enter into force, as in 2001 the George W. Bush administration withdrew the USA from the Protocol, and other big greenhouse gas emitters hesitated.[26] Finally, after ratification by Russia, the Kyoto Protocol entered into force, and its first meeting of the parties took place in Montreal in 2005. The next emission reduction period should have been negotiated but this has been continually postponed from meeting to meeting. In 2007, the Bali Roadmap was accomplished, with the ambitious objective to improve the treaty system and to include both the United States and the major developing nations in the joint work towards reducing emissions.

The 2009 Copenhagen Conference failed badly to achieve this objective, however, and the USA led the creation of the last-minute non-binding

Copenhagen Accord. Its participants politically undertook certain measures to reduce emissions. The problem after the Copenhagen Conference was that no one knew whether the Kyoto Protocol would have a next commitment period, how long it could be and how the major actors could be involved in the climate change regime. There was even uncertainty after the Copenhagen Conference about whether the regime would continue under the auspices of the UN. The Cancun Conference again tried to 'rescue' the climate change regime from its crisis. The resulting new attempt took place in the 2011 Durban Climate Conference; its accomplishments will be discussed in Chapter 7 (see 'Achievements of the Durban Conference', pp. 201–203).

The success of the ozone regime and the failure of the climate regime

The ozone regime is justly regarded as a success story: it has managed to contain a global environmental problem through innovative regulation measures involving the entire international community. There are several reasons for this. One reason is that the only (at least for now) superpower, the USA, had begun to control the manufacture and use of CFC compounds even before the international measures commenced; it applied strong pressure on other countries to follow suit and limit and eliminate CFC compounds.

The activity of the United States can be traced to a very clear view within the scientific community that ozone depletion is caused by the use of CFC compounds and that ozone depletion causes, among other things, skin cancer in humans. It was also significant that CFC compounds were manufactured by a relatively small number of companies in a few countries. That was easy compared with the enormous challenge faced in climate change: nearly all human activity around the globe has an impact on the climate. The innovative regulation systems – implementation committee, science mechanism and flexible amendment procedures, for example – contribute to the expectation that the ozone layer will actually recover in a few decades. The ozone regime was touted as a model for getting climate change under control.

The climate regime itself – and the people who work in its secretariat – is functioning well. Many legal innovations have been made, within the limits that states set to the system, of course. Cost-effective ways of mitigating climate change with flexible mechanisms are carefully considered and well justified, and have contributed to the know-how of developing nations and their knowledge about climate change. Checking that the states report their emissions and carbon sinks[27] correctly guarantees the reliability of the reporting system and states' awareness as to how widely they are responsible for climate change. The Kyoto Protocol compliance committee has the greatest authority to penalize a state that fails to observe the rules – and the compliance committee was established by a decision of the meeting of the parties only.

The problem with the functioning of the climate regime does not lie within the regime system itself but with the factors that cause climate change. While ozone depletion was caused by a few big companies that only operated in some countries, there are much wider issues behind climate change. We could say that one of the cornerstones of our modern lifestyle is the use of fossil fuels: they provide a great deal of our heating and electrical energy but they also produce enormous amounts of carbon dioxide. Although the drawbacks of fossil fuels were discovered a long time ago, we have since become more rather than less dependent on them.

A major cause of climate change is land use, especially the use of forests, which are the most important carbon sinks for absorption of carbon from the atmosphere through photosynthesis. When a forest burns or is burnt down, the carbon is released back to the atmosphere. Logging forests for wood production and planting forests are, therefore, decisive measures from the climate change perspective.

The tropical rainforests are a focus of concern, because they grow rapidly, absorbing much carbon – and because they are being destroyed at a colossal rate in many developing and middle-income countries. One problem with the original Framework Convention on Climate Change is that it does not mention forests specifically. The climate regime is now devising various methods of conserving tropical forests; the most significant project is Reducing Emissions from Deforestation and Forest Degradation (REDD) and its varieties.

Considering such further problems as our modern deeply ingrained prioritization of continuous economic growth, population growth, and inadequate technological development in the problems that the climate regime is facing, we can quickly see that climate change does not compare with any environmental problem we have experienced thus far.

To understand why the ozone regime is a success and the climate regime is not, we do not even need the explanation of the loss of US leadership. The truth is that the United States has, at least internationally, assumed a line that emerges from its domestic political reality: the USA will not join in international climate work until China and other rapidly developing economies commit themselves to at least some binding emission reductions. The issue for the USA and its businesses is about equality in competition: they fear that countries that are not committed to reducing greenhouse gas emissions could overtake the USA even further (because their product prices do not have to factor in the costs of reduction).

Connections between ozone depletion and climate change

Most gases that cause ozone depletion are also powerful causes of climate change. The ozone regime has already greatly aided the climate regime by eliminating the use of certain greenhouse gases. Experts estimate that the ozone layer will recover by the middle of this century at the present rate.

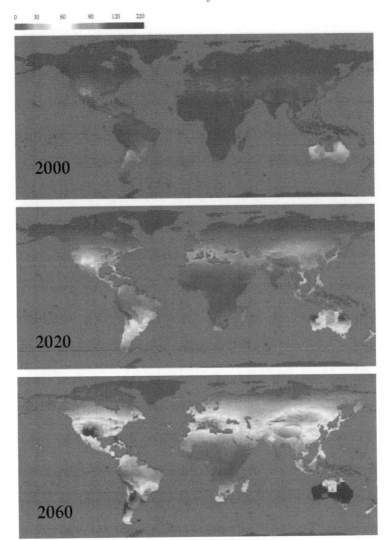

Figure 5.3 An assessment of the development of skin cancer cases in relation to UV radiation in the world. The estimation is that a reduction of 10 per cent in the ozone layer would cause 4,500 cases of melanoma (the most dangerous form of skin cancer) and 300,000 other skin cancer cases annually over the present level.Source: Emmanuelle Bournay, UNEP/GRID-Arendal, http://www.grida.no/graphicslib/detail/number-of-extra-skin-cancer-cases-related-to-uv-radiation_1456.

Meanwhile, ozone depletion is also accelerating climate change. Increased UV radiation damages plants and marine organisms, such as plant plankton, reducing their ability to absorb carbon, which intensifies climate change. Yet, climate change is evening out the score: it causes the average earth surface temperature to rise, cooling the stratosphere, which again hampers the recovery of the ozone layer. NASA estimates that by 2030, the greatest ozone destroyer will no longer be CFC compounds but climate change.

Perhaps the greatest single problem in the success story of the ozone regime is that it seems to have had the side effect of obstructing the fight against climate change. HFC gases (hydrofluorocarbons) were developed to replace the ozone-depleting gases, but they have significant capacity to warm the atmosphere. They are now in great demand, as the need for cooling and air-conditioning has grown and because the ozone regime aims to eliminate HCFC gases (hydrochlorofluorocarbons) so rapidly. Paradoxically, the success of the ozone regime has caused a real challenge to the fight against climate change.

Connections between particular substances and environmental problems such as these inevitably provoke the question of whether the problems could be more effectively managed together. For instance, the UN Convention on the Law of the Sea, Part XII, bases the conservation of the marine environment on this principle: 'In taking measures to prevent, reduce and control pollution of the marine environment, States shall act so as not to transfer, directly or indirectly, damage or hazards from one area to another or transform one type of pollution into another.' This is the benefit we could achieve by implementing a system of gradually evolving atmosphere protection law.

Questions and research tasks

1   How could the coherence of international environmental law be improved, other than through textbooks or cooperation between treaty secretariats?
2   We know that biological diversity suffers as a result of both climate change and ozone depletion. How do these environmental problems affect biodiversity? How does biodiversity (its richness or its poverty) influence climate change? How could these treaty systems cooperate better, being interrelated?
3   Try and consider, by yourself at first, what benefits and drawbacks could result from establishing a big international environmental organization analogous to the WTO which could be responsible for combining the various environmental regimes. Find arguments for and against this on the internet.
4   As we have seen, international environmental law consists of an abundance of self-standing treaties with relatively little cross-referencing between them and a complete absence of comprehensive institutional oversight (in other words, there are many institutions operating but no single institution). However, can you see any common principles that you think apply across all or most of those that we have studied? Do you think that there should be any such principles that form a foundation for international environmental law? Could these principles help make international environmental law seem more coherent and less fragmented?
5   Are there benefits in developing an implementation agreement to the UNCLOS that would conserve biodiversity in areas beyond national jurisdiction? What components should there be in such an agreement?

Notes

1 Ecosystems and Human Well-Being, Synthesis, p. 31, http://www.maweb.org/documents/document.356.aspx.pdf
2 1 nautical mile = 1.852 kilometres.
3 International Convention for the Prevention of Pollution of the Sea by Oil, http://www.admiraltylawguide.com/conven/oilpol1954.html
4 Convention on the Territorial Sea and Contiguous Zone, 1958, http://untreaty.un.org/ilc/texts/instruments/english/conventions/8_1_1958_territorial_sea.pdf
5 Convention on the High Seas, 1958, http://untreaty.un.org/ilc/texts/instruments/english/conventions/8_1_1958_high_seas.pdf
6 Convention on the Continental Shelf, 1958, http://untreaty.un.org/ilc/texts/instruments/english/conventions/8_1_1958_continental_shelf.pdf
7 Convention on Fishing and Conservation of the Living Resources of the High Seas, 1958, http://untreaty.un.org/ilc/texts/instruments/english/conventions/8_1_1958_fishing.pdf
8 Agreement Relating to the Implementation of Part XI of the UN Convention on the Law of the Seas, http://www.un.org/Depts/los/convention_agreements/convention_overview_part_xi.htm
9 Convention on the Protection of the Marine Environment of the Baltic Sea, Helsinki, 1974, http://www.helcom.fi/Convention/
10 Convention on the Protection of the Marine Environment of the Baltic Sea Area, Helsinki, 1992, http://www.helcom.fi/Convention/
11 Agreement for the Implementation of the Provisions of the UNCLOS for the Conservation and Management of Straddling Fish Stocks and Highly Migratory Fish Stocks, http://www.un.org/Depts/los/convention_agreements/convention_overview_fish_stocks.htm
12 Convention on Fishing and Conservation of the Living Resources in the Baltic Sea and the Belts, http://www.ecolex.org/ecolex/ledge/view/RecordDetails?id=TRE-000535&index=treaties
13 Convention on the Protection and Use of Transboundary Watercourses and International Lakes, http://www.unece.org/env/water/
14 Convention on the Law of the Non-navigational Uses of International Watercourses, http://untreaty.un.org/ilc/texts/instruments/english/conventions/8_3_1997.pdf
15 Draft articles on the Law of Transboundary Aquifers, http://untreaty.un.org/ilc/texts/instruments/english/draft%20articles/8_5_2008.pdf
16 Agreement on the Conservation of Small Cetaceans of the Baltic, North East Atlantic, Irish and North Seas, http://www.ascobans.org/
17 Convention on the Conservation of Migratory Species of Wild Animals, http://www.cms.int/
18 International Plant Protection Convention, https://www.ippc.int/
19 Convention on Wetlands of International Importance especially as Waterfowl Habitat, http://www.ramsar.org/cda/en/ramsar-documents-texts-convention-on/main/ramsar/1-31-38%5E20671_4000_0
20 Convention Concerning the Protection of the World Cultural and Natural Heritage, http://whc.unesco.org/en/conventiontext/
21 UN Convention to Combat Desertification in Those Countries Experiencing Serious Drought and/or Desertification, especially in Africa, http://treaties.un.org/Pages/ViewDetails.aspx?src=TREATY&mtdsg_no=XXVII-10&chapter=27&lang=en
22 Convention on International Trade in Endangered Species of Wild Fauna and Flora, http://www.cites.org/
23 If the continental shelf of a state extends beyond 200 nautical miles, the state is also entitled to regulate the conservation of the biodiversity on the seabed within the limits of law of the sea and the UN Convention on the Law of the Sea.

24 Cartagena Protocol on Biosafety related to the Biodiversity Convention, 2000, http://bch.cbd.int/protocol/
25 The Nagoya Protocol on Access to Genetic Resources and the Fair and Equitable Sharing of Benefits Arising from their Utilization to the Convention on Biological Diversity, 2011, http://www.cbd.int/abs/doc/protocol/nagoya-protocol-en.pdf
26 This was because Article 25(1) requires a sufficient number of the major polluters to become parties to the Convention, instead of a simple number of states: 'This Protocol shall enter into force on the ninetieth day after the date on which not less than 55 Parties to the Convention, incorporating Parties included in Annex I which accounted in total for at least 55 per cent of the total carbon dioxide emissions for 1990 of the Parties included in Annex I, have deposited their instruments of ratification, acceptance, approval of accession.'
27 Carbon sinks are carbon dioxide reservoirs. The soil, forests and the surface layers of seas naturally absorb carbon dioxide from the atmosphere.

Further reading

Fitzmaurice, M., 'Compliance with the 1992 Convention on the Protection of the Environment of the Baltic Sea Area (the "Helsinki Convention")', in U. Beyerlin, P. Stoll and R. Wolfrum (eds), *Ensuring Compliance with Multilateral Environmental Agreements: Academic Analysis and Views from Practice*, Leiden: Koninklijke Brill, 2006.

Hakapää, K., *Marine Pollution in International Law: Material Obligations and Jurisdiction with Special Reference to the Third United Nations Conference on the Law of the Sea*, Finnish Academy of Science and Letters, 1981.

International Law Commission, *Conclusions of the Work of the Study Group on the Fragmentation of International Law: Difficulties arising from the Diversification and Expansion of International Law*, 2006, at http://untreaty.un.org/ilc/texts/instruments/english/draft%20articles/1_9_2006.pdf

Keohane, R. and Victor, D., *The Regime Complex for Climate Change*, 2010, http://belfercenter.ksg.harvard.edu/files/Keohane_Victor_Final_2.pdf

Koskenniemi, M. and Leino, P., 'Fragmentation of International Law? Postmodern Anxieties', *Leiden Journal of International Law*, 15, 2002, pp. 553–79.

Melkas, E., *Kyoto Protocol Flexibility Mechanisms and the Changing Role of Sovereign States*, University of Turku, 2008, http://www.doria.fi/bitstream/handle/10024/38581/B309.pdf?sequence=1

Rothwell, D.R. and Stephens, T., *The International Law of the Sea*, Oxford: Hart Publishing, 2010.

Warner, R. and Schofield, C. (eds), *Climate Change and the Oceans*, Cheltenham: Edward Elgar, 2012.

Websites

Professor Cymie R. Payne's video lectures on international environmental law: http://www.cosmolearning.com/courses/international-environmental-law-293/

United Nations Framework Convention on Climate Change: http://unfccc.int/2860.php

6 Legal responsibility for environmental damage

The core issue in law is who is liable when things go wrong. Trainee lawyers are advised to always prepare for the worst. If you were working on a cooperation agreement between two companies, you would be sure to make note of any contentious points that could lead to disputes or litigation right from the outset. The same is true of international environmental law. When an international environmental treaty is negotiated, lawyers will be present as part of the broader team, but should the negotiations turn to compensation for environmental damage, almost all the negotiators in the room will be lawyers.

This tends to make lawyers 'masters of precaution': we always prepare for the worst. We require any risks to be assessed before any project is implemented, lest further down the line there is a chance of liability for damages. How might the 'master of precaution' title be applied to the prevention of climate change? All of humanity is at risk, and solutions are expected from the scholars and practitioners of international environmental law.

There are those who have risen to the challenge. In the 2005 Montreal Climate Conference, the then chair of the Inuit Circumpolar Council, Sheila Watt-Cloutier, announced that her organization had filed a human rights petition with the Inter-American Human Rights Commission against the United States. The organization considered that the irresponsible climate policy of the USA had violated many of the human rights of the Inuit. Watt-Cloutier called the human rights petition against the USA 'the most loving deed of her life'.

I admired her courage, notwithstanding my doubts about the likely success of the petition. We are still living in a time when legal liability in the international community is largely defined on the basis of the compensation principles of general international law and these, as we will see, are difficult to apply to the consequences of climate change. Legal liability can be applied most easily in more tangible circumstances: for example, when a large factory on one side of a border pollutes the environment across the border, or when an oil disaster contaminates a coast.

This chapter discusses the legal responsibility that results when environmental damage is caused. The first question to consider is whether international environmental law has succeeded in developing rules and principles that are applicable to all kinds of environmental damage. The second point to note is that the general international law principle of no-harm continues to be the essential norm according to which inter-state environmental damage is assessed. The next factor is strict liability. Many human functions are intrinsically hazardous: however carefully a nuclear power plant, for instance, is managed, there will always be the risk of catastrophic harm. States have negotiated strict-liability agreements to cover operations such as these; the originator of any damage is generally liable irrespective of how carefully the plant is operated. Finally, we take a look at how the liability rules in international environmental law have developed in recent years. We will see that discussion has at least started as to the legal responsibility of states for the environmental damage caused by climate change.

Difficulties in enacting general liability rules

Assigning responsibility for environmental damage is problematic. The damage caused by climate change is not easily proven to be attributable to a single actor, state or private enterprise. When diffuse pollution is generated by multiple actors – for example, many small companies or millions of cars – it is difficult to identify a guilty party to compensate for the damage incurred by a state or its citizens. Major state contaminators and contributors to climate change can, of course, be identified, such as the USA or China, but they are still just two among many, so it would be difficult to hold only them responsible.

Establishing legal responsibility is challenging enough even in relatively straightforward cases, such as when multiple people in an area might claim to be suffering from the pollution emitted by a single polluting factory. The various types of pollution carried by air or water can be difficult to detect, although environmental sciences and monitoring programmes have facilitated the monitoring of the stages of contamination. How can one prove that a particular contaminant has emanated from a particular factory, given that the environmental problems we are facing are so many and so varied? How can a petitioner prove the causal connection between a factory and the injury they are complaining of? Generally, it is the petitioner that bears the burden of proof: they have to demonstrate that this is likely to be the case. Advances in natural science have helped us to appreciate that science can seldom prove anything with absolute certainty, but nonetheless, the courts require a relatively high certainty as to the causal connection.

In the 1980s and the 1990s, the UN International Law Commission's State Responsibility Project considered whether the widespread pollution of seas and the atmosphere by a state could be deemed state crime, but the project ended up abandoning the idea of state criminal responsibility.[1] The concept of state crime is disputed in international law, while the criminal liability of individuals for breaches of international law has advanced enormously.

Through treaties, states have resolved legal responsibility mainly in cases of intrinsically hazardous operations, for example nuclear power plants. It has turned out to be much more difficult to make rules for industries that are inherently polluting, slowly and cumulatively. An effort has been made to tailor the rules to encompass all environmentally hazardous projects, but this has also been problematic.

The law of state responsibility in cases of environmental damage has developed very little in international environmental law. The Stockholm 1972 Conference declaration initially encouraged states to develop liability rules for environmental damage, and this was reiterated by the Rio Conference 20 years later. The International Law Commission (ILC) had started work as early as 1978 with the objective to formulate a distinct set of liability rules applicable to environmental damage.

This project was kept apart from the Commission's long-term objectives to codify the law of state responsibility in general international law, which were to apply to any violations of international law. In retrospect, this has not proven an effective strategy. After many stages, the special project for environmental liability was split into two parts. Paradoxically, the first stage focused on rules to prevent transboundary environmental damage. These 'preventative rules' of 1999 are now used by international courts, and their status is quite different from that of the rules that were the initial objective: the 'liability rules', which facilitate access to compensation for victims of environmental damage. These draft environmental liability rules were compiled in 2006. They were meant to define who pays whom, and how, in cases of environmental damage.

The environmental liability rules have not been accepted by the international community as widely and clearly as the preventive rules. Why is this? There was widespread criticism of the notion that separate liability rules should be constructed during the ILC process for the creation of environmental liability rules. Why would separate environmental liability rules be necessary if the widely accepted international law of state responsibility was to apply to environmental damage as well? The ILC had worked for decades on the general rules of state responsibility (the actual work started in 1955 but the academic groundwork had begun even before the founding of the United Nations), and they were finally adopted in 2001. The majority of these draft articles are considered to reflect customary international law, as the UN International Court of Justice among others has stated in many of its decisions.

Once the rules of state responsibility had been codified in 2001, it was clear that they also covered environmental damage – just as many critics had claimed. Although the International Law Commission accepted the environmental liability principles in 2006, they focused largely on ensuring access to compensation for private citizens and communities subjected to environmental damage. These principles sought, *inter alia*, to eliminate obstacles in domestic legal systems preventing individuals from seeking compensation in a court of the state from which the pollution originates, even if they themselves were resident in another state. The 2006 environmental liability principles are based on a model that has actually worked in state practice: industries are encouraged to take out comprehensive insurance against environmental damage so that they would actually be in a position to pay the compensation if the worst happens. Similarly, the principles require a state to contribute to the compensation regime if a private enterprise, notwithstanding its insurance, cannot meet its liabilities in full. The principles even imply that if the environment in another state has been damaged, it should be restored. However, the draft principles remained hopelessly general. This is one of the reasons why the principle of no-harm continues to be the essential set of legal responsibility rules.[2]

The role of the international law commission in promoting environmental damage rules

The UN International Law Commission has carried out the preparatory work for several international legally binding agreements. It can also influence the development of international law in other ways, as was the case with the international law of state responsibility.

After more than 50 years of work, the ILC finalized a set of articles on state responsibility and a decision was made to annex them to a resolution of the General Assembly (a non-binding adoption of the rules) but to delay, indefinitely, the negotiations that would develop them into a binding treaty. This was a wise decision. If treaty negotiations had started on the basis of the ILC's draft articles, they would probably have dragged on for years, if not decades, and the contents of the rules would have been totally changed as states sought to water down their substantive content.

As it is, the ILC state responsibility rules are, in name, draft rules only, but as they were generated by an authoritative body over a long time, they are interpreted by the international courts as largely codifying the (binding) customary law of state responsibility. The same was true of the preventive principles – and, it is possible, will also be true of the development of the 2006 environmental liability principles. Although they are draft principles only, the international community may gradually begin to regard them as customary law.

So it seems that, at least in these regulation projects, the ILC is most efficient when it just accepts draft principles instead of subjecting the principles to the logic of inter-state compromise.

Liability based on the principle of due diligence

Despite the long-term efforts of the International Law Commission (ILC) to produce separate state responsibility rules to cover environmental damage, state responsibility is still defined according to the general law of state responsibility codified by the Commission. These general rules only give rough guidelines as to which rules are applicable should a state violate international law – including international environmental law. They define, *inter alia*, what constitutes a violation of international law, what actions can be considered by a state (as opposed to by a private individual or commercial entity), and how states can lawfully respond to violations of international law committed by other states.

The general rules of state responsibility codify customary international law in many respects; many of them reflect the existing general international law. They operate in the same way as the customary law that applies to all treaties: they apply, unless otherwise agreed by the states. The articles do not describe the requirements from states in each case in detail – the so-called 'primary rules' of international law. Instead, the articles focus only on what are called 'secondary rules': that is to say, the consequences of a state's violation of one or more of the primary rules, of a state not doing what is expected of it. The position of the ILC is that although the primary rules vary widely in different fields of international law – including the standard of care that is expected of a state (the degree of diligence due) – in the event that a primary rule is violated, the same secondary rules apply.

The main rule in environmental law is that of legal responsibility based on fault – or negligence. The 'mental' attitude to international law of an individual official or state is unimportant; the first issue to be established is whether, for instance, the principle of due diligence was violated:

- Can state B verify that the pollution damage incurred in its territory is due to certain conduct on the territory or under the jurisdiction of state A?

When this causal connection is clear, the next step will be to find out what measures have been taken in relation to this action:

- Has state A permitted this project, and if so, on what terms?
- Has it examined the possibility of transboundary impacts in advance?
- Has it notified state B of these risks and arranged mutual negotiations?

There is no way of saying exactly when a state has done what is required in terms of diligence in such cases. The higher the probability of serious transboundary impacts, or the more severe the potential damage, the higher the standard of care (diligence) required.

The principle of no-harm in customary law requires similar diligence in cases where environmental damage can be caused to the environment beyond state jurisdiction, for example to the biological diversity of the high seas. Often, the real problem in these cases is that states are not prepared to act for the benefit of the international community as a whole when environmental damage harms them all. As a result, states are predisposed to exercise their legal rights only when there is identifiable damage to their own territory – and even then, only rarely.

Strict-liability agreements

Certain intrinsically hazardous activities are regulated by special agreements. Traditionally, such agreements are related to nuclear power plants and oil transport, while new strict-liability agreements have emerged in recent years. This section first surveys the conventional agreements that impose legal liability for damage to private actors and then looks briefly at the liability obligations in new international environmental agreements.

We already saw in Chapter 2 that since the 1960s, the amount of regulation applying to the use of nuclear power and oil transport has been expanding. The use of nuclear power is especially hazardous and therefore both the Organisation for Economic Co-operation and Development (OECD) and the International Atomic Energy Agency (IAEA) developed conventions in the early 1960s (although there are few contracting parties). Both nuclear treaty systems are based on the same principles:

1   The liability is channelled to the operator of a nuclear power plant: the treaty systems apply the principle of 'polluter pays'.
2   The liability is strict (so there is no need to prove that an operator is at fault), but if the damage is due to *force majeure* (such as war or natural catastrophe), there is no liability to compensate.
3   The liability is limited; it was considered that otherwise nuclear plant operators would find it impossible to obtain insurance because of the inherent risk of disaster (the operator, however, must take out insurance up to the limit of the risk).
4   In both treaty systems, states, and ultimately their taxpayers, bear the liability if the limit is exceeded.

The Joint Protocol Relating to the Application of the Vienna Convention and the Paris Convention[3] was adopted in 1988. It was agreed that both the OECD and the IAEA treaty systems can be applied to nuclear damage incurred by the territory of a state that is party to either of the agreement systems; that is, the systems were interlinked. On the basis of these treaty systems an operator of a nuclear power plant is not expected to compensate environmental damage; this was recently corrected by the 1997 Protocol to Amend the Vienna Convention on Civil Liability for Nuclear Damage. Environmental damage and preventive measures are also subject to compensation under the renewed Vienna system.

Another historically significant aspect of strict liability is the regulation of civil liability for maritime oil transportation. The original oil liability agreements – both the International Convention on Civil Liability for Oil Pollution Damage[4] and the International Convention on the Establishment of an International Fund for Compensation for Oil Pollution Damage[5] – were replaced by protocols adopted in 1992 which concerned oil liability and which established a fund for compensation.[6] The protocols entered into force in 1996. These revised liability conventions extended environmental liability to cover not only compensation for damage but with an additional requirement to restore the environment to its previous state. In 2001, the IMO also produced the Convention on Civil Liability for Bunker Oil Pollution Damage.[7]

These oil transport agreements are based on the principle that strict liability is channelled to the owner of the ship; unless he or she can prove that the damage was not caused by the ship (that is, the burden of proof is reversed). The owner's liability is limited in the same way as with nuclear power plant damage. This is because unless the liability was limited, very few states would have ratified the Convention; on the other hand, this also means that the victims are not always being fully compensated. To secure compensation, a ship's proprietors have the obligation to insure. If the insurance is inadequate, the Fund for Compensation for Oil Pollution Damage kicks in: it supplements the oil liability Convention by collecting contributions both from oil companies operating within the convention parties and from the recipients of oil into a fund from which compensation can be paid.

In 1978, the Amoco Cadiz was responsible for causing significant oil damage to the Brittany coast in France. The parties affected by the damage did not turn to the French court system which would have applied the limitations of liability in the oil liability convention; instead, the plaintiffs went directly to the US court system. The USA was not a party to the convention, so the limitations of liability were not applicable (the tanker was owned by Amoco Corporation of USA). The legal strategy yielded greater compensation to the injured parties compared with what they could have obtained through the French courts.

In these cases, states have prioritized the liability of individual actors and industries for compensating environmental damage (and the secondary liability of states in nuclear liability agreements). There is one agreement by which states have assumed the primary liability for compensation: the Convention on International Liability for Damage Caused by Space Objects.[8]

When the Soviet satellite Kosmos 954 crashed in uninhabited parts of Canada in 1978, scattering radioactivity into the environment and causing other environmental damage, Canada invoked the Convention on International Liability for Damage Caused by Space Objects, since both states were parties to it. However, the Soviet Union contested its applicability, and in the end it was not relied upon. Instead, after lengthy negotiations, the Soviet Union agreed to pay about half of the 6 million dollars that Canada had initially claimed. The Soviet Union did not acknowledge its treaty-based liability for the damage caused by the Kosmos.

Both the Stockholm 1972 Declaration (Principle 22) and the Rio 1992 Environment Declaration (Principle 13) urge states to include compensation rules in any international environmental agreements. Nothing happened in the 20 years between these two declarations, but in 1993, the parties to the Basel 1989 Waste Convention revisited the principle of strict liability. The parties produced a protocol in 1999 that resembled the nuclear liability and oil transport systems: the Basel Protocol on Liability and Compensation.[9]

The 2000 Cartagena Protocol on Biosafety, related to the Biodiversity Convention, regulates living organisms that have been modified by biotechnology. In 2004, the parties commenced negotiations for a protocol on compensation; the Protocol was finally opened for signature on 7 March 2011. The Nagoya-Kuala Lumpur Supplementary Protocol on Liability and Redress to the Cartagena Protocol on Biosafety establishes the strict liability of any actor in control of living organisms modified by biotechnology and their transboundary transportation and who is responsible for damage to biodiversity and its sustainable usage.

The parties to the Stockholm POPs Convention also considered a protocol on compensation, but this has not been achieved, at least to date.

There are also regional strict-liability conventions. A common strict-liability protocol was negotiated in 2003 to the two Helsinki Conventions under the UN Economic Commission for Europe. It applies to both industrial accidents and to damage to transboundary watercourses. Although signed by 24 countries, the protocol is ratified by only one of them, where 16 ratifications are required for the protocol to enter into force.

Similarly, Annex VI to the Madrid Protocol on Environmental Protection to the Antarctic Treaty on Liability was adopted in 2005. The objective is to allocate responsibilities and costs for clean-up following environmental emergencies and to establish strict liability in environmental emergencies. Annex VI will enter into force when all consultative parties have adopted it. To date, only a handful of the 28 consultative parties have adopted it, so it is not likely to enter into force any time soon.

Legal liability in practice

On the whole, it is fair to say that although international law and international environmental law do include general rules on state responsibility based on negligence, such rules have scarcely been applied in real world disputes. One could fill a library with the books written about the *sic tuo utere* principle, neighbourliness, or due diligence, but the surprising fact is, the old *Trail Smelter* decision is the only decision that has held a polluting state (Canada) to be legally liable for transboundary environmental damage.[10]

In other cases, states have admitted causing environmental damage but have not assumed legal liability; compensations have been paid *ex gratia*: that is, a state has expressly denied legal liability. However, in some exceptional cases, functioning compensation rules have been created to encompass environmental damage cases as well.

> In 1990, Iraqi troops invaded Kuwait and were defeated by the US-led and UN Security Council mandated troops in 1991. The Security Council established a fund for compensating for the damage caused in Kuwait; proceeds from Iraqi oil sales contributed to the fund. The United Nations Compensation Commission was established to administer the fund; it was not a court of justice, but a kind of inspector of facts. Its various panels decided who was entitled to compensation for the damage caused by Iraq, and how much.
>
> Iraq's actions caused huge environmental damage – for example, in setting fire to oil wells in occupied Kuwait and by intentionally pumping oil into the Persian Gulf. The Security Council decided to establish a panel devoted entirely to environmental damage. The panel introduced a highly progressive view: among other things, compensation was paid for restoration of the ecological status of environment and for assessing and monitoring environmental damage.

Hazardous operations – the use of nuclear power for energy production and marine transport of nuclear materials – are included in regional and global civil liability to some extent, although few states are party to the agreement.

International declarations encourage states to include liability rules in environmental treaties. The ambitious goal of the UN International Law Commission to achieve general principles of state liability for environmental damage seems to have partly failed, although the draft principles were adopted in 2006. Certain international environmental treaties have tried to create strict-liability civil indemnity rules. To date, not many have tried this and no widely ratified compensation protocols have been created.

The law of state responsibility has so far played a limited role in environmental cases. Instead, the preferred option is the creation of collective mechanisms under which implementation committees softly apply pressure on states to observe their treaty obligations and contribute to the prevention of environmental damage. Compensation for damage in international environmental law is still in its infancy. In practice, only oil damage compensation is relatively well regulated. Recent years have seen an increase in the number of individuals and groups submitting human rights petitions to human rights courts or global quasi-legal bodies, such as the committee monitoring the International Covenant on Civil and Political Rights. Environmental damage cases have been taken to the European Court of Human Rights whereby the claimant cites a violation of the right to home and privacy, or of the right to life. The increasing use of human rights mechanisms has improved the possibilities for individuals to obtain compensation for environmental injuries.

Legal liability for environmental damage has recently been the topic of much discussion in relation to climate change. This is understandable, as climate change has already resulted in tangible effects – especially in the Arctic where snow and ice react to the rapidly warming and changing climate system.

In 2005, the Arctic indigenous peoples, the Inuit (Eskimo) filed a petition against the United States – then the greatest greenhouse gas emitter – with the Inter-American Human Rights Commission. Their objective was to prove that the irresponsible climate politics of the US had violated many of the human rights of the Inuit, including their right to property, life and culture. Climate change is a tangible real threat for the Inuit: will they continue to be a distinct People if they are deprived of their culture which is based on snow and ice?

The petition also refers to the Alaskan village of Shishmaref which has to be relocated because the ice that sheltered the coast from the waves has receded further from the coast and erosion caused by the waves has broken down the soil under the village.

The Inuit human rights petition was based on the fact that all indicators in 2005 showed that the United States, above any other state actor, was responsible for climate change – hence it was also guilty of violating Inuit human rights.[11] The petition was rejected by the Commission but it sparked discussion of who could be held legally responsible for climate change.

On 22 September 2011, the island nation of Palau announced to the UN General Assembly that together with the Marshall Islands, it will call upon the General Assembly to seek an advisory opinion from the International Court of Justice concerning legal responsibility related to climate change. When announcing its intention, Palau referred to the principle of no-harm, for example, which would place liability on those who are most responsible for climate change. The opinion would be non-binding but it would, of course, be highly significant as representing the legal opinion of the International Court of Justice.

All the small Pacific island states, whose territories will sooner or later succumb to rising sea levels, appended a declaration to the Framework Convention on Climate Change and in the Kyoto Protocol. Their declaration was that although they were prepared to be party to these treaties, this would not prejudice their right to sue those states that are held to be mostly responsible for causing climate change.

The importance of the principle of no-harm in international environmental law is also signified by the fact that this is what those small Pacific island states referred to in order to illustrate the legal responsibility of those who are mostly responsible for greenhouse gas emissions. Tuvalu announced in 2002 that it would sue Australia in the International Court of Justice and seek environmental refugee status for its citizens in New Zealand and Australia. Technically, the principle of no-harm justifies such a legal argument: 'States have ... the responsibility to ensure that activities within their jurisdiction or control do not cause damage to the environment of other States'.[12] By any criteria (historical greenhouse gas emissions in the atmosphere, current absolute and per capita emissions), it can be shown that the United States is particularly responsible for climate change, and has therefore also played a part in the damage caused to the environment of e.g. small-island states. The announcement by Tuvalu has not yet been followed up by the commencement of legal action.

There are many who trust and expect the UN International Court of Justice to eventually express a substantive legal opinion on state responsibility for climate change. I do not think that the Court will want to side-step the climate regime, especially because climate change is so genuinely the 'fault' of all states and we will all bear the consequences sooner or later. International environmental problems like this require cooperation from the entire international community.

Figure 6.1 A tomb vault sinking in the sea in the Majuro atoll in the Marshall Islands in 2010. The islands are already suffering from rising sea levels and erosion and their future looks increasingly gloomy. (Photo © Michael Gerrard)

Questions and research tasks

1 What is your overall view of the law of state responsibility in cases of environmental damage? Would a different framework of legal responsibility be better? What might it look like?

2 Find a few treaties based on strict liability and think about the meaning of strict liability. Do the treaties have any other function besides imposing compensation for innocent injured parties? If so, what is the function?

3 Why is it increasingly common to demand that the states bearing the greatest responsibility for climate change should be made legally responsible? Are such efforts realistic? What are their strengths and their weaknesses?

4 Increasingly, individuals and groups are using human rights mechanisms to address environmental issues, including climate change. Do you think this is a positive development? What advantages and disadvantages can you see in relying on individuals to bring such claims, rather than states bringing claims against one another? Can you imagine any benefits of bringing such an action even if the case is ultimately rejected by the court or human rights body?

5 Should a 'global fund' for climate change damage be established by the UN to compensate the inhabitants of islands such as Tuvalu and Palau? Which states should contribute and how would it be administered?

Notes

1 Similarly disputed is a state's right to launch an *actio popularis* (an action on behalf of everyone), for instance against a state that has caused widespread pollution of seas and the atmosphere.

2 The only generally applicable liability agreement resembling the Commission's principles was adopted by the Council of Europe in 1993. It is the highly innovative Convention on Civil Liability for Damage resulting from Activities Dangerous to the Environment. However, it has not yet been ratified by any state and it will probably never enter into force.

3 Joint Protocol Relating to the Application of the Vienna Convention and the Paris Convention, http://www.iaea.org/Publications/Documents/Infcircs/Others/inf402.shtml

4 International Convention on Civil Liability for Oil Pollution Damage, http://www.admiraltylawguide.com/conven/civilpol1969.html. The Convention has been amended a couple of times and was renewed in 1992.

5 International Convention on the Establishment of an International Fund for Compensation for Oil Pollution Damage, http://www.imo.org/about/conventions/listofconventions/pages/international-convention-on-the-establishment-of-an-international-fund-for-compensation-for-oil-pollution-damage-(fund).aspx

6 Protocol of 1992 to Amend the International Convention on Civil Liability for Oil Pollution Damage, http://www.imo.org/about/conventions/listofconventions/pages/international-convention-on-civil-liability-for-oil-pollution-damage-(clc).aspx

7 Convention on Civil Liability for Bunker Oil Pollution Damage, http://www.imo.org/about/conventions/listofconventions/pages/international-convention-on-civil-liability-for-bunker-oil-pollution-damage-(bunker).aspx

8 The Convention on International Liability for Damage Caused by Space Objects entered into force in 1972; http://www.oosa.unvienna.org/oosa/SpaceLaw/liability.html

9 Basel Protocol on Liability and Compensation for Damage Resulting from Transboundary Movements of Hazardous Wastes and their Disposal Basel,

10   December   1999.   http://www.basel.int/Countries/StatusofRatifications/
TheProtocol/tabid/1345/Default.aspx

10 Yet even in this case the arbitral tribunal did not find Canada legally responsible for
the transboundary pollution, since Canada's responsibility had already been established in the agreement submitting the dispute to the tribunal.

11 In 2005, the United States had emitted greenhouse gases into the atmosphere historically more than any other country. Its emissions that year totalled more than any
other country's, and above all, its emissions per capita were the highest.

12 Rio Declaration, Principle 2.

Further reading

Crawford, J., *The International Law Commission's Articles on State Responsibility:
Introduction, Text and Commentaries*, Cambridge: Cambridge University Press, 2002.

Faure, M.G. and Nollkaemper, A., 'International Liability as an Instrument to Prevent
and Compensate for Climate Change', *Stanford Journal of International Law*, 43(A),
2007, p. 123.

Hanqin, X., *Transboundary Damage in International Law*, Cambridge: Cambridge
University Press, 2003.

ILC, Draft articles on Prevention of Transboundary Harm from Hazardous Activities,
with commentaries, 2001, http://untreaty.un.org/ilc/texts/instruments/english/
commentaries/9_7_2001.pdf

ILC, Draft principles on the allocation of loss in the case of transboundary harm arising
out of hazardous activities, with commentaries, 2006, http://untreaty.un.org/ilc/
texts/instruments/english/commentaries/9_10_2006.pdf

ILC, Draft articles on Responsibility of States for Internationally Wrongful Acts,
with commentaries, 2001, http://untreaty.un.org/ilc/texts/instruments/english/
commentaries/9_6_2001.pdf

Koivurova, T., 'Due Diligence', in R. Wolfrum (ed.), *The Max Planck Encyclopedia of
Public International Law*, Oxford: Oxford University Press, 2011, online edition.

Mason, M., *New Accountability: Environmental Responsibility Across Borders*, London:
Earthscan, 2005.

Okowa, P.N., *State Responsibility for Transboundary Air Pollution in International Law*,
Oxford: Oxford University Press, 2000.

Rayfuse, R. and Scott, S. (eds), *International Law in the Era of Climate Change*,
Cheltenham: Edward Elgar, 2012.

Pisillo-Mazzeschi, R., 'The Due Diligence Rule and the Nature of the International
Responsibility of States', *German Yearbook of International Law*, 35, 1992, p. 9.

Tol, R.S.J. and Verheyen, R., 'State Responsibility and Compensation for Climate
Change', *Energy Policy*, 32(9), 2004, pp. 1109–30.

Verheyen, R., *Climate Change Damage and International Law: Prevention Duties and State
Responsibility*, Leiden: Brill, 2004.

Voigt, C., 'State Responsibility for Climate Change Damage', *Nordic Journal of
International Law*, 77(1–2), 2008, pp. 1–22.

Websites

Inuit petition to the Inter American Commission on Human Rights against the United
States: http://www.inuitcircumpolar.com/files/uploads/icc-files/FINALPetitionICC.pdf

Climate Justice Programme, 'Climate Justice: Enforcing Climate Change Law': http://
www.climatelaw.org/

BankTrack (bank sector network of civil society organizations): http://www.banktrack.org/

International Court of Justice: http://www.icj-cij.org/homepage/index.php?lang=en

7   The future of international environmental law

It has been proposed that it is time to commence a completely new phase in international environmental protection. In 1999, I was fortunate enough to have had the interesting experience of hearing the ideas of former Vice President of the International Court of Justice, Christopher Weeramantry, when he visited the University of Lapland's Faculty of Law. He had also taken the opportunity to express his ideas in his dissenting opinions during his tenure at the Court.

Weeramantry's opinion is that our relationship to the environment will only change when most of the world's religion-based belief systems change. He argues that any religion can be interpreted from the holy scriptures in many different ways and that all religions share the same basis when you look deeply enough. If the religions that affect human everyday life choices are not reinterpreted, the status of the environment can never improve, because 95 per cent of the world's population adheres to one religion or another.

The belief systems of most religions make reference to a very basic outline of the human role in creation; they also guide everyday environmental choices. Weeramantry lived as he preached: he was both Christian and Muslim. Weeramantry had many interesting ideas. However, it seemed difficult to believe that Christians and Muslims, for instance, would be able to find any common ground – at least not any time in the near future.

Even though I found Weeramantry's ideas interesting, I am more excited by how quickly our views and conceptions of the environment have changed in a relatively short period of time, for international environmental protection at the state level did not really take off in earnest until the 1970s. The environmental sciences have taken our ideas a long way. We have realized the importance of ecosystems – mostly through increased ecosystem service thinking – and we no longer see ourselves as somehow detached from the ecosystems of which we are intrinsically a part.

When the decision-making generations of the future are educated about our dependence on the biosphere and the functioning of its ecosystems, things will change. The sooner such ideas are adopted in international environmental treaties and other instruments, the more rapid the change will be. We must concede that our attitudes are still largely reactive: we only tend to take environmental measures when a disaster occurs. A long-term change requires new thinking that will only be attained through the education of future generations – although we might want to ask ourselves whether we have the time for this.

This chapter discusses the future of international environmental law, first of all from the perspectives that have been the central motifs in this book. How has international environmental law been able to create administrative mechanisms tailored for the resolution of international environmental problems? Has the classical structure of international law that maintains the Westphalian state-centred political system hindered or restrained the implementation of effective international environmental protection?

Next, we look at the opportunities for creating a more unified institutionally based system of international environmental law and environmental governance; thus far, the international environmental protection measures are highly fragmented. This was a key issue in the Rio 20-year follow-up conference held in June 2012, and will continue to be so. We look at some macro-level ideas of developing international environmental governance and some micro-level goals of finding synergies between those regimes that in part address the same environmental problems. Finally, we consider whether new means that go beyond the present regime could be found to control the gravest environmental problem of our times: climate change.

Where are we now?

Unlike high-level international political problems, international environmental problems have rarely dominated the agendas of international organizations and states. Climate change, of course, has received attention, but it is still being treated just like any other international environmental problem: as a matter for governance and control, not as a crisis to be proactively averted. The future of international environmental law seems to be determined by the development of the international political and economic system.

The UN Environmental Conference in Stockholm 1972 was the catalyst for the development of international environmental law; its recent culmination was the 20-year follow-up conference held in Rio in 1992. A further follow-up conference to Rio 1992, the Rio +20 Conference, took place again in Rio in June 2012. For the first time, two central themes were discussed: the green economy, and institutional changes.

This environmental conference differed from previous UN conferences as it discussed two tangible themes, although a wider environmental and development agenda was also considered through the goals of sustainable development.

Figure 7.1 The representatives of Finland and Cape Verde during a recess in a preparatory meeting for Rio +20 in New York on 19 March 2012. (Photo ©
IISD/Earth Negotiations Bulletin)

The Stockholm Conference created the basis for international environmental
law. Environmental protection was at its hottest in Rio 1992 and much was
accomplished, at least at ideas level. The Johannesburg sustainable development
summit in 2002 then attempted to move forward from words to deeds.

Sustainable development goals were the focus of Rio +20. Generally, it
could be said that Rio +20 aimed at advancing sustainable development
through a pragmatic approach that involved all stakeholders, not just states.
The crucial question of the Conference was whether or not it could revive the
spirit of its predecessor, the Rio 1992 Environment and Development
Conference. This was not to be the case, and many scholars of international
environmental law were as disappointed with Rio +20 as they had been with
the Johannesburg Conference.

A new outlook and new challenges

The world is not yet ready for what many scholars of international environmental law would recommend: a full-scale turn towards the long-term
prioritization of environmental protection rather than short-term economic
benefits. This will only be possible when a new generation of decision-makers
sees the world in a different way, for example in acknowledging the vital
services that are constantly produced by our environment.

A new outlook will ultimately become inevitable. The world population
has exceeded the 7 billion mark, and current estimates of the human population in the year 2100 are around 15 billion. We have recently lurched from

one economic crisis to another, but our faith in economic growth has not been shaken. It is also hard to believe that, at the present rate, technological developments alone will be sufficient to save us from ourselves. We need changes in our attitude and consequently our everyday behaviour.

One of the major challenges for international environmental protection is the gradual geopolitical change caused by the free trade system: many former developing countries have now become very rapidly advancing economies. Asia's emerging economies are causing an increasingly acknowledged challenge to the international legal system. In the 1960s and 1970s, many African and Asian nations openly challenged the legitimacy of international law, which they claimed had been created and developed by Europeans, and they sought to make changes. Similarly, these emerging Asian economies – and China in particular – have started to question whether the present international law system adequately takes their interests and views into account. They are also openly aiming for a standard of living that Western countries have long enjoyed.

We must now find a way of taking both the new geopolitical situation and the different stages of development into account. Professor Yasuaki Onuma of Tokyo University argues that we need to look beyond our own civilization's views as to the rules that should govern the world; we need to open a genuinely equal inter-cultural dialogue. If we fail to do so, many branches within international law will suffer, not least international environmental law, as any real basis for global cooperation will be lacking.

Sustainable development is a great principle, but it has not created the basis for social decision-making that is necessary to protect life within the limited carrying capacity of the ecosystems of our biosphere. The concept of sustainable development has been reduced to mean just taking the environment into account in all social decisions. The increasing number of aggravating environmental problems proves that merely taking the environment into account in decision-making is not enough. The resilience of the biosphere's ecosystems must be protected if we intend to go on living on this planet.

This is what makes the 'ecosystem services' idea so important. It can help human communities realize how completely dependent we are on the functions that the ecosystems in our environment perform and how vital the services are that they provide for us. The ecosystem services idea is also a realistic way of influencing our decision-making. It helps justify our decisions by offering an increase in our well-being, even according to the terms that states understand best: money. This is one of the critical questions for our planet. How can we promote thinking that includes the ecosystem services as part of a wider understanding of the functioning of the green economy?

The divergence of international environmental law from international law

International environmental law as a branch of law seems to be distancing itself further and further from the structures of classical international law. International environmental law has to be able to adapt to a rapidly changing

New ways of thinking are emerging

All over the world, it is being increasingly acknowledged that gross national product is an obsolete concept because it only measures the production of a state that goes through the market and for which a price is paid. We now recognize that well-being should be assessed more widely, considering environmental, social and economic sustainability factors. Creating wider assessments of the well-being of states and regions will also help to understand the importance of environmental protection in developing our societies.

'Planetary boundaries' is another interesting approach that is gaining attention. The core of this approach is that through industrialization, all of the major environmental changes have been caused by man. These changes, however, have limits. If we exceed these planetary boundaries in nine sectors (ocean acidification, ozone depletion, climate change, land and freshwater use, nitrogen cycle, loss of biodiversity, atmospheric aerosol loading, POP compounds and heavy metals), there is a serious risk of rapid and probably irreversible change. This is a useful concept as it turns our attention away from individual issues or functions towards a more holistic view of all the environmentally hazardous activities that will inevitably reach their limit in various ways:

- chemical pollution (not yet quantified)
- climate change
- ocean acidification
- ozone layer loss
- biogeochemical flow boundary
  - nitrogen cycle
  - phosphorus cycle
- freshwater use
- land use
- loss of biodiversity
- atmospheric aerosol loading (not yet quantified).

world. The global economy is changing the world at such a rapid rate that international environmental protection is now regulated by multiple administrative layers – not merely by states. It is likely that in the future, international environmental law will focus increasingly on the interaction of those regulatory levels.

The new generation of international environmental law professionals is no longer primarily concerned with transboundary environmental regulation. Rather, the focus now is on how the various levels (international, regional and national environmental law) can regulate a particular environmental problem, how commercial policy actions can promote environmental protection, and how soft-law organizations or general regulation can promote environmental protection so that the principles of good governance are heeded (for example,

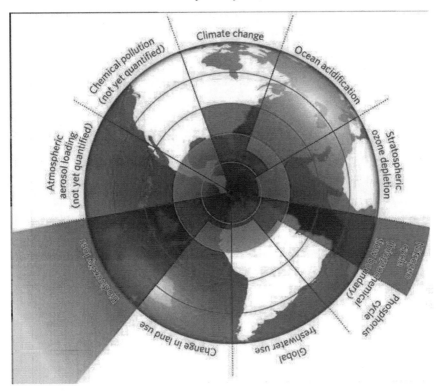

Figure 7.2 The boundaries of our planet. The two innermost circles show the safe
levels. The further out from the centre, the worse the problems (climate
change, disturbed nitrogen cycle, for example). Once outside the circle,
the tipping point is exceeded, causing irreversible consequences. Climate
change is on the third circle already, but we can still bring it under control.

Source: Azote Images/Stockholm Resilience Centre

securing better access to environmental decision-making and to appealing against
environmentally unfavourable decisions). Increasingly, new and innovative
methods of regulation and control for the protection of the environment are
being sought. Instead of observing international environmental law as part of
international law, scholars are increasingly considering it as part of a global
environmental administration in which environmental regulation is observed
as a multi-layer phenomenon.

This book has considered the extent to which international environmental
law has been able to separate itself from classical international law. This seems
to be inevitable, as the international political community gradually established
by the Peace of Westphalia (1648) – and maintained by classical international
law – is unable to meet the challenges of international environmental law,
which requires the following:

1   Collective decision mechanisms, by which humankind has the flexibility to make scientifically based decisions in order to avert environmental problems.
2   An extensive understanding of who is able to participate in international environmental protection, and how.
3   Acceptance of the principles and mechanisms that give access to decision-making to those who may be affected by the decision, and the requirement that all human activity should be environmentally sustainable.
4   Strict liability for environmental damage. The operator must compensate for any harm caused to the environment without the affected party having to prove the operator's negligence. Strict liability also has a pre-ventive function. Operators who know that they will be obliged to compensate for any injuries will take a more diligent attitude to their operations.

How successful has international environmental law been in distancing itself from classical international law and in adopting a new approach? The main difference is that international environmental law has developed its own methods for the negotiation and enactment of international environmental protection rules. International environmental regulation has to be quick to respond to changes as new scientific data emerges. It is also important to create administrative structures in which states focus less on defending their sovereignty than on considering themselves parts of a collective that makes the decisions that are best for our shared environment. The soft-law instrument offers a good way of reacting quickly to an environmental problem. It allows states and other actors to adopt tentative regulation rapidly and flexibly, without the challenges and procedures involved in international treaties, which protect state sovereignty. This method sustains a fast, tentative, non-binding international environmental regulation that evolves gradually over time into internationally binding law.

The ability of international environmental law to create novel ways of reacting to international environmental problems is best shown by the fact that treaty regimes have become the prominent method of regulating international environmental problems. The objective is to create a collective decision–making body that, instead of penalizing individual members of the regime, focuses on encouraging the parties to work with various actor groups on the basis of scientific research to resolve an environmental problem. Interestingly, regimes are being constructed on the basis of both legal rules and principles and soft-law norms. Non-binding decisions by meetings of parties are often more effective than treaty amendments in affecting the reaction to an environmental problem; they can be made quickly and by consensus and they are considered acceptable in international environmental law since all parties have been involved with their creation. Compliance committees have proven effective in reacting to problems relating to the compliance of individual states. It is essential that the treaty community first helps a party to return to the path of compliance. International treaty regimes have been able to create powerful scientific institutions that can influence the decisions taken by the various actor groups within the regime.

International environmental law has also widened the concept of the 'actor' from the classical international law understanding, which is strongly based on states and their domination in international politics and law-making. States are the main actors in international environmental law as well, but their status has become inevitably more relative. Scientific institutions play an important role in defining the political alternatives that are open to states in resolving an international environmental problem. Today, a variety of groups of actors affected by international environmental problems can, in different ways, influence the decision-making process in environmental treaty negotiations. Access of these types of actor groups to the functioning of international environmental regimes is now increasingly considered a human right – the right to influence environmental decisions internationally.

Classic international law has significantly influenced international environmental protection through its principles. It is important to remember that classic international law maintains a world in which sovereign states are at the heart of international politics and law. On the basis of the principles of international law, states are entitled to implement the environmental law and politics of their choice within their own territory within the limits of international law.

The environment in the areas beyond state jurisdiction is not defended by anyone, except for the International Seabed Authority in its own limited Area and within the scope of its own limited mandate (to ensure protection of the Area from the harmful effects of seabed mining activities). The UN Environment Programme (UNEP) has no such mandate, and individual states seem reluctant to protect the environment within these common areas unless their own interests are at stake. It is typical for serious environmental problems such as climate change or loss of biodiversity to be managed according to the principle of 'common concern of humankind'. This principle is based on state sovereignty: it obligates states only to do something to avert these threats, not even to bind themselves to an international treaty.

Nonetheless, new principles, approaches and guidance methods are being developed in international and national environmental law at an accelerating pace to meet the challenges revealed by scientific research into environmental problems.

International environmental law has not been able to make any significant advances in creating responsibility and liability rules for environmental damage beyond general international law. The principle of no-harm is still the most important principle, even though some specific strict-liability treaties have been concluded. Classical international law is also reflected in the settlement of environmental disputes between states, which are still principally being decided on the basis of the same rules as were applied in the 1941 *Trail Smelter* case.

International environmental regimes have managed thus far, however, to avoid the kind of disputes that might threaten inter-state relations; hence, only a few regimes have developed an obligatory dispute settlement system. Instead, they have set up compliance committees to support or delicately pressure the parties in order to comply with their treaty obligations. A few international environmental regimes even contain an article on liability for environmental damage.

Improving international environmental governance

International environmental law is governed by a diverse array of different intergovernmental organizations and international global and regional treaties. Their bodies and meetings of the parties produce both overlapping and sometimes contradictory decisions and rules. The UN International Court of Justice established a specific Chamber in which to process environmental disputes, but even when submitting an environmental dispute to the International Court of Justice, states were unwilling to resort to it. The UN Environment Programme (UNEP) has perhaps been the most significant body to take up and promote the settlement of international environmental problems, but it is only a UN programme – not even a UN specialized agency – and it lacks the resources and the competence to coordinate the fragmented field of international environmental law. The idea of a world environmental organization corresponding to the WTO that could unify the highly fragmented field of international environmental law has been proposed time and again. However, there is just not sufficient political will to establish such an organization.

One of the most high-profile aspects of the Rio +20 preparatory process was the debate regarding the institutional changes required to enhance the governance of international environmental protection. The institutions of international environmental law will have to be altered sooner or later, so the discussion on the institutional changes is likely to remain on the agenda for some time. Environmental protection is not the only objective of social decision-making, and it has to be matched with the goals of sustainable development. Various international treaty systems ought to recognize each other's objectives and take them into account.

It is widely acknowledged that the measures required to conserve biological diversity and to avert climate change would result in different policies. For the aversion of climate change, it is important to produce efficient carbon sinks by planting trees that bind carbon efficiently, or to maintain seagrass beds, mangroves and salt marshes to bind blue carbon efficiently, for example. From the biodiversity perspective, this is problematic, as monoplantations (plantations of a single species) are very poor in terms of genetic diversity.

So we see that cooperation between the treaty regimes is essential. Such synergies are already being explored in the UNEP hazardous waste and chemicals cooperation between the Rotterdam, Basel and Stockholm Conventions (see below, 'A model example: chemical regimes', p. 198), and between the environmental regimes of the UN Economic Commission for Europe. We must avoid replacing one environmental problem with another; this is formulated in Article 195 of the UNCLOS: 'In taking measures to prevent, reduce and control pollution of the marine environment, states shall act so as not to transfer, directly or indirectly, damage or hazards from one area to another or transform one type of pollution into another.'

There have been well-known cases where factories raised the height of their chimneys so that their pollutants were no longer harmful to those in the immediate vicinity, but instead dispersed the damage among more distant environments and communities. The same logic can be seen in the way in which atmospheric substances impact on various different environmental problems. The better the governance mechanisms for environmental problems and their sources are coordinated – or common decision-making measures are created – the better the chances are of avoiding the replacement of one emission problem with another.

A vast number of treaty regimes regulate international environmental problems, of which only a few coordinate their actions with each other. A significant exception is the deepening cooperation between the Basel, Rotterdam and Stockholm Conventions: the synergies between these three treaty systems are being enhanced in several different ways and should serve as an example for other treaty regimes that regulate partly overlapping environmental problems.

It is imperative that these international objectives are matched within the national context: the way in which each state implements its international environmental treaty obligations. Unless it is coordinated at the national level, the significance of these treaties will remain limited. The treaties can only work when they are implemented nationally. The resources and capacity for environmental protection of developing nations should be better coordinated. One of the objectives for most global environmental treaties is to improve the ability of developing nations to understand the causes and effects of their environmental problems and to advance their management of them. It is vital that the programmes of the various international environmental treaties and UNEP programmes are unified so that resources are not wasted and know-how is shared more efficiently.

The latest scientific research on an environmental problem's status is essential to the decision-making of the majority of international environmental treaty regimes, and so it cannot be beneficial that the Intergovernmental Panel on Climate Change (IPCC) was separated from the climate change regime itself. When science is filtered into the international environmental protection treaties efficiently and objectively, the decision-makers' prospects of making more sustainable decisions are greatly improved.

A world environmental organization (WEO)

When institutional changes for international environmental law and policy are debated, the idea of an organization comparable with the World Trade Organization (WTO) is often proposed: a 'world environmental organization' (WEO). If an organization were created along the lines of the WTO, all the global environmental protection treaties could be integrated under its governance. This would certainly enhance the scope for synergies between the treaties that currently operate on overlapping tasks. If a WEO had an automatic dispute settlement system comparable to the WTO, states could take each other to WEO dispute settlement panels, gradually creating the foundation for a unified regulation of international environmental law.

Most international environmental law professionals are broadly in favour of establishing a WEO in theory, although different scholars have different ideas as to how it would be constituted and operate. In October 2011, environmental lawyers signed an appeal in Limoges, France, which was sent to the UN and its member states.[1] This ambitious appeal supported the establishment of a WEO. The idea was debated at the Rio +20 preparatory meetings, alongside a UN 'Environment Organization' (UNEO), which would have also been an autonomous intergovernmental organization. Proposals to strengthen the UNEP to make it a specialized agency rather than a subsidiary body of the UN General Assembly also received a lot of attention.

These proposals are all too ambitious to be realized at the moment, however. There is simply not sufficient will to establish any extensive new international organization, especially in the sphere of environmental protection, which is not a top priority for the international community. Few of the present international environmental treaty secretariats would probably be ready for such a change. They already have their own objectives for the areas they have been assigned to by the creators of their respective regimes, the states. Consideration should also be given to how the establishment of such an organization would relate to the WTO, to existing human rights monitoring bodies, and to other institutions important for the promotion of sustainable development. In Rio +20, the most viable solution proposed was to strengthen and upgrade the UNEP by expanding its governing body from the current 58 members to universal membership.

There are others who propose that a WEO might be established by changing the status of the UN Environment Programme into a separate specialized UN agency. It might then be assigned more tasks in the coordination of international environmental treaties. As it is, cooperation between the treaties that monitor waste and hazardous chemicals is already taking place under the auspices of the UNEP. The UNEP will certainly one day require a new enhanced status for this coordination work, as the field of international environmental protection is so badly fragmented. At the very least, an increase in the cooperation between the secretariats and meetings of the parties of environmental treaties would be very promising.

The pressure for change to the international environmental administration also comes from the WTO dispute settlement procedure. The capacity of the WTO dispute settlement procedure to make decisions affecting international environmental protection has become increasingly problematic. WTO members can automatically take each other to the dispute settlement procedure while there is no such opportunity in international environmental law. Most environmental treaties do not contain an automatic legal dispute settlement procedure, so it is difficult to bring disputes into legal procedures. From the free trade perspective, environmental protection is often seen as commercial protectionism, against which the WTO rules are designed.

Although the Appellate Body in WTO dispute settlement has in some decisions made it possible to consider environmental issues, the problem is structural. The dispute settlement panels and Appellate Body of the WTO generally interpret intergovernmental disputes primarily from the point of view of promoting free trade. Environmental protection is permissible, but it is an exception from the main rule and as such is interpreted narrowly. This friction will likely increase the pressure to unify the fragmented field of international environmental law.

Searching for synergies between regimes

The benefits of synergy between different international environmental regimes are already being explored. As the regime that comprehensively promotes the conservation of species and habitats, the biodiversity convention has good prospects of unifying the international regulation related to biological diversity. Much has been done already. Cooperation grows closer between the biodiversity regime and three kinds of treaty systems: the treaties relevant to biological diversity, the Rio treaties, and other treaties.

The cooperation between the biodiversity regime and five other diversity treaties has advanced furthest: the Bonn Migratory Species Convention, the CITES, the Ramsar Wetlands Convention, the Plant Genetic Resources Convention, and the World Heritage Convention. These six treaty regimes aim at coordinating their operations nationally, regionally and globally so that the agreed objectives of protection and sustainable use can be achieved. They have already developed many common approaches, such as the ecosystem-based approach, and ways to implement their common objectives in practice (such as work programmes, multilateral systems related to availability and benefit-sharing, and regional agreements).

To complement the conventions accepted in Rio in 1992, a Joint Liaison Group was established in 2001 to increase synergies and to reduce overlapping activities. This is a flexible method of cooperation allowing the group to exchange information, promote synergies, and enhance coordination between the treaty regimes.

The biodiversity regime is also cooperating with many other treaty regimes: for example, the International Plant Protection Convention (IPPC), the Berne Convention on the Conservation of Wildlife, and the Convention for the Protection and Development of the Marine Environment of the Wider Caribbean Region (Cartagena, 1983). The Biodiversity Convention is gradually evolving into an umbrella convention, bringing together the fragmented body of treaty systems protecting and regulating various species and ecosystems.

A model example: chemical regimes

Three UNEP-connected chemical treaties have established close cooperation: the Basel Convention on the Control of Transboundary Movements of Hazardous Wastes and their Disposal, the Rotterdam Convention on the Prior Informed Consent Procedure for Certain Hazardous Chemicals and Pesticides in International Trade,[2] and the Stockholm Convention on Persistent Organic Pollutants. Their common goal is to protect human health and the environment from hazardous chemicals and wastes. The cooperation and coordination of the practical implementation of these three treaty regimes provides an example for other international treaty regimes, proving that synergies can be created between treaty regimes where their regulatory functions are overlapping.

The Basel Convention[3] was adopted in 1989 and entered into force in 1992 as the first of these three conventions related to hazardous chemicals and pesticides. There was an underlying fear that businesses in industrial countries were transporting their hazardous wastes to developing countries. The Convention aims at reducing the generation of hazardous waste, improving its environmentally sustainable management and limiting its transboundary movement, unless it is environmentally sustainable. The Convention does not itself ban transporting hazardous waste from OECD countries to developing countries. The Basel Convention meeting of the parties in 1994 introduced the ban, which was later adopted as an amendment. The amendment, however, has not entered into force yet, although the tenth meeting of the parties in October 2011 brought this closer to reality.

The Convention prohibits the transportation of hazardous waste to Antarctica, any non-member state, or a state that has banned the import of hazardous waste. The Convention also establishes a regulatory mechanism for transporting hazardous waste to another country when this is permissible according to the Convention. The authorities in the exporting country must notify the importing country and any transit countries in writing in advance, giving the details of the planned transportation. Exporting hazardous waste is permitted only if both the transit countries and the importing country agree in writing.

The Rotterdam Convention was adopted in 1998 and entered into force in 2004. The pressure to negotiate the Convention came partly from the fear that hazardous chemicals were being transported without controls to developing countries, and partly from the exponential increase in the export and import of chemicals. The parties to the Rotterdam Convention are obligated to obtain prior informed consent when exporting Annex III substances. The parties also commit themselves to informing the target country of the export of chemicals not listed in Annex III which are otherwise nationally banned or strictly controlled. The prior consent procedure is not applicable in these cases.

Any additions to the list of chemicals in Annex III are proposed to the meeting of parties by the Rotterdam Convention Chemical Review Committee (CRC); additions require the consensus agreement of the parties.

Developing nations and transition economies are also entitled to propose additions of hazardous pesticides.

The Stockholm Convention[4] was adopted in 2001, and entered into force in 2004. At the time when the regional persistent organic pollutants (POP) Protocol was adopted to the LRTAP Convention in 1998, there was a demand for universal control of these chemicals. Above all, the 'dirty dozen' among POP compounds was to be eliminated, including, for example, PCB and aldrin. The introduction to the Convention states that they 'possess toxic properties, resist degradation, bioaccumulate and are transported, through air, water and migratory species, across international boundaries and deposited far from their place of release, where they accumulate in terrestrial and aquatic ecosystems'. The parties committed to ban the production and usage, and the import and export, of the 12 POP compounds listed in Annex A, and to limit the production and usage of chemicals listed in Annex B. Measures to reduce or eliminate emissions unintentionally produced (Annex C) require a plan of action by the parties.

These three Conventions have much in common. Their objective is to protect human health and the environment and each of them applies to most POP compounds and to a large number of pesticides. They also contain import and export rules. The Basel and Stockholm Conventions include rules related to waste processing and management. They were negotiated under the auspices of the UNEP and they are institutionally connected with it. The Rotterdam Convention was negotiated under the auspices of the UNEP and the UN Food and Agriculture Organization (FAO).

The Conventions stipulate that technical assistance must be provided to developing countries. The Basel and Stockholm Conventions have established regional centres for education and technology, while the Rotterdam Convention operates through the regional offices of FAO and UNEP. The Basel and Stockholm Conventions have the greater number of parties (Basel 179, and Stockholm 178), but cooperation between the treaty regimes is expected to increase the number of parties to the Rotterdam Convention (150) as well.[5]

The meetings of the parties to all these conventions have similar duties, such as assessing whether the conventions are efficiently implemented. They share similar technical-scientific bodies: the Stockholm Persistent Organic Pollutants Review Committee, the Rotterdam Chemical Review Committee, and the Basel Open-ended Working Group. The Basel Convention has had a compliance committee established since 2002 and the two other Conventions are in the process of developing similar committees. The dispute settlement procedures of the Conventions are similar and the secretariats have roughly similar tasks.

Cooperation began in 2006 when the three meetings of the parties established the Ad Hoc Joint Working Group on enhancing cooperation and coordination among the Basel, Rotterdam and Stockholm Conventions (AHJWG). It was composed of representatives of 15 countries that were party to all three Conventions; the process was led by Chile, China and Finland,

and the group met three times, the most recent meeting taking place in March 2008. The working group agreed on a set of recommendations for promoting inter-treaty synergies nationally, regionally and globally. On the basis of these recommendations, almost identical draft decisions were produced, which were accepted with small exceptions by the meetings of the parties to all three Conventions in 2008 and 2009 (the synergy decision). These decisions resulted in the establishment of service units. More importantly, however, they led to a historic meeting of the parties to all three Conventions in February 2010 in Bali.

The synergy decision resulted in some interesting proposals, of which only a few can be considered here. Coordination will be increased at the national level: for example, through processes initiated by the parties to implement all three conventions; focal points will be named, and joint preparations will take place for the meetings of the parties of all three regimes. The parties are encouraged to adopt a programme of both national and regional cooperation and to include an action strategy in their national development plans. In this way, they are able to implement all three conventions and to clarify their own national priorities in implementation.

The Convention secretariats are encouraged to submit proposals to the meetings of the parties as to how the compliance committees (once they are all operational) could function in a more coordinated way. The synergy decision gives such examples as shared secretariat services for the compliance committees, and the presence of the compliance committee chairs at each other's meetings; the decision also encourages the nomination in the compliance committees of one person who has experience of the compliance committees of other conventions. The secretariats of the three regimes are expected to work jointly in communication and education, and in developing systems for the exchange of information on environmental and health impacts, and joint representation in other international processes.

The synergy decision also encourages administrative reform: for example, whether to appoint a single secretary-general to supervise all three secretariats (this has now been adopted). Further, the three are encouraged to join their services, such as legal services, and to arrange meetings of the parties in a coordinated way. These decisions were agreed and refined in a shared meeting of the parties in 2010. The cooperation between these three treaty regimes will most likely prove a significant example for other international environmental treaties.

How can we solve the most urgent environmental problem: climate change?

To date, the climate change regime has not been able to rise to the challenge of climate change. There are several reasons for this: climate change calls for a restructuring of the foundations of modern economies, especially their energy systems.

Figure 7.3 The chairs of the meetings of the parties to the Basel, Rotterdam and Stockholm Conventions made their historic decision on 24 February 2010 in Bali, Indonesia. (Photo © IISD/Earth Negotiations Bulletin)

The UN Human Development Report clearly shows that climate change is different from all the other problems currently faced by humanity because it requires us to change our ways of thinking so fundamentally. Above all, the report emphasizes that climate change forces us to accept the fact that in order to survive, we must accept that humans are interdependent. In one sense, climate change reminds us that we have a single common denominator – our planet – and that all individuals and all nations share the one and only atmosphere.

Achievements of the Durban Conference

After the 2009 Copenhagen Conference, the Cancun Conference in 2010 once again introduced measures to try to save the climate regime. Since the Cancun and Durban Conferences, there have been signs that the climate regime is recovering. The 17th meeting of the parties to the Climate Change Convention took place in Durban in December 2011. There were many difficult issues to negotiate, perhaps, above all, how the states of the world could be made to commit themselves legally to the reduction of greenhouse gas emissions.

The main problem is that only a small proportion of greenhouse gas emitters have legally committed themselves to reducing their emissions under the Kyoto Protocol. Many of the worst emitters, such as the United States or the emerging Asian powers (China and India), have not committed themselves to legally binding reductions.

The Durban Conference has already been evaluated in both pessimistic and optimistic terms. For the majority the Durban Conference managed to actually accomplish much more than had been anticipated.

First, the decision was taken to negotiate another commitment period to the Kyoto Protocol of five to eight years. Many issues remain open – for instance, what reductions the Kyoto Protocol parties would be prepared to commit themselves to – but a consensus to another commitment period alone was considered an accomplishment. (In the 2012 Doha Climate Conference, the parties managed to agree on a second commitment period lasting until 2020, but with the commitment of fewer states than the first commitment period.)

Second, and perhaps most importantly, the parties agreed to negotiate 'a protocol, another legal instrument or an agreed outcome with legal force under the Convention applicable to all Parties'. The wording does not make it clear what kind of a legal outcome the parties actually committed themselves to. The goal of this negotiation process is to set binding emission reductions on all parties after 2020 – not only for industrialized countries – and extending also to include the United States. The principle of common but differentiated responsibilities seems to be gradually releasing its grip on the climate regime.

Few had believed that the Durban Conference could revive the Kyoto Protocol in the short term and initiate serious negotiations on the reduction of emissions for all world states. This was a real achievement. The developing world's share of greenhouse gas emissions has increased exponentially, and the fact that both the developing nations and the United States committed themselves to the same negotiation process for legally binding reductions is a great success. The EU played a significant role as the mediator for this 'roadmap'. The EU's condition for agreeing to another commitment period was that other large economies commit themselves to negotiating a legally binding agreement. Industrial nations, African states and small island nations all supported the EU's approach, increasing the pressure on other significant negotiating parties and resulting in a real achievement. The Durban Conference also made many other important decisions.

However, since the Durban Climate Conference it has become apparent that the world community will struggle to keep the rise in the global temperature below two degrees. According to the climate change regime, this is the limit we cannot exceed if we are to observe the objective recorded in the Framework Convention on Climate Change: stabilization of greenhouse gas concentrations in the atmosphere at a level that would prevent dangerous anthropogenic interference with the climate system (Article 2). Most scientific evaluations state that if we are to keep the temperature rise from pre-industrial levels below two degrees, global emissions should reach their peak in 2015 and then start to decrease steadily. Emissions had increased by 6 per cent in 2010 – the highest annual increase to date – and new binding targets will probably not enter into force until 2020.

Another problem is that the parties only committed themselves to a new 'roadmap', as they had done in Bali 2010. Many observers are concerned that the failure of the Bali process will end up repeating itself.

The Durban Conference established another set of new processes with ambitious goals, while the actual reduction of emissions was postponed. Small wonder that various actor groups are becoming frustrated that the climate change regime seems to be progressing at such a slow pace, while the effects of climate change still threaten to destroy living conditions in large parts of the world. It is only natural that those countries that are suffering the most from climate change should be seeking ways to enhance the climate change regime both through legal and through other more unconventional methods. It also seems that disputes related to climate and energy policy (especially to renewable energy sources) are being brought more and more frequently to the WTO dispute settlement procedure.

From the perspective of the WTO free trade rules, the most dramatic measure was that the EU decided to require foreign airlines to participate in the implementation of its emissions trading scheme: for any planes departing from or arriving at an EU airport, the airlines must have the correct amount of emission rights defined by the directive. This requirement has caused serious disputes between the EU and a number of other states; there have even been speculations of a trade war!

Several of the small island states have long been thinking about legal strategies to enhance the climate change regime since rising sea levels resulting from climate change are threatening their very existence. They have begun taking steps to require the International Court of Justice to determine who is legally responsible for climate change and its consequences.

Some of the states have considered taking the worst polluters to the International Court of Justice in contentious proceedings; others are canvassing support from a sufficient number of states to request an advisory opinion from the Court on the matter through the UN General Assembly.

Interestingly, some of these small island states are engaged in a global 'legal struggle' against climate change. For example, the Federated States of Micronesia participated in the environmental impact assessment of the Prunerov coal power plant extension project in the Czech Republic. From Micronesia's point of view, power plants such as this one are essentially accelerating climate change. Micronesia's action at least managed to demonstrate the complicity of power plants in causing climate change.

Figure 7.4 During the Durban Climate Conference, on 10 December 2011, civic organizations demonstrated outside the plenary hall. Representatives witnessed the anger of these civic organizations: little had been accomplished while Africa and other affected areas were becoming increasingly endangered. This demonstration took place before the conference had accomplished any tangible results. (Photos © Vernon Rive)

New ways of containing climate change

Could new ways be found to contain and resolve climate change? From the political–legal angle, three major approaches have been presented. The version that has provoked the most discussion and received the most attention to date is the utilitarian **cost-benefit model** on the global scale. The best-known option is the so-called 'contraction and convergence' model presented by the Global Commons Institute.

The basic idea is that states should first agree on what constitutes safe levels of atmospheric greenhouse gases. Once this is settled, emission rights are divided among the states according to what their per capita emissions are. This would mean that developing countries with their low per capita emissions would receive high emission rights. This in turn results in convergence: as the developing nations would receive much higher emission rights, they would be able to develop economically, but at the same time their per capita greenhouse gas emissions would increase and they would have to start limiting their emissions. Meanwhile, the industrialized nations would receive much lower emission rights and would therefore be under pressure to reduce their per capita emissions from the outset. Sooner or later, the per capita emission rights of states would reach the same level globally, and the total emissions would remain below the agreed safe levels.

The **human rights model** is critical of this cost-benefit model, because it continues to divide the emission reduction loads among states on the basis of states' relative wealth rather than the needs and capacities of individuals. In principle, the contraction and convergence model allows states like Bangladesh, for instance, high emission rights at first because of its low per capita emissions, but it fails to take into account the enormous gaps between the rich and the poor within developing countries. Emissions rights and targets are calculated according to a state's gross national product and population size, but these, of course, provide only crude averages and do not distinguish between the obligations on the very rich in poor countries or the very poor in rich or middle-income countries.

Professor Simon Caney[6] argues that the best solution would be to allocate emission burdens on the basis of human rights. Caney sees two advantages in the human rights model compared with the cost-benefit model. First of all, the human rights violations caused by climate change generally affect certain population groups worst: generally the poor within existing states. As states already have global human rights legal obligations, both states and the international community at large are liable for the protection at the very least of the core of essential human rights – to ensure that climate change does not result in death or sickness of the population. It is not necessary to protect everyone's human rights, because the wealthy can generally protect themselves against the worst impacts of climate change. Caney argues that the second advantage of the human rights approach is that the affected parties are entitled to compensation from those who contribute the most to climate change. This viewpoint is not endorsed by the current climate change regime, which only concentrates on reducing greenhouse gas emissions into the atmosphere and on preparing to adapt to the effects of climate change.

The third alternative is **turning climate change into a security issue**. Climate change is generally thought to be an environmental problem that can be controlled and administered. If, however, science proves that the phenomenon is threatening the future of our planet, should it not be considered as a security policy issue, thus assigning it a totally different weight and resourcing in international politics? The UK, for instance, arranged a special session on climate change as a security policy issue in the UN Security Council during its presidency. However, the problem might be that if climate change were to become a security policy field, it could be administered by armies and security forces.

To date, none of these models seems to have gained much momentum in international politics. Climate change is not considered a security policy issue and not really a human rights issue. There are several opinions about which model could reduce greenhouse gas emissions into the atmosphere, while the Durban 'roadmap' is the only vague plan for the future.

An essential change in our world-view

There is little room for doubt that climate change is the environmental problem that threatens humankind most severely. Its effects are so dramatic and inclusive that if we are not prepared to change our way of life, and states do not reassess their deeply held political and economic values, the future predicted by scientists is difficult even to imagine. Climate change is also the most difficult environmental problem to solve. The earth's surface temperature is likely to rise only gradually, so it is difficult to create the kind of pressure for regulation that normally follows a catastrophic environmental disaster.

Containing climate change will require intervention with the basics of modern economies: first and foremost, a radical reduction in the use of all fossil fuels. With a few exceptions, all current energy policy decisions result in an increase of the use of fossil fuels. The International Energy Agency goes as far as to predict that we will use considerably more fossil fuels in 2030 than we do now. This will accelerate climate change, as more carbon dioxide is released into the atmosphere, causing the earth's surface temperature to rise and the climate to change. The worst-case scenario is that we exceed the so-called tipping point, after which even a slight rise in temperature will cause dramatic changes to the climate system through self-sustaining feedback loops.

The most serious effects of climate change, such as desertification and rising sea levels, are likely to afflict poorer developing countries in the South (and first and foremost the poorest people in the poorest countries), who are already battling multiple social problems. They do not have the know-how, the resources, or in some cases the governmental stability to adapt to the consequences of climate change.

An all-inclusive phenomenon, climate change is revolutionizing our worldview. All those of us who live on this planet and all our communities will have to make gradual changes in our lives as measures are taken to contain the effects of climate change. The entire biosphere and its biological diversity will change and we will need to adapt accordingly to a completely new world.

The positive effect of climate change is that it challenges existing human communities to view things in a holistic way. Since our entire way of existence, both public and private, will be affected by climate change, we can no longer delude ourselves that our existing highly specialized modern societies in which various policies and actors only view matters from the perspectives of their respective agendas can be maintained. As a result of the all-inclusive effects of climate change, nature is forcing us to recognize that we form just one small part of the biosphere. Hopefully, we will see that every human being is sitting in the same boat; no one is spared from the dramatic effects of climate change, although in the short term, those on the front line of climate change are the world's poorest, and there will even be some (short-lived) 'winners' from climate change.

If industrial countries continue to fight for their way of life and standard of living, and if developing countries continue to aspire towards the same standard of living in the long term, we can be fairly sure that the battle will be lost before it has even begun. In this battle our only opponents are ourselves – ourselves and the limited time available to us to make a change. It is vital that we fully take on board that there is still hope of averting climate change and its horrific effects with the choices that we make.

Questions and research tasks

1   What do you think are the greatest future challenges for international environmental law? How should international environmental work prioritize its reactions to different problems?

2   What do you consider to have been the major accomplishments of the Rio +20 Conference towards improving international environmental governance? Consider, in a wider perspective, how international environmental governance could and should be changed.

3   What do you think is the most crucial challenge that humanity faces, among all of our global problems? What is the most difficult environmental problem? What is the major cause of this environmental problem? What could we do to resolve the problem?

4   Some scholars promote the attachment of economic values to environmental goods so that they can be better taken into account by the international economic systems that dominate contemporary international relations. What do you think might be the advantages and disadvantages of this approach?

Notes

1 Call for Action from Lawyers and Environmental Law Organizations can be found at http://greenlaw.blogs.law.pace.edu/2011/11/08/limoges-rio-20-preparatory-conference/
2 Rotterdam Convention on the Prior Informed Consent Procedure for Certain Hazardous Chemicals and Pesticides in International Trade, http://www.pic.int/
3 Basel Convention on the Control of Transboundary Movements of Hazardous Wastes and their Disposal, http://www.basel.int/Portals/4/Basel%20Convention/docs/text/BaselConventionText-e.pdf
4 Stockholm Convention on Persistent Organic Pollutants, http://chm.pops.int/default.aspx
5 Status of ratification according to the United Nations Treaty Collection as of 18 January 2013.
6 Simon Caney, 'Climate Change, Human Rights and Moral Thresholds', in S. Humphreys (ed.), *Human Rights and Climate Change*, pp. 69–90, Cambridge: Cambridge University Press, 2009.

Further reading

Allott, P., *Eunomia: New Order for a New World*, Oxford: Oxford University Press, 2001.
Desai, B.H., 'Mapping the Future of International Environmental Governance', *Yearbook of International Environmental Law*, 13, 2002, http://www.yale.edu/gegdialogue/docs/dialogue/oct03/papers/Desai.pdf)
Desai, B.H., 'UNEP: A Global Environmental Authority?', *Environmental Policy & Law*, 36(3–4), 2006, pp. 137–57.
Leary, D. and Pisupati, B. (eds), *The Future of International Environmental Law*, Tokyo: United Nations University Press, 2010.
Onuma, Y., *A Transcivilizational Perspective on International Law*, Leiden: Nijhoff, 2010.
Posner, E.A. and Yoo, J., 'International Law and The Rise of China', *Chicago Journal of International Law*, 7, 2006, http://works.bepress.com/johnyoo/36
Weeramantry, C.G., *The Lord's Prayer: Bridge to a Better World*, Liguori, MO: Liguori/Triumph, 1998.
Yang, T. and Percival, R., 'The Emergence of Global Environmental Law', *Ecology Law Quarterly*, 36, 2009, p. 615, http://digitalcommons.law.umaryland.edu/cgi/viewcontent.cgi?article=1847&context=fac_pubs

Websites

Rio +20, United Nations Conference on Sustainable Development (homepage): http://www.uncsd2012.org/rio20/
Audiovisual Library of International Law, Lecture Series (Edith Brown Weiss): http://untreaty.un.org/cod/avl/ls/Weiss_EL.html

Index